Lectures On The French Revolution

By

John Emerich Edward Dalberg Acton

Lectures on the French Revolution
by John Emerich Edward Dalberg Acton

Copyright © 2024

All Rights reserved.

No part of this publication may be reproduced, stored in a retrieval system, or transmitted in any form or by any means, electronic, mechanical, photocopying or Otherwise, without the written permission of the publisher.
The author/editor asserts the moral right to be identified as the author/editor of this work.

ISBN: 978-93-63050-31-0

Published by

DOUBLE 9 BOOKS

2/13-B, Ansari Road
Daryaganj, New Delhi – 110002
info@double9books.com
www.double9books.com
Tel. 011-40042856

This book is under public domain

ABOUT THE AUTHOR

John Emerich Edward Dalberg-Acton, also known as Lord Acton, was an English Catholic historian, politician, and writer. He is well known for remarking in a letter to an Anglican bishop in 1887: "Power tends to corrupt, and absolute power corrupts absolutely." Acton was the only son of Sir Ferdinand Dalberg-Acton, 7th Baronet, and grandson of the Neapolitan admiral and prime minister Sir John Acton, 6th Baronet (who succeeded to the baronetcy and estates held by another branch of the Acton family in Shropshire in 1791). From 1837 to 1869, he was known as Sir John Dalberg-Acton, 8th Baronet. Acton's father, Richard, married Marie Louise Pelline, the only daughter of Emmerich Joseph, 1st Duc de Dalberg, a naturalized French nobility of old German ancestry who served under Napoleon and represented Louis XVIII at the Congress of Vienna in 1814. After Sir Richard Acton died in 1837, she married the 2nd Earl Granville (1840). Marie Louise Pelline de Dalberg was the heiress of Herrnsheim, Germany. She became the mother of John Dalberg-Acton, born in Naples.

CONTENTS

PREFATORY NOTE		7
I	THE HERALDS OF THE REVOLUTION	8
II	THE INFLUENCE OF AMERICA	23
III	THE SUMMONS OF THE STATES-GENERAL	38
IV	THE MEETING OF THE STATES-GENERAL	52
V	THE TENNIS-COURT OATH	61
VI	THE FALL OF THE BASTILLE	68
VII	THE FOURTH OF AUGUST	82
VIII	THE CONSTITUTIONAL DEBATES	93
IX	THE MARCH TO VERSAILLES	106
X	MIRABEAU	118
XI	SIEYÈS AND THE CONSTITUTION CIVILE	132
XII	THE FLIGHT TO VARENNES	144
XIII	THE FEUILLANTS AND THE WAR	158
XIV	DUMOURIEZ	172
XV	THE CATASTROPHE OF MONARCHY	183
XVI	THE EXECUTION OF THE KING	195
XVII	THE FALL OF THE GIRONDE	207
XVIII	THE REIGN OF TERROR	217
XIX	ROBESPIERRE	229
XX	LA VENDÉE	242
XXI	THE EUROPEAN WAR	254
XXII	AFTER THE TERROR	265
APPENDIX		276
INDEX		299

PREFATORY NOTE

The following Lectures were delivered by Lord Acton as Regius Professor of Modern History at Cambridge in the academical years 1895-96, 1896-97, 1897-98, 1898-99. The French Revolution, 1789-95, was in those years one of the special subjects set for the Historical Tripos, and this determined the scope of the course. In addition some discussion of the literature of the Revolution generally took place either in a conversation class or as an additional lecture. Such connected fragments of these as remain have been printed as an appendix. For the titles of the Lectures the editors are responsible.

J. N. F.
R. V. L.
August 10, 1910

I
THE HERALDS OF THE REVOLUTION

The revenue of France was near twenty millions when Lewis XVI., finding it inadequate, called upon the nation for supply. In a single lifetime it rose to far more than one hundred millions, while the national income grew still more rapidly; and this increase was wrought by a class to whom the ancient monarchy denied its best rewards, and whom it deprived of power in the country they enriched. As their industry effected change in the distribution of property, and wealth ceased to be the prerogative of a few, the excluded majority perceived that their disabilities rested on no foundation of right and justice, and were unsupported by reasons of State. They proposed that the prizes in the Government, the Army, and the Church should be given to merit among the active and necessary portion of the people, and that no privilege injurious to them should be reserved for the unprofitable minority. Being nearly an hundred to one, they deemed that they were virtually the substance of the nation, and they claimed to govern themselves with a power proportioned to their numbers. They demanded that the State should be reformed, that the ruler should be their agent, not their master.

That is the French Revolution. To see that it is not a meteor from the unknown, but the product of historic influences which, by their union were efficient to destroy, and by their division powerless to construct, we must follow for a moment the procession of ideas that went before, and bind it to the law of continuity and the operation of constant forces.

If France failed where other nations have succeeded, and if the passage from the feudal and aristocratic forms of society to the industrial and democratic was attended by convulsions, the cause was not in the men of that day, but in the ground on which they stood. As long as the despotic kings were victorious abroad, they were accepted at home. The first signals of revolutionary thinking lurk dimly among the oppressed minorities during intervals of disaster. The Jansenists were loyal and patient; but their famous jurist Domat was a philosopher, and is remembered as the writer who restored the supremacy of reason in the chaotic jurisprudence of the time. He had learnt from St. Thomas, a great name in the school he belonged to, that legislation ought to be for the people and by the people, that the cashiering of bad kings may be not only a right but a duty. He insisted that law shall proceed from common sense, not from custom, and shall draw its precepts from an eternal code. The principle of the higher law signifies Revolution. No government founded on positive enactments only can stand before it, and it points the way to that system of primitive, universal, and indefeasible rights which the lawyers of the Assembly, descending from Domat, prefixed to their constitution.

Under the edict of Nantes the Protestants were decided royalists; so that, even after the Revocation, Bayle, the apostle of Toleration, retained his loyalty in exile at Rotterdam. His enemy, Jurieu, though intolerant as a divine, was liberal in his politics, and contracted in the neighbourhood of William of Orange the temper of a continental Whig. He taught that sovereignty comes from the people and reverts to the people. The Crown forfeits powers it has made ill use of. The rights of the nation cannot be forfeited. The people alone possess an authority which is legitimate without conditions, and their acts are valid even when they are wrong. The most telling of Jurieu's seditious propositions, preserved in the transparent amber of Bossuet's reply, shared the immortality of a classic, and in time contributed to the doctrine that the democracy is irresponsible and must have its way.

Maultrot, the best ecclesiastical lawyer of the day, published three volumes in 1790 on the power of the people over kings, in which, with accurate research among sources very familiar to him and to nobody else, he explained how the Canon Law approves the principles of 1688 and rejects the modern invention of divine right. His book explains still better the attitude of the clergy in the Revolution, and their brief season of popularity.

The true originator of the opposition in literature was Fénelon. He was neither an innovating reformer nor a discoverer of new truth; but as a singularly independent and most intelligent witness, he was the first who saw through the majestic hypocrisy of the court, and knew that France was on the road to ruin. The revolt of conscience began with him before the glory of the monarchy was clouded over. His views grew from an extraordinary perspicacity and refinement in the estimate of men. He learnt to refer the problem of government, like the conduct of private life, to the mere standard of morals, and extended further than any one the plain but hazardous practice of deciding all things by the exclusive precepts of enlightened virtue. If he did not know all about policy and international science, he could always tell what would be expected of a hypothetically perfect man. Fénelon feels like a citizen of Christian Europe, but he pursues his thoughts apart from his country or his church, and his deepest utterances are in the mouth of pagans. He desired to be alike true to his own beliefs, and gracious towards those who dispute them. He approved neither the deposing power nor the punishment of error, and declared that the highest need of the Church was not victory but liberty. Through his friends, Fleury and Chevreuse, he favoured the recall of the Protestants, and he advised a general toleration. He would have the secular power kept aloof from ecclesiastical concerns, because protection leads to religious servitude and persecution to religious hypocrisy. There were moments when his steps seemed to approach the border of the undiscovered land where Church and State are parted.

He has written that a historian ought to be neutral between other countries and his own, and he expected the same discipline in politicians, as patriotism cannot absolve a man from his duty to mankind. Therefore no war can be just, unless a war to which we are compelled in the sole cause of freedom. Fénelon wished that France should surrender the ill-gotten conquests of which she was so proud, and especially that she should withdraw from Spain. He declared that the Spaniards were degenerate and imbecile, but that nothing could make that right which was contrary to the balance of power and the security of nations. Holland seemed to him the hope of Europe, and he thought the allies justified in excluding the French dynasty from Spain for the same reason that no claim of law could have made it right that Philip II. should occupy England. He hoped that his country would be thoroughly humbled, for he dreaded the effects of success on the temperament of the victorious French. He deemed it only fair that Lewis should be compelled to dethrone his grandson with his own guilty hand.

In the judgment of Fénelon, power is poison; and as kings are nearly always bad, they ought not to govern, but only to execute the law. For it is the mark of barbarians to obey precedent and custom. Civilised society must be regulated by a solid code. Nothing but a constitution can avert arbitrary power. The despotism of Lewis XIV. renders him odious and contemptible, and is the cause of all the evils which the country suffers. If the governing power which rightfully belonged to the nation was restored, it would save itself by its own exertion; but absolute authority irreparably saps its foundations, and is bringing on a revolution by which it will not be moderated, but utterly destroyed. Although Fénelon has no wish to sacrifice either the monarchy or the aristocracy, he betrays sympathy with several tendencies of the movement which he foresaw with so much alarm. He admits the state of nature, and thinks civil society not the primitive condition of man, but a result of the passage from savage life to husbandry. He would transfer the duties of government to local and central assemblies; and he demands entire freedom of trade, and education provided by law, because children belong to the State first and to the family afterwards. He does not resign the hope of making men good by act of parliament, and his belief in public institutions as a means of moulding individual character brings him nearly into touch with a distant future.

He is the Platonic founder of revolutionary thinking. Whilst his real views were little known, he became a popular memory; but some complained that his force was centrifugal, and that a church can no more be preserved by suavity and distinction than a state by liberty and justice. Lewis XVI., we are often told, perished in expiation of the sins of his forefathers. He perished, not because the power he inherited from them had been carried to excess, but because it had been discredited and undermined. One author of this discredit was Fénelon. Until he came, the ablest men, Bossuet and even Bayle, revered the monarchy. Fénelon struck it at the zenith, and treated Lewis XIV. in all his grandeur more severely than the disciples of Voltaire treated Lewis XV. in all his degradation. The season of scorn and shame begins with him. The best of his later contemporaries followed his example, and laid the basis of opposing criticism on motives of religion. They were the men whom Cardinal Dubois describes as dreamers of the same dreams as the chimerical archbishop of Cambray. Their influence fades away before the great change that came over France about the middle of the century.

From that time unbelief so far prevailed that even men who were not professed assailants, as Montesquieu, Condillac, Turgot, were estranged from Christianity. Politically, the consequence was this: men who did not attribute any deep significance to church questions never acquired definite notions on Church and State, never seriously examined under what conditions religion may be established or disestablished, endowed or disendowed, never even knew whether there exists any general solution, or any principle by which problems of that kind are decided. This defect of knowledge became a fact of importance at a turning-point in the Revolution. The theory of the relations between states and churches is bound up with the theory of Toleration, and on that subject the eighteenth century scarcely rose above an intermittent, embarrassed, and unscientific view. For religious liberty is composed of the properties both of religion and of liberty, and one of its factors never became an object of disinterested observation among actual leaders of opinion. They preferred the argument of doubt to the argument of certitude, and sought to defeat intolerance by casting out revelation as they had defeated the persecution of witches by casting out the devil. There remained a flaw in their liberalism, for liberty apart from belief is liberty with a good deal of the substance taken out of it. The problem is less complicated and the solution less radical and less profound. Already, then, there were writers who held somewhat superficially the conviction, which Tocqueville made a corner-stone, that nations that have not the self-governing force of religion within them are unprepared for freedom.

The early notions of reform moved on French lines, striving to utilise the existing form of society, to employ the parliamentary aristocracy, to revive the States-General and the provincial assemblies. But the scheme of standing on the ancient ways, and raising a new France on the substructure of the old, brought out the fact that whatever growth of institutions there once had been had been stunted and stood still. If the mediæval polity had been fitted to prosper, its fruit must be gathered from other countries, where the early notions had been pursued far ahead. The first thing to do was to cultivate the foreign example; and with that what we call the eighteenth century began. The English superiority, proclaimed first by Voltaire, was further demonstrated by Montesquieu. For England had recently created a government which was stronger than the institutions that had stood on antiquity. Founded upon fraud and treason, it had yet established the security of law more firmly than it had ever existed under the system of legitimacy, of prolonged inheritance, and of religious sanction. It flourished on the unaccustomed belief that theological dissensions need not detract from the power of the State, while political dissensions are the very secret of its prosperity. The men of questionable character who accomplished the change and had governed for the better part of sixty years, had successfully maintained public order, in spite of conspiracy and rebellion; they had built up an enormous system of national credit, and had been victorious in continental war. The Jacobite doctrine, which was the basis of European monarchy, had been backed by the arms of France, and had failed to shake the newly planted throne. A great experiment had been crowned by a great discovery. A novelty that defied the wisdom of centuries had made good its footing, and revolution had become a principle of stability more sure than tradition.

Montesquieu undertook to make the disturbing fact avail in political science. He valued it because it reconciled him with monarchy. He had started with the belief that kings are an evil, and not a necessary evil, and that their time was running short. His visit to Walpolean England taught him a plan by which they might be reprieved. He still confessed that a republic is the reign of virtue; and by virtue he meant love of equality and renunciation of self. But he had seen a monarchy that throve by corruption. He said that the distinctive principle of monarchy is not virtue but honour, which he once described as a contrivance to enable men of the world to commit almost every offence with impunity. The praise of England was made less injurious to French patriotism by the famous theory that explains institutions and character by the barometer and the latitude. Montesquieu looked about him, and abroad, but not far ahead. His admirable skill in supplying reason for every positive fact sometimes confounds the cause which produces with the argument that defends. He knows so many pleas for privilege that he almost overlooks the class that has none; and having no friendship for the clergy, he approves their immunities. He thinks that aristocracy alone can preserve monarchies, and makes England more free than any commonwealth. He lays down the great conservative maxim, that success generally depends on knowing the time it will take; and the most purely Whig maxim in his works, that the duty of a citizen is a crime when it obscures the duty of man, is Fénelon's. His liberty is of a Gothic type, and not insatiable. But the motto of his work, *Prolem sine matre creatam*, was intended to signify that the one thing wanting was liberty; and he had views on taxation, equality, and the division of powers that gave him a momentary influence in 1789. His warning that a legislature may be more dangerous than the executive remained unheard. The *Esprit des lois* had lost ground in 1767, during the ascendancy of Rousseau. The mind of the author moved within the conditions of society familiar to him, and he did not heed the coming democracy. He assured Hume that there would be no revolution, because the nobles were without civic courage.

There was more divination in d'Argenson, who was Minister of Foreign Affairs in 1745, and knew politics from the inside. Less acquiescent than his brilliant contemporary, he was perpetually contriving schemes of fundamental change, and is the earliest writer from whom we can extract the system of 1789. Others before him had perceived the impending revolution; but d'Argenson foretold that it would open with the slaughter of priests in the streets of Paris. Thirty-eight years later these words came true at the gate of St. Germain's Abbey. As the supporter of the Pretender he was quite uninfluenced by admiration for England, and imputed, not to the English Deists and Whigs but to the Church and her divisions and intolerance, the unbelieving spirit that threatened both Church and State. It was conventionally understood on the Continent that 1688 had been an uprising of Nonconformists, and a Whig was assumed to be a Presbyterian down to the death of Anne. It was easy to infer that a more violent theological conflict would lead to a more violent convulsion. As early as 1743 his terrible foresight discerns that the State is going to pieces, and its doom was so certain that he began to think of a refuge under other masters. He would have deposed the noble, the priest, and the lawyer, and given their power to the masses. Although the science of politics was in its infancy, he relied on the dawning enlightenment to establish rational liberty, and the equality between classes and religions which is the perfection of politics. The world ought to be governed not by parchment and vested rights, but by plain reason, which proceeds from the complex to the simple, and will sweep away all that interposes between the State and the democracy, giving to each part of the nation the management of its own affairs. He is eager to change everything, except the monarchy which alone can change all else. A deliberative assembly does not rise above the level of its average members. It is neither very foolish nor very wise. All might be well if the king made himself the irresistible instrument of philosophy and justice, and wrought the reform. But his king was Lewis XV. D'Argenson saw so little that was worthy to be preserved that he did not shrink from sweeping judgments and abstract propositions. By his rationalism, and his indifference to the prejudice of custom and the claim of possession; by his maxim that every man may be presumed to understand the things in which his own interest and responsibility are involved; by his zeal for democracy, equality, and simplicity, and his dislike of intermediate authorities, he belongs to a generation later than his own. He heralded events without preparing them, for the best of all he wrote only became known in our time.

Whilst Montesquieu, at the height of his fame as the foremost of living writers, was content to contemplate the past, there was a student in the Paris seminary who taught men to fix hope and endeavour on the future, and led the world at twenty-three. Turgot, when he proclaimed that upward growth and progress is the law of human life, was studying to become a priest. To us, in an age of science, it has become difficult to imagine Christianity without the attribute of development and the faculty of improving society as well as souls. But the idea was acquired slowly. Under the burden of sin, men accustomed themselves to the consciousness of degeneracy; each generation confessed that they were unworthy children of their parents, and awaited with impatience the approaching end. From Lucretius and Seneca to Pascal and Leibniz we encounter a few dispersed and unsupported passages, suggesting advance towards perfection, and the flame that brightens as it moves from hand to hand; but they were without mastery or radiance. Turgot at once made the idea habitual and familiar, and it became a pervading force in thoughtful minds, whilst the new sciences arose to confirm it. He imparted a deeper significance to history, giving it unity of tendency and direction, constancy where there had been motion, and development instead of change. The progress he meant was moral as much as intellectual; and as he professed to think that the rogues of his day would have seemed sanctified models to an earlier century, he made his calculations without counting the wickedness of men. His analysis left unfathomed depths for future explorers, for Lessing and still more for Hegel; but he taught mankind to expect that the future would be unlike the past, that it would be better, and that the experience of ages may instruct and warn, but cannot guide or control. He is eminently a benefactor to historical study; but he forged a weapon charged with power to abolish the product of history and the existing order. By the hypothesis of progress, the new is always gaining on the old; history is the embodiment of imperfection, and escape from history became the watchword of the coming day. Condorcet, the master's pupil, thought that the world might be emancipated by burning its records.

Turgot was too discreet for such an excess, and he looked to history for the demonstration of his law. He had come upon it in his theological studies. He renounced them soon after, saying that he could not wear a mask. When Guizot called Lamennais a malefactor, because he threw off his cassock and became a freethinker, Scherer, whose course had been some way parallel, observed: "He little knows how much it costs." The abrupt transition seems to have been accomplished by Turgot without a struggle. The *Encyclopædia*, which was the largest undertaking since the invention of printing, came out at that time, and Turgot wrote for it. But he broke off, refusing to be connected with a party professedly hostile to revealed religion; and he rejected the declamatory paradoxes of Diderot and Raynal. He found his home among the Physiocrats, of all the groups the one that possessed the most compact body of consistent views, and who already knew most of the accepted doctrines of political economy, although they ended by making way for Adam Smith. They are of supreme importance to us, because they founded political science on the economic science which was coming into existence. Harrington, a century before, had seen that the art of government can be reduced to system; but the French economists precede all men in this, that holding a vast collection of combined and verified truths on matters contiguous to politics and belonging to their domain, they extended it to the whole, and governed the constitution by the same fixed principles that governed the purse. They said: A man's most sacred property is his labour. It is anterior even to the right of property, for it is the possession of those who own nothing else. Therefore he must be free to make the best use of it he can. The interference of one man with another, of society with its members, of the state with the subject, must be brought down to the lowest dimension. Power intervenes only to restrict intervention, to guard the individual from oppression, that is from regulation in an interest not his own. Free labour and its derivative free trade are the first conditions of legitimate government. Let things fall into their natural order, let society govern itself, and the sovereign function of the State will be to protect nature in the execution of her own law. Government must not be arbitrary, but it must be powerful enough to repress arbitrary action in others. If the supreme power is needlessly limited, the secondary powers will run riot and oppress. Its supremacy will bear no check. The problem is to enlighten the ruler, not to restrain him; and one man is more easily enlightened than many. Government by opposition, by balance and control, is contrary to principle; whereas absolutism might be requisite to the attainment of their higher purpose. Nothing less than concentrated power could overcome the obstacles to such beneficent reforms as they meditated. Men who sought only the general good must wound every distinct and separate interest of class, and would be mad to break up the only force that they could count upon, and thus to throw away the means of preventing the evils that must follow if things were left to the working of opinion and the feeling of masses. They had no love for absolute power in itself, but they computed that, if they had the use of it for five years, France would be free. They distinguished an arbitrary monarch and the irresistible but impersonal state.

    It was the era of repentant monarchy. Kings had become the first of public servants, executing, for the good of the people, what the people were unable to do for themselves; and there was a reforming movement on foot which led to many instances of prosperous and intelligent administration. To men who knew what unutterable suffering and wrong was inflicted by bad laws, and who lived in terror of the uneducated and inorganic masses, the idea of reform from above seemed preferable to parliamentary government managed by Newcastle and North, in the interest of the British landlord. The economists are outwardly and avowedly less liberal than Montesquieu, because they are incomparably more impressed by the evils of the time, and the need of immense and fundamental changes. They prepared to undo the work of absolutism by the hand of absolutism. They were not its opponents, but its advisers, and hoped to convert it by their advice. The indispensable liberties are those which constitute the wealth of nations; the rest will follow. The disease had lasted too long for the sufferer to heal himself: the relief must come from the author of his sufferings. The power that had done the wrong was still efficient to undo the wrong. Transformation, infinitely more difficult in itself than preservation, was not more formidable to the economists because it consisted mainly in revoking the godless work of a darker age. They deemed it their mission not to devise new laws, for that is a task which God has not committed to man, but only to declare the inherent laws of the existence of society and enable them to prevail.

The defects of the social and political organisation were as distinctly pointed out by the economists as by the electors of the National Assembly, twenty years later, and in nearly all things they proposed the remedy. But they were persuaded that the only thing to regenerate France was a convulsion which the national character would make a dreadful one. They desired a large scheme of popular education, because commands take no root in soil that is not prepared. Political truths can be made so evident that the opinion of an instructed public will be invincible, and will banish the abuse of power. To resist oppression is to make a league with heaven, and all things are oppressive that resist the natural order of freedom. For society secures rights; it neither bestows nor restricts them. They are the direct consequence of duties. As truth can only convince by the exposure of errors and the defeat of objections, liberty is the essential guard of truth. Society is founded, not on the will of man, but on the nature of man and the will of God; and conformity to the divinely appointed order is followed by inevitable reward. Relief of those who suffer is the duty of all men, and the affair of all.

Such was the spirit of that remarkable group of men, especially of Mercier de la Rivière, of whom Diderot said that he alone possessed the true and everlasting secret of the security and the happiness of empires. Turgot indeed had failed in office; but his reputation was not diminished, and the power of his name exceeded all others at the outbreak of the Revolution. His policy of employing the Crown to reform the State was at once rejected in favour of other counsels; but his influence may be traced in many acts of the Assembly, and on two very memorable occasions it was not auspicious. It was a central dogma of the party that land is the true source of wealth, or, as Asgill said, that man deals in nothing but earth. When a great part of France became national property, men were the more easily persuaded that land can serve as the basis of public credit and of unlimited assignats. According to a weighty opinion which we shall have to consider before long, the parting of the ways in the Revolution was on the day when, rejecting the example both of England and America, the French resolved to institute a single undivided legislature. It was the Pennsylvanian model and Voltaire had pronounced Pennsylvania the best government in the world. Franklin gave the sanction of an oracle to the constitution of his state, and Turgot was its vehement protagonist in Europe.

A king ruling over a level democracy, and a democracy ruling itself through the agency of a king, were long contending notions in the first Assembly. One was monarchy according to Turgot, the other was monarchy adapted to Rousseau; and the latter, for a time, prevailed. Rousseau was the citizen of a small republic, consisting of a single town, and he professed to have applied its example to the government of the world. It was Geneva, not as he saw it, but as he extracted its essential principle, and as it has since become, Geneva illustrated by the Forest Cantons and the Landesgemeinde more than by its own charters. The idea was that the grown men met in the market-place, like the peasants of Glarus under their trees, to manage their affairs, making and unmaking officials, conferring and revoking powers. They were equal, because every man had exactly the same right to defend his interest by the guarantee of his vote. The welfare of all was safe in the hands of all, for they had not the separate interests that are bred by the egotism of wealth, nor the exclusive views that come from a distorted education. All being equal in power and similar in purpose, there can be no just cause why some should move apart and break into minorities. There is an implied contract that no part shall ever be preferred to the whole, and minorities shall always obey. Clever men are not wanted for the making of laws, because clever men and their laws are at the root of all mischief. Nature is a better guide than civilisation, because nature comes from God, and His works are good; culture from man, whose works are bad in proportion as he is remoter from natural innocence, as his desires increase upon him, as he seeks more refined pleasures, and stores up more superfluity. It promotes inequality, selfishness, and the ruin of public spirit.

By plausible and easy stages the social ideas latent in parts of Switzerland produced the theory that men come innocent from the hands of the Creator, that they are originally equal, that progress from equality to civilisation is the passage from virtue to vice and from freedom to tyranny, that the people are sovereign, and govern by powers given and taken away; that an individual or a class may be mistaken and may desert the common cause and the general interest, but the people, necessarily sincere, and true, and incorrupt, cannot go wrong; that there is a right of resistance to all governments that are fallible, because they are partial, but none against government of the people by the people, because it has no master and no judge, and decides in the last instance and alone; that insurrection is the law of all unpopular societies founded on a false principle and a broken contract, and submission that of the only legitimate societies, based on the popular will; that there is no privilege against the law of nature, and no right against the power of all. By this chain of reasoning, with little infusion of other ingredients, Rousseau applied the sequence of the ideas of pure democracy to the government of nations.

Now the most glaring and familiar fact in history shows that the direct self-government of a town cannot be extended over an empire. It is a plan that scarcely reaches beyond the next parish. Either one district will be governed by another, or both by somebody else chosen for the purpose. Either plan contradicts first principles. Subjection is the direct negation of democracy; representation is the indirect. So that an Englishman underwent bondage to parliament as much as Lausanne to Berne or as America to England if it had submitted to taxation, and by law recovered his liberty but once in seven years. Consequently Rousseau, still faithful to Swiss precedent as well as to the logic of his own theory, was a federalist. In Switzerland, when one half of a canton disagrees with the other, or the country with the town, it is deemed natural that they should break into two, that the general will may not oppress minorities. This multiplication of self-governing communities was admitted by Rousseau as a preservative of unanimity on one hand, and of liberty on the other. Helvétius came to his support with the idea that men are not only equal by nature but alike, and that society is the cause of variation; from which it would follow that everything may be done by laws and by education.

Rousseau is the author of the strongest political theory that had appeared amongst men. We cannot say that he reasons well, but he knew how to make his argument seem convincing, satisfying, inevitable, and he wrote with an eloquence and a fervour that had never been seen in prose, even in Bolingbroke or Milton. His books gave the first signal of a universal subversion, and were as fatal to the Republic as to the Monarchy. Although he lives by the social contract and the law of resistance, and owes his influence to what was extreme and systematic, his later writings are loaded with sound political wisdom. He owes nothing to the novelty or the originality of his thoughts. Taken jointly or severally, they are old friends, and you will find them in the school of Wolf that just preceded, in the dogmatists of the Great Rebellion and the Jesuit casuists who were dear to Algernon Sidney, in their Protestant opponents, Duplessis Mornay, and the Scots who had heard the last of our schoolmen, Major of St. Andrews, renew the speculations of the time of schism, which decomposed and dissected the Church and rebuilt it on a model very propitious to political revolution, and even in the early interpreters of the Aristotelian Politics which appeared just at the era of the first parliament.

Rousseau's most advanced point was the doctrine that the people are infallible. Jurieu had taught that they can do no wrong: Rousseau added that they are positively in the right. The idea, like most others, was not new, and goes back to the Middle Ages. When the question arose what security there is for the preservation of traditional truth if the episcopate was divided and the papacy vacant, it was answered that the faith would be safely retained by the masses. The maxim that the voice of the people is the voice of God is as old as Alcuin; it was renewed by some of the greatest writers anterior to democracy, by Hooker and Bossuet, and it was employed in our day by Newman to prop his theory of development. Rousseau applied it to the State.

The sovereignty of public opinion was just then coming in through the rise of national debts and the increasing importance of the public creditor. It meant more than the noble savage and the blameless South Sea islander, and distinguished the instinct that guides large masses of men from the calculating wisdom of the few. It was destined to prove the most serious of all obstacles to representative government. Equality of power readily suggests equality of property; but the movement of Socialism began earlier, and was not assisted by Rousseau. There were solemn theorists, such as Mably and Morelly, who were sometimes quoted in the Revolution, but the change in the distribution of property was independent of them.

A more effective influence was imported from Italy; for the Italians, through Vico, Giannone, Genovesi, had an eighteenth century of their own. Sardinia preceded France in solving the problem of feudalism. Arthur Young affirms that the measures of the Grand Duke Leopold had, in ten years, doubled the produce of Tuscany; at Milan, Count Firmian was accounted one of the best administrators in Europe. It was a Milanese, Beccaria, who, by his reform of criminal law, became a leader of French opinion. Continental jurisprudence had long been overshadowed by two ideas: that torture is the surest method of discovering truth, and that punishment deters not by its justice, its celerity, or its certainty, but in proportion to its severity. Even in the eighteenth century the penal system of Maria Theresa and Joseph II. was barbarous. Therefore no attack was more surely aimed at the heart of established usage than that which dealt with courts of justice. It forced men to conclude that authority was odiously stupid and still more odiously ferocious, that existing governments were accursed, that the guardians and ministers of law, divine and human, were more guilty than their culprits. The past was branded as the reign of infernal powers, and charged with long arrears of unpunished wrong. As there was no sanctity left in law, there was no mercy for its merciless defenders; and if they fell into avenging hands, their doom would not exceed their desert. Men afterwards conspicuous by their violence, Brissot and Marat, were engaged in this campaign of humanity, which raised a demand for authorities that were not vitiated by the accumulation of infamy, for new laws, new powers, a new dynasty.

As religion was associated with cruelty, it is at this point that the movement of new Ideas became a crusade against Christianity. A book by the Curé Meslier, partially known at that time, but first printed by Strauss in 1864, is the clarion of vindictive unbelief; and another abbé, Raynal, hoped that the clergy would be crushed beneath the ruins of their altars.

Thus the movement which began, in Fénelon's time, with warnings and remonstrance and the zealous endeavour to preserve, which produced one great scheme of change by the Crown and another at the expense of the Crown, ended in the wild cry for vengeance and a passionate appeal to fire and sword. So many lines of thought converging on destruction explain the agreement that existed when the States-General began, and the explosion that followed the reforms of '89, and the ruins of '93. No conflict can be more irreconcilable than that between a constitution and an enlightened absolutism, between abrogation of old laws and multiplication of new, between representation and direct democracy, the people controlling and the people governing, kings by contract and kings by mandate.

Yet all these fractions of opinion were called Liberal: Montesquieu, because he was an intelligent Tory; Voltaire, because he attacked the clergy; Turgot, as a reformer; Rousseau, as a democrat; Diderot, as a freethinker. The one thing common to them all is the disregard for liberty.

II
THE INFLUENCE OF AMERICA

The several structures of political thought that arose in France, and clashed in the process of revolution, were not directly responsible for the outbreak. The doctrines hung like a cloud upon the heights, and at critical moments in the reign of Lewis XV. men felt that a catastrophe was impending. It befell when there was less provocation, under his successor; and the spark that changed thought into action was supplied by the Declaration of American Independence. It was the system of an international extra-territorial universal Whig, far transcending the English model by its simplicity and rigour. It surpassed in force all the speculation of Paris and Geneva, for it had undergone the test of experiment, and its triumph was the most memorable thing that had been seen by men.

The expectation that the American colonies would separate was an old one. A century before, Harrington had written: "They are yet babes, that cannot live without sucking the breasts of their mother-cities; but such as I mistake if, when they come of age, they do not wean themselves; which causes me to wonder at princes that like to be exhausted in that way." When, in 1759, the elder Mirabeau announced it, he meant that the conquest of Canada involved the loss of America, as the colonists would cling to England as long as the French were behind them, and no longer. He came very near to the truth, for the war in Canada gave the signal. The English colonies had meditated the annexation of the French, and they resented that the king's government undertook the expedition, to deprive them of the opportunity for united action. Fifty years later President Adams said that the treatment of American officers by the British made his blood boil.

The agitation began in 1761, and by the innovating ideas which it flung abroad it is as important as the Declaration itself, or the great constitutional debate. The colonies were more advanced than Great Britain in the way of free institutions, and existed only that they might escape the vices of the mother country. They had no remnants of feudalism to cherish or resist. They possessed written constitutions, some of them remarkably original, fit roots of an immense development. George III. thought it strange that he should be the sovereign of a democracy like Rhode Island, where all power reverted annually to the people, and the authorities had to be elected anew. Connecticut received from the Stuarts so liberal a charter, and worked out so finished a scheme of local self-government, that it served as a basis for the federal constitution. The Quakers had a plan founded on equality of power, without oppression, or privilege, or intolerance, or slavery. They declared that their holy experiment would not have been worth attempting if it did not offer some very real advantage over England. It was to enjoy freedom, liberty of conscience, and the right to tax themselves, that they went into the desert. There were points on which these men anticipated the doctrines of a more unrestrained democracy, for they established their government not on conventions, but on divine right, and they claimed to be infallible. A Connecticut preacher said in 1638: "The choice of public magistrates belongs unto the people, by God's own allowance. They who have the power to appoint officers and magistrates, it is in their power, also, to set the bounds and limitations of the power and place unto which they call them." The following words, written in 1736, appear in the works of Franklin: "The judgment of a whole people, especially of a free people, is looked upon to be infallible. And this is universally true, while they remain in their proper sphere, unbiassed by faction, undeluded by the tricks of designing men. A body of people thus circumstanced cannot be supposed to judge amiss on any essential points; for if they decide in favour of themselves, which is extremely natural, their decision is just, inasmuch as whatever contributes to their benefit is a general benefit, and advances the real public good." A commentator adds that this notion of the infallible perception by the people of their true interest, and their unerring pursuit of it, was very prevalent in the provinces, and for a time in the States after the establishment of American independence.

In spite of their democratic spirit, these communities consented to have their trade regulated and restricted, to their own detriment and the advantage of English merchants. They had protested, but they had ended by yielding. Now Adam Smith says that to prohibit a great people from making all they can of every part of their own produce, or from employing their stock and industry in the way that they judge most advantageous for themselves, is a manifest violation of the most sacred rights of mankind. There was a latent sense of injury which broke out when, in addition to interference with the freedom of trade, England exercised the right of taxation. An American lately wrote: "The real foundation of the discontent which led to the Revolution was the effort of Great Britain, beginning in 1750, to prevent diversity of occupation, to attack the growth of manufactures and the mechanic arts, and the final cause before the attempt to tax without representation was the effort to enforce the navigation laws." When England argued that the hardship of regulation might be greater than the hardship of taxation, and that those who submitted to the one submitted, in principle, to the other, Franklin replied that the Americans had not taken that view, but that, when it was put before them, they would be willing to reject both one and the other. He knew, however, that the ground taken up by his countrymen was too narrow. He wrote to the French economist, Morellet: "Nothing can be better expressed than your sentiments are on this point, where you prefer liberty of trading, cultivating, manufacturing, etc., even to civil liberty, this being affected but rarely, the other every hour."

These early authors of American independence were generally enthusiasts for the British Constitution, and preceded Burke in the tendency to canonise it, and to magnify it as an ideal exemplar for nations. John Adams said, in 1766: "Here lies the difference between the British Constitution and other forms of government, namely, that liberty is its end, its use, its designation, drift and scope, as much as grinding corn is the use of a mill." Another celebrated Bostonian identified the Constitution with the law of Nature, as Montesquieu called the Civil Law, written Reason. He said: "It is the glory of the British prince and the happiness of all his subjects, that their constitution hath its foundation in the immutable laws of Nature; and as the supreme legislative, as well as the supreme executive, derives its authority from that constitution, it should seem that no laws can be made or executed that are repugnant to any essential law in Nature." The writer of these words, James Otis, is the founder of the revolutionary doctrine. Describing one of his pamphlets, the second President says: "Look over the declaration of rights and wrongs issued by Congress in 1774; look into the declaration of independence in 1776; look into the writings of Dr. Price and Dr. Priestley; look into all the French constitutions of government; and, to cap the climax, look into Mr. Thomas Paine's *Common Sense, Crisis,* and *Rights of Man*. What can you find that is not to be found in solid substance in this 'Vindication of the House of Representatives'?" When these men found that the appeal to the law and to the constitution did not avail them, that the king, by bribing the people's representatives with the people's money, was able to enforce his will, they sought a higher tribunal, and turned from the law of England to the law of Nature, and from the king of England to the King of kings. Otis, in 1762, 1764 and 1765, says: "Most governments are, in fact, arbitrary, and consequently the curse and scandal of human nature; yet none are of right arbitrary. By the laws of God and nature, government must not raise taxes on the property of the people without the consent of the people or their deputies. There can be no prescription old enough to supersede the law of Nature and the grant of God Almighty, who has given all men a right to be free. If a man has but little property to protect and defend, yet his life and liberty are things of some importance." About the same time Gadsden wrote: "A confirmation of our essential and common rights as Englishmen may be pleaded from charters clearly enough; but any further dependence on them may be fatal. We should stand upon the broad common ground of those natural rights that we all feel and know as men and as descendants of Englishmen."

The primitive fathers of the United States began by preferring abstract moral principle to the letter of the law and the spirit of the Constitution. But they went farther. Not only was their grievance difficult to substantiate at law, but it was trivial in extent. The claim of England was not evidently disproved, and even if it was unjust, the injustice practically was not hard to bear. The suffering that would be caused by submission was immeasurably less than the suffering that must follow resistance, and it was more uncertain and remote. The utilitarian argument was loud in favour of obedience and loyalty. But if interest was on one side, there was a manifest principle on the other—a principle so sacred and so clear as imperatively to demand the sacrifice of men's lives, of their families and their fortune. They resolved to give up everything, not to escape from actual oppression, but to honour a precept of unwritten law. That was the transatlantic discovery in the theory of political duty, the light that came over the ocean. It represented liberty not as a comparative release from tyranny, but as a thing so divine that the existence of society must be staked to prevent even the least constructive infraction of its sovereign right. "A free people," said Dickinson, "can never be too quick in observing nor too firm in opposing the beginnings of alteration either in form or reality, respecting institutions formed for their security. The first kind of alteration leads to the last. As violations of the rights of the governed are commonly not only specious, but small at the beginning, they spread over the multitude in such a manner as to touch individuals but slightly. Every free state should incessantly watch, and instantly take alarm at any addition being made to the power exercised over them." Who are a free people? Not those over whom government is reasonably and equitably exercised; but those who live under a government so constitutionally checked and controlled that proper provision is made against its being otherwise exercised. The contest was plainly a contest of principle, and was conducted entirely on principle by both parties. "The amount of taxes proposed to be raised," said Marshall, the greatest of constitutional lawyers, "was too inconsiderable to interest the people of either country." I will add the words of Daniel Webster, the great expounder of the Constitution, who is the most eloquent of the Americans, and stands, in politics, next to Burke: "The Parliament of Great Britain asserted a right to tax the Colonies in all cases whatsoever; and it was precisely on this question that they made the Revolution turn. The amount of taxation was trifling, but the claim itself was inconsistent with liberty, and that was in their eyes enough. It was against the recital of an act of Parliament, rather than against any suffering under its enactment, that they took up arms. They went to war against a preamble. They fought seven years against a declaration. They saw in the claim of the British Parliament a seminal principle of mischief, the germ of unjust power."

The object of these men was liberty, not independence. Their feeling was expressed by Jay in his address to the people of Great Britain: "Permit us to be as free as yourselves, and we shall ever esteem a union with you to be our greatest glory and our greatest happiness." Before 1775 there was no question of separation. During all the Revolution Adams declared that he would have given everything to restore things as before with security; and both Jefferson and Madison admitted in the presence of the English minister that a few seats in both Houses would have set at rest the whole question.

In their appeal to the higher law the Americans professed the purest Whiggism, and they claimed that their resistance to the House of Commons and the jurisprudence of Westminster only carried forward the eternal conflict between Whig and Tory. By their closer analysis, and their fearlessness of logical consequences, they transformed the doctrine and modified the party. The uprooted Whig, detached from his parchments and precedents, his leading families and historic conditions, exhibited new qualities; and the era of compromise made way for an era of principle. Whilst French diplomacy traced the long hand of the English opposition in the tea riots at Boston, Chatham and Camden were feeling the influence of Dickinson and Otis, without recognising the difference. It appears in a passage of one of Chatham's speeches, in 1775: "This universal opposition to your arbitrary system of taxation might have been foreseen. It was obvious from the nature of things, and from the nature of man, and, above all, from the confirmed habits of thinking, from the spirit of Whiggism flourishing in America. The spirit which now pervades America is the same which formerly opposed loans, benevolences, and ship-money in this country, is the same spirit which roused all England to action at the Revolution, and which established at a remote era your liberties, on the basis of that grand fundamental maxim of the Constitution, that no subject of England shall be taxed but by his own consent. To maintain this principle is the common cause of the Whigs on the other side of the Atlantic, and on this. It is the alliance of God and Nature, immutable, eternal, fixed as the firmament of heaven. Resistance to your acts was necessary as it was just; and your vain declarations of the omnipotence of parliament, and your imperious doctrines of the necessity of submission will be found equally impotent to convince or enslave your fellow-subjects in America."

The most significant instance of the action of America on Europe is Edmund Burke. We think of him as a man who, in early life, rejected all generalities and abstract propositions, and who became the most strenuous and violent of conservatives. But there is an interval when, as the quarrel with the Colonies went on, Burke was as revolutionary as Washington. The inconsistency is not as flagrant as it seems. He had been brought forward by the party of measured propriety and imperative moderation, of compromise and unfinished thought, who claimed the right of taxing, but refused to employ it. When he urged the differences in every situation and every problem, and shrank from the common denominator and the underlying principle, he fell into step with his friends. As an Irishman, who had married into an Irish Catholic family, it was desirable that he should adopt no theories in America which would unsettle Ireland. He had learnt to teach government by party as an almost sacred dogma, and party forbids revolt as a breach of the laws of the game. His scruples and his protests, and his defiance of theory, were the policy and the precaution of a man conscious of restraints, and not entirely free in the exertion of powers that lifted him far above his tamer surroundings. As the strife sharpened and the Americans made way, Burke was carried along, and developed views which he never utterly abandoned, but which are difficult to reconcile with much that he wrote when the Revolution had spread to France.

In his address to the Colonists he says: "We do not know how to qualify millions of our countrymen, contending with one heart for an admission to privileges which we have ever thought our own happiness and honour, by odious and unworthy names. On the contrary, we highly revere the principles on which you act. We had much rather see you totally independent of this crown and kingdom, than joined to it by so unnatural a conjunction as that of freedom and servitude. We view the establishment of the English Colonies on principles of liberty, as that which is to render this kingdom venerable to future ages. In comparison of this, we regard all the victories and conquests of our warlike ancestors, or of our own times, as barbarous, vulgar distinctions, in which many nations, whom we look upon with little respect or value, have equalled, if not far exceeded us. Those who have and who hold to that foundation of common liberty, whether on this or on your side of the ocean, we consider as the true and the only true Englishmen. Those who depart from it, whether there or here, are attainted, corrupted in blood, and wholly fallen from their original rank and value. They are the real rebels to the fair constitution and just supremacy of England. A long course of war with the administration of this country may be but a prelude to a series of wars and contentions among yourselves, to end at length (as such scenes have too often ended) in a species of humiliating repose, which nothing but the preceding calamities would reconcile to the dispirited few who survived them. We allow that even this evil is worth the risk to men of honour when rational liberty is at stake, as in the present case we confess and lament that it is."

At other times he spoke as follows:—"Nothing less than a convulsion that will shake the globe to its centre can ever restore the European nations to that liberty by which they were once so much distinguished. The Western world was the seat of freedom until another, more Western, was discovered; and that other will probably be its asylum when it is hunted down in every other part. Happy it is that the worst of times may have one refuge still left for humanity. If the Irish resisted King William, they resisted him on the very same principle that the English and Scotch resisted King James. The Irish Catholics must have been the very worst and the most truly unnatural of rebels, if they had not supported a prince whom they had seen attacked, not for any designs against their religion or their liberties, but for an extreme partiality for their sect. Princes otherwise meritorious have violated the liberties of the people, and have been lawfully deposed for such violation. I know no human being exempt from the law. I consider Parliament as the proper judge of kings, and it is necessary that they should be amenable to it. There is no such thing as governing the whole body of the people contrary to their inclination. Whenever they have a feeling they commonly are in the right. Christ appeared in sympathy with the lowest of the people, and thereby made it a firm and ruling principle that their welfare was the object of all government.

"In all forms of government the people is the true legislator. The remote and efficient cause is the consent of the people, either actual or implied, and such consent is absolutely essential to its validity. Whiggism did not consist in the support of the power of Parliament or of any other power, but of the rights of the people. If Parliament should become an instrument in invading them, it was no better in any respect, and much worse in some, than any other instrument of arbitrary power. They who call upon you to belong wholly to the people are those who wish you to belong to your proper home, to the sphere of your duty, to the post of your honour. Let the Commons in Parliament assembled be one and the same thing with the Commons at large. I see no other way for the preservation of a decent attention to public interest in the representatives, but the interposition of the body of the people itself, whenever, it shall appear by some flagrant and notorious act, by some capital innovation, that those representatives are going to overleap the fences of the law and to introduce an arbitrary power. This interposition is a most unpleasant remedy; but if it be a legal remedy, it is intended on some occasion to be used—to be used then only when it is evident that nothing else can hold the Constitution to its true principles. It is not in Parliament alone that the remedy for parliamentary disorders can be completed; hardly, indeed, can it begin there. A popular origin cannot therefore be the characteristic distinction of a popular representative. This belongs equally to all parts of government, and in all forms. The virtue, spirit, and essence of a House of Commons consists in its being the express image of the feelings of the nation. It was not instituted to be a control upon the people. It was designed as a control for the people. Privilege of the crown and privilege of Parliament are only privilege so long as they are exercised for the benefit of the people. The voice of the people is a voice that is to be heard, and not the votes and resolutions of the House of Commons. He would preserve thoroughly every privilege of the people, because it is a privilege known and written in the law of the land; and he would support it, not against the crown or the aristocratic party only, but against the representatives of the people themselves. This was not a government of balances. It would be a strange thing if two hundred peers should have it in their power to defeat by their negative what had been done by the people of England. I have taken my part in political connections and political quarrels for the purpose of advancing justice and the dominion of reason, and I hope I shall never prefer the means, or any feelings growing out of the use of those means, to the great and substantial end itself. Legislators can do what lawyers can not, for they have no other rules to bind them but the great principles of reason and equity and the general sense of mankind. All human laws are, properly speaking, only declaratory; they may alter the mode and application, but have no power over the substance, of original justice. A conservation and secure enjoyment of our natural rights is the great and ultimate purpose of civil society.

"The great inlet by which a colour for oppression has entered into the world is by one man's pretending to determine concerning the happiness of another. I would give a full civil protection, in which I include an immunity from all disturbance of their public religious worship, and a power of teaching in schools as well as temples, to Jews, Mahometans, and even Pagans. The Christian religion itself arose without establishment, it arose even without toleration, and whilst its own principles were not tolerated, it conquered all the powers of darkness, it conquered all the powers of the world. The moment it began to depart from these principles, it converted the establishment into tyranny, it subverted its foundation from that very hour. It is the power of government to prevent much evil; it can do very little positive good in this, or perhaps in anything else. It is not only so of the State and statesman, but of all the classes and descriptions of the rich: they are the pensioners of the poor, and are maintained by their superfluity. They are under an absolute, hereditary, and indefeasible dependence on those who labour and are miscalled the poor. That class of dependent pensioners called the rich is so extremely small, that if all their throats were cut, and a distribution made of all they consume in a year, it would not give a bit of bread and cheese for one night's supper to those who labour, and who in reality feed both the pensioners and themselves. It is not in breaking the laws of commerce, which are the laws of nature and consequently the laws of God, that we are to place our hope of softening the divine displeasure. It is the law of nature, which is the law of God."

I cannot resist the inference from these passages that Burke, after 1770, underwent other influences than those of his reputed masters, the Whigs of 1688. And if we find that strain of unwonted thought in a man who afterwards gilded the old order of things and wavered as to toleration and the slave trade, we may expect that the same causes would operate in France.

When the *Letters of a Pennsylvanian Farmer* became known in Europe, Diderot said that it was madness to allow Frenchmen to read such things, as they could not do it without becoming intoxicated and changed into different men. But France was impressed by the event more than by the literature that accompanied it. America had made herself independent under less provocation than had ever been a motive of revolt, and the French Government had acknowledged that her cause was righteous and had gone to war for it. If the king was right in America, he was utterly wrong at home, and if the Americans acted rightly, the argument was stronger, the cause was a hundredfold better, in France itself. All that justified their independence condemned the Government of their French allies. By the principle that taxation without representation is robbery, there was no authority so illegitimate as that of Lewis XVI. The force of that demonstration was irresistible, and it produced its effect where the example of England failed. The English doctrine was repelled at the very earliest stage of the Revolution, and the American was adopted. What the French took from the Americans was their theory of revolution, not their theory of government—their cutting, not their sewing. Many French nobles served in the war, and came home republicans and even democrats by conviction. It was America that converted the aristocracy to the reforming policy, and gave leaders to the Revolution. "The American Revolution," says Washington, "or the peculiar light of the age, seems to have opened the eyes of almost every nation in Europe, and a spirit of equal liberty appears fast to be gaining ground everywhere." When the French officers were leaving, Cooper, of Boston, addressed them in the language of warning: "Do not let your hopes be inflamed by our triumphs on this virgin soil. You will carry our sentiments with you, but if you try to plant them in a country that has been corrupt for centuries, you will encounter obstacles more formidable than ours. Our liberty has been won with blood; you will have to shed it in torrents before liberty can take root in the old world." Adams, after he had been President of the United States, bitterly regretted the Revolution which made them independent, because it had given the example to the French; although he also believed that they had not a single principle in common.

Nothing, on the contrary, is more certain than that American principles profoundly influenced France, and determined the course of the Revolution. It is from America that Lafayette derived the saying that created a commotion at the time, that resistance is the most sacred of duties. There also was the theory that political power comes from those over whom it is exercised, and depends upon their will; that every authority not so constituted is illegitimate and precarious; that the past is more a warning than an example; that the earth belongs to those who are upon it, not to those who are underneath. These are characteristics common to both Revolutions.

At one time also the French adopted and acclaimed the American notion that the end of government is liberty, not happiness, or prosperity, or power, or the preservation of an historic inheritance, or the adaptation of national law to national character, or the progress of enlightenment and the promotion of virtue; that the private individual should not feel the pressure of public authority, and should direct his life by the influences that are within him, not around him.

And there was another political doctrine which the Americans transmitted to the French. In old colonial days the executive and the judicial powers were derived from a foreign source, and the common purpose was to diminish them. The assemblies were popular in origin and character, and everything that added to their power seemed to add security to rights. James Wilson, one of the authors and commentators of the constitution, informs us that "at the Revolution the same fond predilection, and the same jealous dislike, existed and prevailed. The executive, and the judicial as well as the legislative authority, was now the child of the people, but to the two former the people behaved like stepmothers. The legislature was still discriminated by excessive partiality." This preference, historic but irrational, led up naturally to a single chamber. The people of America and their delegates in Congress were of opinion that a single Assembly was every way adequate to the management of their federal concerns, and when the Senate was invented, Franklin strongly objected. "As to the two chambers," he wrote, "I am of your opinion that one alone would be better; but, my dear friend, nothing in human affairs and schemes is perfect, and perhaps this is the case of our opinions."

Alexander Hamilton was the ablest as well as the most conservative of the American statesmen. He longed for monarchy, and he desired to establish a national government and to annihilate state rights. The American spirit, as it penetrated France, cannot well be described better than it was by him: "I consider civil liberty, in a genuine, unadulterated sense, as the greatest of terrestrial blessings. I am convinced that the whole human race is entitled to it, and that it can be wrested from no part of them without the blackest and most aggravated guilt. The sacred rights of mankind are not to be rummaged for among old parchments or musty records. They are written, as with a sunbeam, in the whole volume of human nature, by the hand of the Divinity itself, and can never be erased or obscured by mortal power."

But when we speak in the gross of the American Revolution we combine different and discordant things. From the first agitation in 1761 to the Declaration of Independence, and then to the end of the war in 1782, the Americans were aggressive, violent in their language, fond of abstractions, prolific of doctrines universally applicable and universally destructive. It is the ideas of those earlier days that roused the attention of France, and were imported by Lafayette, Noailles, Lameth, and the leaders of the future revolution who had beheld the lowering of the British flag at Yorktown. The America of their experience was the America of James Otis, of Jefferson, of *The Rights of Man*.

A change followed in 1787, when the Convention drew up the Constitution. It was a period of construction, and every effort was made, every scheme was invented, to curb the inevitable democracy. The members of that assembly were, on the whole, eminently cautious and sensible men. They were not men of extraordinary parts, and the genius of Hamilton failed absolutely to impress them. Some of their most memorable contrivances proceeded from no design, but were merely half measures and mutual concessions. Seward has pointed out this distinction between the revolutionary epoch and the constituent epoch that succeeded: "The rights asserted by our forefathers were not peculiar to themselves. They were the common rights or mankind. The basis of the Constitution was laid broader by far than the superstructure which the conflicting interests and prejudices of the day suffered to be erected. The Constitution and laws of the Federal Government did not practically extend those principles throughout the new system of government; but they were plainly promulgated in the Declaration of Independence."

Now, although France was deeply touched by the American Revolution, it was not affected by the American Constitution. It underwent the disturbing influence, not the conservative.

The Constitution, framed in the summer of 1787, came into operation in March 1789, and nobody knew how it worked, when the crisis came in France. The debates, which explain every intention and combination, remained long hidden from the world. Moreover, the Constitution has become something more than the original printed paper. Besides amendments, it has been interpreted by the courts, modified by opinion, developed in some directions, and tacitly altered in others. Some of its most valued provisions have been acquired in this way, and were not yet visible when the French so greatly needed the guiding lessons of other men's experience. Some of the restrictions on the governing power were not fully established at first.

The most important of these is the action of the Supreme Court in annulling unconstitutional laws. The Duke of Wellington said to Bunsen that by this institution alone the United States made up for all the defects of their government. Since Chief Justice Marshall, the judiciary undoubtedly obtained immense authority, which Jefferson, and others besides, believed to be unconstitutional; for the Constitution itself gives no such power. The idea had grown up in the States, chiefly, I think, in Virginia. At Richmond, in 1782, Judge Wythe said: "Tyranny has been sapped, the departments kept within their own spheres, the citizens protected, and general liberty promoted. But this beneficial result attains to higher perfection when, those who hold the purse and the sword differing as to the powers which each may exercise, the tribunals, who hold neither, are called upon to declare the law impartially between them, if the whole legislature—an event to be deprecated—should attempt to overleap the boundaries prescribed to them by the people, I, in administering the justice of the country, will meet the united powers at my seat in this tribunal, and, pointing to the Constitution, will say to them: 'Here is the limit of your authority; hither shall you go, but no further.'" The Virginian legislature gave way, and repealed the act.

After the Federal Constitution was drawn up, Hamilton, in the seventy-eighth number of the *Federalist*, argued that the power belonged to the judiciary; but it was not constitutionally recognised until 1801. "This," said Madison, "makes the judiciary department paramount, in fact, to the legislature, which was never intended, and can never be proper. In a government whose vital principle is responsibility, it never will be allowed that the legislative and executive departments should be completely subjected to the judiciary, in which that characteristic feature is so faintly seen." Wilson, on the other hand, justified the practice on the principle of the higher law: "Parliament may, unquestionably, be controlled by natural or revealed law, proceeding from divine authority. Is not this superior authority binding upon the courts of justice? When the courts of justice obey the superior authority, it cannot be said with propriety that they control the inferior one; they only declare, as it is their duty to declare, that this inferior one is controlled by the other, which is superior. They do not repeal an act of

Parliament; they pronounce it void, because contrary to an overruling law." Thus the function of the judiciary to be a barrier against democracy, which, according to Tocqueville, it is destined to be, was not apparent. In the same manner religious liberty, which has become so much identified with the United States, is a thing which grew by degrees, and was not to be found imposed by the letter of the law.

The true natural check on absolute democracy is the federal system, which limits the central government by the powers reserved, and the state governments by the powers they have ceded. It is the one immortal tribute of America to political science, for state rights are at the same time the consummation and the guard of democracy. So much so that an officer wrote, a few months before Bull Run: "The people in the south are evidently unanimous in the opinion that slavery is endangered by the current of events, and it is useless to attempt to alter that opinion. As our government is founded on the will of the people, when that will is fixed our government is powerless." Those are the words of Sherman, the man who, by his march through Georgia, cut the Confederacy into two. Lincoln himself wrote, at the same time: "I declare that the maintenance inviolate of the rights of the states, and especially the right of each state to order and control its own domestic institutions according to its own judgment exclusively, is essential to that balance of powers on which the perfection and endurance of our political fabric depend." Such was the force with which state rights held the minds of abolitionists on the eve of the war that bore them down.

At the Revolution there were many Frenchmen who saw in federalism the only way to reconcile liberty and democracy, to establish government on contract, and to rescue the country from the crushing preponderance of Paris and the Parisian populace. I do not mean the Girondins, but men of opinions different from theirs, and, above all, Mirabeau. He planned to save the throne by detaching the provinces from the frenzy of the capital, and he declared that the federal system is alone capable of preserving freedom in any great empire. The idea did not grow up under American influence; for no man was more opposed to it than Lafayette; and the American witness of the Revolution, Morris, denounced federalism as a danger to France.

Apart from the Constitution, the political thought of America influenced the French next to their own. And it was not all speculation, but a system for which men died, which had proved entirely practical, and strong enough to conquer all resistance, with the sanction and encouragement of Europe.

It displayed to France a finished model of revolution, both in thought and action, and showed that what seemed extreme and subversive in the old world, was compatible with good and wise government, with respect for social order, and the preservation of national character and custom. The ideas which captured and convulsed the French people were mostly ready-made for them, and much that is familiar to you now, much of that which I have put before you from other than French sources, will meet us again next week with the old faces, when we come to the States-General.

III
THE SUMMONS OF THE STATES-GENERAL

The condition of France alone did not bring about the overthrow of the monarchy and the convulsion that ensued. For the sufferings of the people were not greater than they had been before; the misgovernment and oppression were less, and a successful war with England had largely wiped out the humiliations inflicted by Chatham.

But the confluence of French theory with American example caused the Revolution to break out, not in an excess of irritation and despair, but in a moment of better feeling between the nation and the king. The French were not mere reckless innovators; they were confiding followers, and many of the ideas with which they made their venture were those in which Burke agreed with Hamilton, and with his own illustrious countrymen, Adam Smith and Sir William Jones. When he said that, compared to England, the government of France was slavery, and that nothing but a revolution could restore European liberty, Frenchmen, saying the same thing, and acting upon it, were unconscious of extravagance, and might well believe that they were obeying precepts stored in the past by high and venerable authority. Beyond that common ground, they fell back on native opinion in which there was wide divergence, and an irrepressible conflict arose. We have to deal with no unlikely motives, with no unheard of theories, and, on the whole, with convinced and average men.

The States-General were convoked because there was no other way of obtaining money for the public need. The deficit was a record of bad government, and the first practical object was the readjustment of taxes. From the king's accession, the revival of the old and neglected institution had been kept before the country as a remedy, not for financial straits only, but for all the ills of France.

The imposing corporation of the judiciary had constantly opposed the Crown, and claimed to subject its acts to the judgment of the law. The higher clergy had raised objections to Turgot, to Necker, to the emancipation of Protestants; and the nobles became the most active of all the parties of reform. But the great body of the people had borne their trouble in patience. They possessed no recognised means of expressing sentiments. There was no right of public meeting, no liberty for the periodical press; and the privileged newspapers were so tightly swaddled in their official character that they had nothing to say even of an event like the oath in the Tennis Court. The feelings that stirred the multitude did not appear, unless they appeared in the shape of disorder. Without it France remained an unknown quantity. The king felt the resistance of the privileged and interested classes which was the source of his necessity, but he was not apprehensive of a national opposition. He was prepared to rely on the Third Estate with hopefulness, if not with confidence, and to pay a very high price for their support. In a certain measure their interest was the same. The penury of the State came from the fact that more than half the property of France was not taxed in its proportion, and it was essential for the government to abolish the exception, and to bring nobles and clergy to surrender their privilege, and pay like the rest. To that extent the object of the king was to do away with privilege and to introduce equality before the law. So far the Commons went along with him. They would be relieved of a heavy burden if they ceased to pay the share of those who were exempt, and rejected the time-honoured custom that the poor should bear taxation for the rich. An alliance, therefore, was indicated and natural. But the extinction of privilege, which for monarchy and democracy alike meant fiscal equality, meant for the democracy a great deal more. Besides the money which they were required to pay in behalf of the upper class and for their benefit and solace, money had to be paid to them. Apart from rent for house or land, there were payments due to them proceeding from the time, the obscure and distant time, when power went with land, and the focal landholder was the local government, the ruler and protector of the people, and was paid accordingly. And there was another category of claims, proceeding indirectly from the same historic source, consisting of commutation and compensation for ancient rights, and having therefore a legal character, founded upon contract, not upon force.

Every thinking politician knew that the first of these categories, the beneficial rights that were superfluous and oppressive, could not be maintained, and that the nobles would be made to give up not only that form of privilege which consisted in exemption from particular taxes, but that composed of superannuated demands in return for work no longer done, or value given. Those, on the other hand, which were not simply mediæval, but based upon contract, would be treated as lawful property, and would have to be redeemed. Privilege, in the eyes of the state, was the right of evading taxes. To the politician it meant, furthermore, the right of imposing taxes. For the rural democracy it had a wider significance. To them, all these privileges were products of the same principle, ruins of the same fabric. They were relics and remnants of feudalism, and feudalism meant power given to land and denied to capital and industry. It meant class government, the negation of the very idea of the state and of the nation; it meant conquest and subjugation by a foreign invader. None denied that many great families had won their spurs in the service of their country; everybody indeed knew that the noblest of all, Montmorency, bore the arms of France because, at the victory of Bouvines, where their ancestor was desperately wounded, the king laid his finger on the wound and drew with his blood the lilies upon his shield. When we come, presently, to the Abbé Sieyès, we shall see how firmly men believed that the nobles were, in the mass, Franks, Teutonic tyrants, and spoilers of the Celtic native. They intended that feudalism should not be trimmed but uprooted, as the cause of much that was infinitely odious, and as a thing absolutely incompatible with public policy, social interests, and right reason. That men should be made to bear suffering for the sake of what could only be explained by very early history and very yellow parchments was simply irrational to a generation which received its notion of life from Turgot, Adam Smith, or Franklin.

Although there were three interpretations of feudal privilege, and consequently a dangerous problem in the near future, the first step was an easy one, and consisted in the appeal by the Crown to the Commons for aid in regenerating the State. Like other princes of his time, Lewis XVI. was a reforming monarch. At his accession, his first choice of a minister was Machault, known to have entertained a vast scheme of change, to be attempted whenever the throne should be occupied by a serious prince. Later, he appointed Turgot, the most profound and thorough reformer of the century. He appointed Malesherbes, one of the weakest but one of the most enlightened of public men; and after having, at the Coronation, taken an oath to persecute, he gave office to Necker, a Protestant, an alien, and a republican. When he had begun, through Malesherbes, to remove religious disabilities, he said to him, "Now you have been a Protestant, and I declare you a Jew"; and began to prepare a measure for the relief of Jews, who, wherever they went, were forced to pay the same toll as a pig. He carried out a large and complicated scheme of law reform; and he achieved the independence of revolted America. In later days the Elector of Cologne complained to an *émigré* that his king's policy had been deplorable, and that, having promoted resistance to authority in the Colonies, in Holland, and in Brabant, he had no claim on the support of European monarchs.

But the impulse in the direction of liberal improvement was intermittent, and was checked by a natural diffidence and infirmity of purpose. The messenger who was to summon Machault was recalled as he mounted his horse. Turgot was sacrificed to gratify the queen. Necker's second administration would have begun a year and a half earlier, but, at the last moment, his enemies intervened. The war minister, Saint Germain, was agreeable to the king, and he wished to keep him. "But what can I do?" he wrote; "his enemies are bent on his dismissal, and I must yield to the majority." Maurepas, at his death, left a paper on which were the names of four men whom he entreated his master not to employ. Lewis bestowed the highest offices upon them all. He regarded England with the aversion with which Chatham, and at that time even Fox, looked upon France, and he went to war in the just hope of avenging the disgrace of the Seven Years' War, but from no sympathy with the American cause. When he was required to retrench his personal expenditure, he objected, and insisted that much of the loss should be made to fall on his pensioners. The liberal concessions which he allowed were in many cases made at the expense, not of the Crown, but of powers that were obstructing the Crown. By the abolition of torture he incurred no loss, but curbed the resources of opposing magistrates. When he emancipated the Protestants and made a Swiss Calvinist his principal adviser, he displeased the clergy; but he cared little for clerical displeasure. The bishops, finding that he took no notice of them, disappeared from his *levée*. He objected to the appointment of French cardinals. English travellers at Versailles, Romilly and Valpy, observed that he was inattentive at mass, and talked and laughed before all the court. At the Council he would fall asleep, and when the discussion was distasteful, he used to snore louder than when he slept. He said to Necker that he desired the States-General because he wanted a guide. When, in 1788, after skirmishing with magistrates and prelates, he took the memorable resolution to call in the outer people, to compel a compromise with the class that filled his court, that constituted society, that ruled opinion, it was the act of a man destitute of energy, and gifted with an uncertain and indistinct enlightenment. And Necker said, "You may lend a man your ideas, you cannot lend him your strength of will."

The enterprise was far beyond the power and quality of his mind, but the lesson of his time was not lost upon him, and he had learnt something since the days when he spoke the unchanging language of absolutism. He showed another spirit when he emancipated the serfs of the Crown, when he introduced provincial and village councils, when he pronounced that to confine local government to landowners was to offend a still larger class, when he invited assistance in reforming the criminal code in order that the result might be the work, not of experts only, but of the public. All this was genuine conviction. He was determined that the upper class should lose its fiscal privileges with as little further detriment as possible. And, to accomplish this necessary and deliberate purpose, he offered terms to the Commons of France such as no monarch ever proposed to his subjects. He declared in later days, and had a right to declare, that it was he who had taken the first step to concert with the French people a permanent constitution, the abolition of arbitrary power, of pecuniary privilege, of promotion apart from merit, of taxation without consent. When he heard that the Notables had given only one vote in favour of increased representation of the Third Estate, he said, "You can add mine." Malouet, the most high-minded and sagacious statesman of the Revolution, testifies to his sincerity, and declares that the king fully shared his opinions.

The tributary elements of a free constitution which were granted by Lewis XVI., not in consultation with deputies, not even always with public support, included religious toleration, Habeas Corpus, equal incidence of taxes, abolition of torture, decentralisation and local self-government, freedom of the press, universal suffrage, election without official candidates or influence, periodical convocation of parliament, right of voting supplies, of initiating legislation, of revising the constitution, responsibility of ministers, double representation of the Commons at the States-General. All these concessions were acts of the Crown, yielding to dictates of policy more than to popular demand. It is said that power is an object of such ardent desire to man, that the voluntary surrender of it is absurd in psychology and unknown in history. Lewis XVI. no doubt calculated the probabilities of loss and gain, and persuaded himself that his action was politic even more than generous. The Prussian envoy rightly described him in a despatch of July 31, 1789. He says that the king was willing to weaken the executive at home, in order to strengthen it abroad; if the ministers lost by a better regulated administration, the nation would gain by it in resource, and a limited authority in a more powerful state seemed preferable to absolute authority which was helpless from its unpopularity and the irreparable disorder of finance. He was resolved to submit the arbitrary *government of his ancestors to the rising forces of the* day. The royal initiative was pushed so far on the way to established freedom that it was exhausted, and the rest was left to the nation. As the elections were not influenced, as the instructions were not inspired, the deliberations were not guided or controlled. The king abdicated before the States-General. He assigned so much authority to the new legislature that none remained with the Crown, and its powers, thus practically suspended, were never recovered. The rival classes, that only the king could have reconciled and restrained, were abandoned to the fatal issue of a trial of strength.

In 1786 the annual deficit amounted to between four and five millions, and the season for heroic remedies had evidently come. The artful and evasive confusion of accounts that shrouded the secret could not be maintained, and the minister of finance, Calonne, convoked the Notables for February 1787. The Notables were a selection of important personages, chiefly of the upper order, without legal powers or initiative. It was hoped that they would strengthen the hands of the government, and that what they agreed to would be accepted by the class to which they belonged. It was an experiment to avert the evil day of the States-General. For the States-General, which had not been seen for one hundred and seventy-five years, were the features of a bygone stage of political life, and could neither be revived as they once had been, nor adapted to modern society. If they imposed taxes, they would impose conditions, and they were an auxiliary who might become a master. The Notables were soon found inadequate to the purpose, and the minister, having failed to control them, was dismissed. Necker, his rival and obvious successor, was sent out of the way, and the Archbishop of Toulouse, afterwards of Sens, who was appointed in his place, got rid of the Assembly. There was nothing left to fall back upon but the dreaded States-General. Lafayette had demanded them at the meeting of the Notables, and the demand was now repeated far and wide.

On August 8, 1788, the king summoned the States-General for the following year, to the end, as he proclaimed, that the nation might settle its own government in perpetuity. The words signified that the absolute monarchy of 1788 would make way for a representative monarchy in 1789. In what way this was to be done, and how the States would be constituted, was unknown. The public were invited to offer suggestions, and the press was practically made free for publications that were not periodical. Necker, the inevitable minister of the new order of things, was immediately nominated to succeed the Archbishop, and the funds rose 30 per cent in one day. He was a foreigner, independent of French tradition and ways of thought, who not only stood aloof from the Catholics, as a Genevese, but also from the prevailing freethinkers, for Priestley describes him as nearly the only believer in religion whom he found in intellectual society at Paris. He was the earliest foreign statesman who studied and understood the modern force of opinion; and he identified public opinion with credit, as we should say, with the city. He took the views of capitalists as the most sensitive record of public confidence; and as Paris was the headquarters of business, he contributed, in spite of his declared federalism, to that predominance of the centre which became fatal to liberty and order.

Necker was familiar with the working of republican institutions, and he was an admirer of the British model; but the king would not hear of going to school to the people whom he had so recently defeated, and who owed their disgrace as much to political as to military incapacity. Consequently Necker repressed his zeal in politics, and was not eager for the States-General. They would never have been wanted, he said, if he had been called to succeed Calonne, and had had the managing of the Notables. He was glad now that they should serve to bring the entire property of the country, on equal terms, under the tax-gatherer, and if that could have been effected at once, by an overwhelming pressure of public feeling, his practical spirit would not have hungered for further changes.

The *Third* Estate was *Invoked* for a *great fiscal* operation. If it brought the upper class to the necessary sense of their own obligations and the national claims, that was enough for the keeper of the purse, and he would have deprecated the intrusion of other formidable and absorbing objects, detrimental to his own. Beyond that was danger, but the course was clear towards obtaining from the greater assembly what he would have extracted from the less if he had held office in 1787. That is the secret of Necker's unforeseen weakness in the midst of so much power, and of his sterility when the crisis broke and it was discovered that the force which had been calculated equal to the carrying of a modest and obvious reform was as the rush of Niagara, and that France was in the resistless rapids.

Everything depended on the manner in which the government decided that the States should be composed, elected, and conducted. To pronounce on this, Necker caused the Notables to be convoked again, exposed the problem, and desired their opinion. The nobles had been lately active on the side of liberal reforms, and it seemed possible that their reply might relieve him of a dreaded responsibility and prevent a conflict. The Notables gave their advice. They resolved that the Commons should be elected, virtually, by universal suffrage without conditions of eligibility; that the parish priests should be electors and eligible; that the lesser class of nobles should be represented like the greater. They extended the franchise to the unlettered multitude, because the danger which they apprehended came from the middle class, not from the lower. But they voted, by three to one, that each order should be equal in numbers. The Count of Provence, the king's next brother, went with the minority, and voted that the deputies of the Commons should be as numerous as those of the two other orders together. This became the burning question. If the Commons did not predominate, there was no security that the other orders would give way. On the other hand, by the important innovation of admitting the parish clergy, and those whom we should call provincial gentry, a great concession was made to the popular element. The antagonism between the two branches of the clergy, and between the two branches of the *noblesse*, was greater than that between the inferior portion of each and the Third Estate, and promised a contingent to the liberal cause. It turned out, at the proper time, that the two strongest leaders of the democracy were, one, an ancient noble; the other, a canon of the cathedral of Chartres. The Notables concluded their acceptable labours on December 12. On the 5th the magistrates who formed the parliament of Paris, after solemnly enumerating the great constitutional principles, entreated the king to establish them as the basis of all future legislation. The position of the government was immensely simplified. The walls of the city had fallen, and it was doubtful where any serious resistance would come from.

Meantime, the agitation in the provinces, and the explosion of pent-up feeling that followed the unlicensed printing of political tracts, showed that public opinion moved faster than that of the two great conservative bodies. It became urgent that the Government should come to an early and resolute decision, and should occupy ground that might be held against the surging democracy. Necker judged that the position would be impregnable if he stood upon the lines drawn by the Notables, and he decided that the Commons should be equal to either order singly, and not jointly to the two. In consultation with a statesmanlike prelate, the Archbishop of Bordeaux, he drew up and printed a report, refusing the desired increase. But as he sat anxiously watching the winds and the tide, he began to doubt; and when letters came, warning him that the nobles would be butchered if the decision went in their favour, he took alarm. He said to his friends, "If we do not multiply the Commons by two, they will multiply themselves by ten." When the Archbishop saw him again at Christmas, Necker assured him that the Government was no longer strong enough to resist the popular demand. But he was also determined that the three houses should vote separately, that the Commons should enjoy no advantage from their numbers in any discussion where privilege was at stake, or the interest of classes was not identical. He hoped that the nobles would submit to equal taxation of their own accord, and that he would stand between them and any exorbitant claim of equal political power.

On December 27 Necker's scheme was adopted by the Council. There was some division of opinion; but the king overruled it, and the queen, who was present, showed, without speaking, that she was there to support the measure. By this momentous act Lewis XVI., without being conscious of its significance, went over to the democracy. He said, in plain terms, to the French people: "Afford me the aid I require, so far as we have a common interest, and for that definite and appropriated assistance you shall have a princely reward. For you shall at once have a constitution of your own making, which shall limit the power of the Crown, leaving untouched the power and the dignity and the property of the upper classes, beyond what is involved in an equal share of taxation." But in effect he said; "Let us combine to deprive the aristocracy of those privileges which are injurious to the Crown, whilst we retain those which are offensive only to the people." It was a tacit compact, of which the terms and limits were not defined; and where one thought of immunities, the other was thinking of oppression. The organisation of society required to be altered and remodelled from end to end to sustain a constitution founded on the principle of liberty. It was no arduous problem to adjust relations between the people and the king. The deeper question was between the people and the aristocracy. Behind a political reform there was a social revolution, for the only liberty that could avail was liberty founded on equality. Malouet, who was at this moment Necker's best adviser, said to him: "You have made the Commons equal in influence to the other orders. Another revolution has to follow, and it is for you to accomplish it—the levelling of onerous privilege." Necker had no ambition of the kind, and he distinctly guarded privilege in all matters but taxation.

The resolution of the king in Council was received with loud applause; and the public believed that everything they had demanded was now obtained, or was at least within reach. The doubling of the Commons was illusory if they were to have no opportunity of making their numbers tell. The Count of Provence, afterwards Lewis XVIII., had expressly argued that the old States-General were useless because the Third Estate was not suffered to prevail in them. Therefore he urged that the three orders should deliberate and vote as one, and that the Commons should possess the majority. It was universally felt that this was the real meaning of the double representation, and that there was a logic in it which could not be resisted. The actual power vested in the Commons by the great concession exceeded their literal and legal power, and it was accepted and employed accordingly.

The mode of election was regulated on January 24. There were to be three hundred deputies for the clergy, three hundred for the nobles, six hundred for the Commons. There were to be no restrictions and no exclusions; but whereas the greater personages voted directly, the vote of the lower classes was indirect; and the rule for the Commons was that one hundred primary voters chose an elector. Besides the deputy, there was the deputy's deputy, held in reserve, ready in case of vacancy to take his place. It was on this peculiar device of eventual representatives that the Commons relied, if their numbers had not been doubled. They would have called up their substitutes. The rights and charters of the several provinces were superseded, and all were placed on the same level.

A more sincere and genuine election has never been held. And on the whole it was orderly. The clergy were uneasy, and the nobles more openly alarmed. But the country in general had confidence in what was coming; and some of the most liberal and advanced and outspoken manifestations proceeded from aristocratic and ecclesiastical constituencies. On February 9 the Venetian envoy reports that the clergy and nobles are ready to accept the principle of equality in taxation. The elections were going on for more than two months, from February to the beginning of May.

In accordance with ancient custom, when a deputy was a plenipotentiary more than a representative, it was ordained that the preliminary of every election was the drawing up of instructions. Every corner of France was swept and searched for its ideas. The village gave them to its elector, and they were compared and consolidated by the electors in the process of choosing their member. These instructions, the characteristic bequest to its successors of a society at the point of death, were often the work of conspicuous public men, such as Malouet, Lanjuinais, Dupont, the friend of Turgot and originator of the commercial treaty of 1786; and one paper, drawn up by Sieyès, was circulated all over France by the duke of Orleans.

In this way, by the lead which was taken by eminent and experienced men, there is an appearance of unanimity. All France desired the essential institutions of limited monarchy, in the shape of representation and the division of power, and foreshadowed the charter of 1814. There is scarcely a trace of the spirit of departing absolutism; there is not a sign of the coming republic. It is agreed that precedent is dead, and the world just going to begin. There are no clear views on certain grave matters of detail, on an Upper House, Church and State, and primary education. Free schools, progressive taxation, the extinction of slavery, of poverty, of ignorance, are among the things advised. The privileged orders are prepared for a vast surrender in regard to taxes, and nobody seems to associate the right of being represented in future parliaments with the possession of property. On nine-tenths of all that is material to a constitution there is a general agreement. The one broad division is that the Commons wish that the States-General shall form a single united Assembly, and the other orders wish for three. But on this supreme issue the Commons are all agreed, and the others are not. An ominous rift appears, and we already perceive the minority of nobles and priests, who, in the hour of conflict, were to rule the fate of European society. From all these papers, the mandate of united France, it was the function of true statesmanship to distil the essence of a sufficient freedom.

These instructions were intended to be imperative. Nine years before, Burke, when he retired from the contest at Bristol, had defined the constitutional doctrine on constituency and member; and Charles Sumner said that he legislated when he made that speech. But the ancient view, on which instructions are founded, made the deputy the agent of the deputing power, and much French history turns on it. At first the danger was unfelt; for the instructions were often compiled by the deputy himself, who was to execute them. They were a pledge even more than an order.

The nation had responded to the royal appeal, and there was agreement between the offer and the demand. The upper classes had opposed and resisted the Crown; the people were eager to support it, and it was expected that the first steps would be taken together. The comparative moderation and serenity of the Instructions disguised the unappeasable conflict of opinion and the furious passion that raged below.

The very cream of the upper and middle class were elected; and the Court, in its prosperous complacency, abandoned to their wisdom the task of creating the new institutions and permanently settling the financial trouble. It persisted in non-interference, and had no policy but expectation. The initiative passed to every private member. The members consisted of new men, without connection or party organisation. They wanted time to feel their way, and missed a moderator and a guide. The governing power ceased, for the moment, to serve the supreme purpose of government; and monarchy transformed itself into anarchy to see what would come of it, and to avoid committing itself on either side against the class by which it was always surrounded or the class which seemed ready with its alliance.

The Government renounced the advantage which the elections and the temperate instructions gave them; and in the hope that the elect would be at least as reasonable as the electors, they threw away their greatest opportunity. There was a disposition to underrate dangers that were not on the surface. Even Mirabeau, who, if not a deep thinker, was a keen observer, imagined that the entire mission of the States-General might have been accomplished in a week. Few men saw the ambiguity hidden in the term Privilege, and the immense difference that divided fiscal change from social change. In attacking feudalism, which was the survival of barbarism, the middle class designed to overthrow the condition of society which gave power as well as property to a favoured minority. The assault on the restricted distribution of power involved an assault on the concentration of wealth. The connection of the two ideas is the secret motive of the Revolution. At that time the law by which power follows property, which has been called the most important discovery made by man since the invention of printing, was not clearly known. But the underground forces at work were recognised by the intelligent conservatives, and they were assuming the defensive, in preparation for the hour when they would be deserted by the king. It was therefore impossible that the object for which the States-General were summoned should be attained while they were divided into three. Either they must be dissolved, or the thing which the middle-class deputies could not accomplish by use of forms would be attempted by the lower class, their masters and employers, by use of force.

Before the meeting Malouet once more approached the minister with weighty counsel. He said: "You now know the wishes of France; you know the instructions, you do not know the deputies. Do not leave all things to the arbitrament of the unknown. Convert at once the demands of the people into a constitution, and give them force of law. Act while you have unfettered power of action. Act while your action will be hailed as the most magnificent concession ever granted by a monarch to a loyal and expectant nation. To-day you are supreme and safe. It may be too late to-morrow."

In particular, Malouet advised that the Government should regulate the verification of powers, leaving only contested returns to the judgment of the representatives. Necker abided by his meditated neutrality, and preferred that the problem should work itself out with entire freedom. He would not take sides lest he should offend one party without being sure of the other, and forfeit his chance of becoming the accepted arbitrator. Whilst, by deciding nothing, he kept the enemy at bay, the upper classes might yet reach the wise conclusion that, in the midst of so much peril to royalty and to themselves, it was time to place the interest of the state before their own, and to accept the duties and the burdens of undistinguished men.

Neither party could yield. The Commons could not fail to see that time was on their side, and that, by compelling the other orders to merge with them, they secured the downfall of privilege and played the game of the court. The two other orders were, by the imperative mandate of many constituencies, prohibited from voting in common. Their resistance was legitimate, and could only be overcome by the intervention either of the Crown or the people. Their policy might have been justified if they had at once made their surrender, and had accomplished with deliberation in May what had to be done with tumult in August. With these problems and these perils before them, the States-General met on that memorable 5th of May. Necker, preferring the abode of financiers, wished them to meet at Paris; and four or five other places were proposed. At last the king, breaking silence, said that it could be only at Versailles, on account of his hunting. At the time he saw no cause for alarm in the proximity of the capital. Since then, the disturbances in one or two places, and the open language of some of the electors, had begun to make him swerve.

On the opening day the queen was received with offensive silence; but she acknowledged a belated cheer with such evident gladness and with such stately grace that applause followed her. The popular groups of deputies were cheered as they passed—all but the Commons of Provence, for they had Mirabeau among them. He alone was hissed. Two ladies who watched the procession from the same window were the daughter of Necker and the wife of the Foreign Minister, Montmorin. One thought with admiration that she was a witness of the greatest scene in modern history; and the other was sad with evil forebodings. Both were right; but the feeling of confidence and enthusiasm pervaded the crowd. Near relations of my own were at Rome in 1846, during the excitement at the reforms of the new Pope, who, at that moment, was the most popular sovereign in Europe. They asked an Italian lady who was with them why all the demonstrations only made her more melancholy. She answered: "Because I was at Versailles in 1789."

Barentin, the minister who had opposed Necker's plans and viewed the States-General with apprehension and disgust, spoke after the king. He was a French judge, with no heart for any form of government but the ancient one enjoyed by France. Nevertheless he admitted that joint deliberation was the reasonable solution. He added that it could only be adopted by common consent; and he urged the two orders to sacrifice their right of exemption. Necker perplexed his hearers by receding from the ground which the Chancellor had taken. He assured the two orders that they need not apprehend absorption in the third if, while voting separately, they executed the promised surrender. He spoke as their protector, on the condition that they submitted to the common law, and paid their taxes in arithmetical proportion. He implied, but did not say, that what they refused to the Crown would be taken by the people. In his financial statement he under-estimated the deficit, and he said nothing of the Constitution. The great day ended badly. The deputies were directed to hand in their returns to the Master of Ceremonies, an official of whom we shall soon see more. But the Master of Ceremonies was not acceptable to the Commons, because he had compelled them to withdraw, the day before, from their places in the nave of the church. Therefore the injunction was disregarded; and the verification of powers, which the Government might have regulated, was left to the deputies themselves, and became the lever by which the more numerous order overthrew the monarchy, and carried to an end, in seven weeks, the greatest constitutional struggle that has ever been fought out in the world by speech alone.

IV
THE MEETING OF THE STATES-GENERAL

The argument of the drama which opened on May 6, 1789, and closed on June 27, is this:—The French people had been called to the enjoyment of freedom by every voice they heard—by the king; by the notables, who proposed unrestricted suffrage; by the supreme judiciary, who proclaimed the future Constitution; by the clergy and the aristocracy, in the most solemn pledges of the electoral period; by the British example, celebrated by Montesquieu and Voltaire; by the more cogent example of America; by the national classics, who declared, with a hundred tongues, that all authority must be controlled, that the masses must be rescued from degradation, and the individual from constraint.

When the Commons appeared at Versailles, they were there to claim an inheritance of which, by universal consent, they had been wrongfully deprived. They were not arrayed against the king, who had been already brought to submission by blows not dealt by them. They desired to make terms with those to whom he was ostensibly opposed. There could be no real freedom for them until they were as free on the side of the nobles as on that of the Crown. The modern absolutism of the monarch had surrendered; but the ancient owners of the soil remained, with their exclusive position in the State, and a complicated system of honours and exactions which humiliated the middle class and pauperised the lower. The educated democracy, acting for themselves, might have been content with the retrenchment of those privileges which put them at a disadvantage. But the rural population were concerned with every fragment of obsolete feudalism that added to the burden of their lives.

The two classes were undivided. Together they had elected their deputies, and the cleavage between the political and the social democrat, which has become so great a fact in modern society, was scarcely perceived. The same common principle, the same comprehensive term, composed the policy of both. They demanded liberty, both in the State and in society, and required that oppression should cease, whether exercised in the name of the king or in the name of the aristocracy. In a word, they required equality as well as liberty, and sought deliverance from feudalism and from absolutism at the same time. And equality was the most urgent and prominent claim of the two, because the king, virtually, had given way, but the nobles had not.

The battle that remained to be fought, and at once commenced, was between the Commons and the nobles; that is, between people doomed to poverty by the operation of law, and people who were prosperous at their expense. And as there were men who would perish from want while the laws remained unchanged, and others who would be ruined by their repeal, the strife was deadly.

The real object of assault was not the living landlord, but the unburied past. It had little to do with socialism, or with high rents, bad times, and rapacious proprietors. Apart from all this was the hope of release from irrational and indefensible laws, such as that by which a patrician's land paid three francs where the plebeian's paid fourteen, because one was noble and the other was not, and it was an elementary deduction from the motives of liberal desire.

The elections had made it unexpectedly evident that when one part of territorial wealth had been taken by the State, another would be taken by the people; and that a free community, making its own laws, would not submit to exactions imposed of old by the governing class on a defenceless population. When the notables advised that every man should have a vote, this consequence was not clear to them. It was perceived as things went on, and no provision for aristocratic interests was included in the popular demands.

In the presence of imminent peril, the privileged classes closed their ranks, and pressed the king to resist changes sure to be injurious to them. They became a Conservative party. The court was on their side, with the Count d'Artois at its head, and the queen and her immediate circle.

The king remained firm in the belief that popularity is the best form of authority, and he relied on the wholesome dread of democracy to make the rich aristocrats yield to his wishes. As long as the Commons exerted the inert pressure of delay, he watched the course of events. When at the end of five tedious and unprofitable weeks they began their attack, he was driven slowly, and without either confidence or sympathy, to take his stand with the nobles, and to shrink from the indefinite change that was impending.

When the Commons met to deliberate on the morning of the 6th of May, the deputies were unknown to each other. It was necessary to proceed with caution, and to occupy ground on which they could not be divided. Their unanimity was out of danger so long as nothing more complex was discussed than the verification of powers. The other orders resolved at once that each should examine its own returns. But this vote, which the nobles carried by a majority of 141, obtained in the clergy a majority of only 19. It was evident at once that the party of privilege was going asunder, and that the priests were nearly as well inclined to the Commons as to the *noblesse*. It became advisable to give them time, to discard violence until the arts of conciliation were exhausted and the cause of united action had been pleaded in vain. The policy of moderation was advocated by Malouet, a man of practical insight and experience, who had grown grey in the service of the State. It was said that he defended the slave trade; he attempted to exclude the public from the debates; he even offered, in unauthorised terms, to secure the claims, both real and formal, of the upper classes. He soon lost the ear of the House. But he was a man of great good sense, as free from ancient prejudice as from modern theory, and he never lost sight of the public interest in favour of a class. The most generous proposals on behalf of the poor afterwards emanated from him, and parliamentary life in France began with his motion for negotiation with the other orders.

He was supported by Mounier, one of the deepest minds of that day, and the most popular of the deputies. He was a magistrate of Grenoble, and had conducted the Estates of Dauphiné with such consummate art and wisdom that all ranks and all parties had worked in harmony. They had demanded equal representation and the vote in common; they gave to their deputies full powers instead of written instructions, only requiring that they should obtain a free government to the best of their ability; they resolved that the chartered rights of their province should not be put in competition with the new and theoretic rights of the nation. Under Mounier's controlling hand the prelate and the noble united to declare that the essential liberties of men are ensured to them by nature, and not by perishable title-deeds. Travellers had initiated him in the working of English institutions, and he represented the school of Montesquieu; but he was an emancipated disciple and a discriminate admirer. He held Montesquieu to be radically illiberal, and believed the famous theory which divides powers without isolating them to be an old and a common discovery. He thought that nations differ less in their character than in their stage of progress, and that a Constitution like the English applies not to a region, but to a time. He belonged to that type of statesmanship which Washington had shown to be so powerful—revolutionary doctrine in a conservative temper. In the centre of affairs the powerful provincial betrayed a lack of sympathy and attraction. He refused to meet Sieyès, and persistently denounced and vilified Mirabeau. Influence and public esteem came to him at once, and in the great constructive party he was a natural leader, and predominated for a time. But at the encounter of defeat, his austere and rigid character turned it into disaster; and as he possessed but one line of defence, the failure of his tactics was the ruin of his cause. Although he despaired prematurely, and was vociferously repentant of his part in the great days of June, parading his sackcloth before Europe, he never faltered in the conviction that the interests of no class, of no family, of no man, can be preferred to those of the nation. Napoleon once said with a sneer: "You are still the man of 1789." Mounier replied: "Yes, sir. Principles are not subject to the law of change."

He desired to adopt the English model, which meant: representation of property; an upper house founded upon merit, not upon descent; royal veto and right of dissolution. This could only be secured by active co-operation on the part of all the conservative elements. To obtain his majority he required that the other orders should come over, not vanquished and reluctant, but under the influence of persuasion. Mirabeau and his friends only wished to put the nobles in the wrong, to expose their obstinacy and arrogance, and then to proceed without them. The plan of Mounier depended on a real conciliation.

The clergy were ready for a conference; and by their intervention the nobles were induced to take part in it. There, on May 23, the Archbishop of Vienne, who was in the confidence of Mounier, declared that the clergy recognised the duty of sharing taxes in equal proportion. The Duke of Luxemburg, speaking for the nobles, made the same declaration. The intention, he said, was irrevocable; but he added that it would not be executed until the problem of the Constitution was solved. The nobles declined to abandon the mode of separate verification which had been practised formerly. And when the Commons objected that what was good in times of civil dissension was inapplicable to the Arcadian tranquillity of 1789, the others were not to blame if they treated the argument with contempt.

The failure of the conference was followed by an event which confirmed Necker in the belief that he was not waiting in vain. He received overtures from Mirabeau. Until that time Mirabeau had been notorious for the obtrusive scandal of his life, and the books he had written under pressure of need did not restore his good name. People avoided him, not because he was brutal and vicious like other men of his rank, but because he was reputed a liar and a thief. During one of his imprisonments he had obtained from Dupont de Nemours communication of an important memoir embodying Turgot's ideas on local government. He copied the manuscript, presented it to the minister as his own work, and sold another copy to the booksellers as the work of Turgot. Afterwards he offered to suppress his letters from Prussia if the Government would buy them at the price he could obtain by publishing them. Montmorin paid what he asked for, on condition that he renounced his candidature in Provence. Mirabeau agreed, spent the money on his canvass, and made more by printing what he had sold to the king. During the contest, by his coolness, audacity, and resource, he soon acquired ascendency. The nobles who rejected him were made to feel his power. When tumults broke out, he appeased them by his presence, and he moved from Marseilles to Aix escorted by a retinue of 200 carriages. Elected in both places by the Third Estate, he came to Versailles hoping to repair his fortune. There it was soon apparent that he possessed powers of mind equal to the baseness of his conduct. He is described by Malouet as the only man who perceived from the first where the Revolution was tending; and his enemy Mounier avows that he never met a more intelligent politician. He was always ready to speak, and always vigorous and adroit. His renowned orations were often borrowed, for he surrounded himself with able men, mostly Genevese, versed in civil strife, who supplied him with facts, mediated with the public, and helped him in the press. Rivarol said that his head was a gigantic sponge, swelled out with other men's ideas. As extempore speaking was a new art, and the ablest men read their speeches, Mirabeau was at once an effective debater—probably the best debater, though not the most perfect orator, that has appeared in the splendid record of parliamentary life in France. His father was one of the most conspicuous economists, and he inherited their belief in a popular and active monarchy, and their preference for a single chamber.

In 1784 he visited London, frequented the Whigs, and supplied Burke with a quotation. He did not love England, but he thought it a convincing proof of the efficacy of paper Constitutions, that a few laws for the protection of personal liberty should be sufficient to make a corrupt and ignorant people prosper.

His keynote was to abandon privilege and to retain the prerogative; for he aspired to sway the monarchy, and would not destroy the power he was to wield. The king, he said, is the State, and can do no wrong. Therefore he was at times the most violent and indiscreet of men, and at times unaccountably moderate and reserved; and both parts were carefully prepared. As he had a fixed purpose before him, but neither principle nor scruple, no emergency found him at a loss, or embarrassed by a cargo of consistent maxims. Incalculable, and unfit to trust in daily life, at a crisis he was the surest and most available force. From the first moment he came to the front. On the opening day he was ready with a plan for a consultation in common, before deciding whether they should act jointly or separately. The next day he started a newspaper, in the shape of a report to his constituents, and when the Government attempted to suppress it, he succeeded, May 19, in establishing the liberty of the press.

The first political club, afterwards that of the Jacobins, was founded, at his instigation, by men who did not know the meaning of a club. For, he said to them, ten men acting together can make a hundred thousand tremble apart from each other. Mirabeau began with caution, for his materials were new and he had no friends. He believed that the king was really identified with the magnates, and that the Commons were totally unprepared to confront either the court or the approaching Revolution. He thought it hopeless to negotiate with his own doomed order, and meant to detach the king from them. When the scheme of conciliation failed, his opportunity came. He requested Malouet to bring him into communication with ministers. He told him that he was seriously alarmed, that the nobles meant to push resistance to extremity, and that his reliance was on the Crown. He promised, if the Government would admit him to their confidence, to support their policy with all his might. Montmorin refused to see him. Necker reluctantly consented. He had a way of pointing his nose at the ceiling, which was not conciliatory, and he received the hated visitor with a request to know what proposals he had to make. Mirabeau, purple with rage at this frigid treatment by the man he had come to save, replied that he proposed to wish him good morning. To Malouet he said, "Your friend is a fool, and he will soon have news of me." Necker lived to regret that he had thrown such a chance away. At the time, the interview only helped to persuade him that the Commons knew their weakness, and felt the need of his succour.

Just then the expected appeal reached him from the ecclesiastical quarter. When it was seen that the nobles could not be constrained by fair words, the Commons made one more experiment with the clergy. On May 27 they sent a numerous and weighty deputation to adjure them, in the name of the God of peace and of the national welfare, not to abandon the cause of united action. The clergy this time invoked the interposition of Government.

On the 30th conferences were once more opened, and the ministers were present. The discussion was as inconclusive as before, and, on June 4, Necker produced a plan of his own. He proposed, in substance, separate verification, the crown to decide in last instance. It was a solution favourable to the privileged orders, one of which had appealed to him. He wanted their money, not their power. The clergy agreed. The Commons were embarrassed what to do, but were quickly relieved; for the nobles replied that they had already decided simply to try their own cases. By this act, on June 9, negotiations were broken off.

The decision had been taken in the apartments of the Duchess of Polignac, the queen's familiar friend, and it made a breach between the court and the minister at the first step he had taken since the Assembly met. Up to this point the aristocracy were intelligible and consistent. They would make no beginning of surrender until they knew how far it would lead them, or put themselves at the mercy of a hostile majority without any assurance for private rights. Malouet offered them a guarantee, but he was disavowed by his colleagues in a way that warned the nobles not to be too trusting.

Nobody could say how far the edifice of privilege was condemned to crumble, or what nucleus of feudal property, however secured by contract and prescription, would be suffered to remain. The nobles felt justified in defending things which were their own by law, by centuries of unquestioned possession, by purchase and inheritance, by sanction of government, by the express will of their constituents. In upholding the interest, and the very existence, of the class they represented, they might well believe that they acted in the spirit of true liberty, which depends on the multiplicity of checking forces, and that they were saving the throne. From the engagement to renounce fiscal exemption, and submit to the equal burden of taxation, they did not recede, and they claimed the support of the king. Montlosier, who belonged to their order, pronounced that their case was good and their argument bad. Twice they gave the enemy an advantage. When they saw the clergy waver, they resolved, by their usual majority of 197 to 44, that each order possessed the right of nullification; so that they would no more yield to the separate vote of the three Estates than to their united vote. Evidently the country would support those who denied the veto and were ready to overrule it, against those who gave no hope that anything would be done. Again, when they declined the Government proposals, they isolated themselves, and became an obstruction. They had lost the clergy. They now repulsed the minister. Nothing was left them except their hopes of the king. They ruined him as well as themselves. It did not follow that, because they supported the monarchy, they were sure of the monarch. And it was a graver miscalculation to think that a regular army is stronger than an undisciplined mob, and that the turbulent Parisians, eight miles off, could not protect the deputies against regiments of horse and foot, commanded by the gallant gentlemen of France, accustomed for centuries to pay the tax of blood, and fighting now in their own cause.

There was nothing more to be done. The arts of peace were exhausted. A deliberate breach with legality could alone fulfil the national decree. The country had grown tired of dilatory tactics and prolonged inaction. Conciliation, tried by the Commons, by the clergy, and by the Government, had been vain. The point was reached where it was necessary to choose between compulsion and surrender, and the Commons must either employ the means at their command to overcome resistance, or go away confessing that the great movement had broken down in their hands, and that the people had elected the wrong men. Inaction and delay had not been a policy, but the preliminary of a policy. It was reasonable to say that they would try every possible effort before resorting to aggression; but it would have been unmeaning to say that they would begin by doing nothing, and that afterwards they would continue to do nothing. Their enemy had been beforehand with them in making mistakes. They might hazard something with less danger now.

Victory indeed was assured by the defection among the nobles and the clergy. Near fifty of the one, and certainly more than one hundred of the others, were ready to come over. Instead of being equal, the parties were now two to one. Six hundred Commons could not control the same number of the deputies of privilege. But eight hundred deputies were more than a match for four hundred. Therefore, on June 10, the Commons opened the attack and summoned the garrison. Mirabeau gave notice that one of the Paris deputies had an important motion to submit. The mover was more important than the motion, for this was the apparition of Sieyès, the most original of the revolutionary statesmen, who, within a fortnight of this, his maiden speech, laid low the ancient monarchy of France. He was a new member, for the Paris elections had been delayed, the forty deputies took their seats three weeks after the opening, and Sieyès was the last deputy chosen. He objected to the existing stagnation, believing that there was no duty to the nobles that outweighed the duty to France. He proposed that the other orders be formally invited to join, and that the House should proceed to constitute itself, and to act with them if they came, without them if they stayed away. The returns were accordingly verified, and Sieyès then moved that they should declare themselves the National Assembly, the proper name for that which they claimed to be.

In spite of Malouet, and even of Mirabeau, on June 17 this motion was carried by 491 to 90. All taxes became dependent on the Assembly. The broad principle on which Sieyès acted was that the Commons were really the nation. The upper classes were not an essential part of it. They were not even a natural and normal growth, but an offending excrescence, a negative quantity, to be subtracted, not to be added up. That which ought not to exist ought not to be represented. The deputies of the Third Estate appeared for the whole. Alone they were sufficient to govern it, for alone they were identified with the common interest.

Sieyès was not solicitous that his invitation should be obeyed, for the accession of the other orders might displace the majority. Those who possessed the plenitude of power were bound to employ it. By axiomatic simplicity more than by sustained argument Sieyès mastered his hearers.

V
THE TENNIS-COURT OATH

We saw last week that much time was spent in fruitless negotiation which ended in a deadlock—the Commons refusing to act except in conjunction with the other orders, and the others insisting on the separate action which had been prescribed by their instructions and by the king.

The Commons altered their policy under the influence of Sieyès, who advised that they should not wait for the others, but should proceed in their absence. In his famous pamphlet he had argued that they were really the nation, and had the right on their side. And his theory was converted into practice, because it now appeared that they had not only the right, but the power. They knew it, because the clergy were wavering. Thursday, June 18, the day after the proclamation of the National Assembly, was a festival. On Friday the clergy divided on the question of joining. The proposal was negatived, but twelve of its opponents stated that they would be on the other side if the vote in common extended only to the verification of returns. The minority at once accepted the condition, and so became the majority. Others thereupon acceded, and by six o'clock in the evening 149 ecclesiastics recorded their votes for the Commons. That 19th of June is a decisive date, for then the priests went over to the Revolution. The Commons, by a questionable and audacious act, had put themselves wrong with everybody when the inferior clergy abandoned the cause of privilege and came to their rescue.

The dauphin had lately died, and the royal family were living in retirement at Marly. At ten o'clock in the evening of the vote, the Archbishops of Paris and Rouen arrived there, described the event to the king, and comforted him by saying that the prelates, all but four, had remained true to their order. They were followed by a very different visitor, whom it behoved the king to hear, for he was a man destined to hold the highest offices of State under many governments, to be the foremost minister of the republic, the empire, and the monarchy, to predominate over European sovereigns at

Vienna, over European statesmen in London, and to be universally feared, and hated, and admired, as the most sagacious politician in the world.

Talleyrand came to Marly at dead of night, and begged a secret audience of the king. He was not a favourite at court. He had obtained the see of Autun only at the request of the assembled clergy of France, and when the pope selected him for a cardinal's hat, Lewis prevented his nomination. He now refused to see him, and sent him to his brother. The Count d'Artois was in bed, but the bishop was his friend, and was admitted. He said it was necessary that the Government should act with vigour. The conduct of the Assembly was illegal and foolish, and would ruin the monarchy unless the States-General were dissolved. Talleyrand would undertake, with his friends, some of whom came with him and were waiting below, to form a new administration. The Assembly, compromised and discredited by the recent outbreak, would be dismissed, a new one would be elected on an altered franchise, and a sufficient display of force would prevent resistance. Talleyrand proposed to reverse the policy of Necker, which he thought feeble and vacillating, and which had thrown France into the hands of Sieyès. With a stronger grasp he meant to restore the royal initiative, in order to carry out the constitutional changes which the nation expected.

The count put on his clothes, and carried the matter to the king. He detested Necker with his concessions, and welcomed the prospect of getting rid of him for a minister of his own making taken from his own circle. He came back with a positive refusal. Then Talleyrand, convinced that it was henceforth vain to serve the king, gave notice that every man must be allowed to shift for himself; and the count admitted that he was right. They remembered that interview after twenty-five years of separation, when one of the two held in his hands the crown of France, which the other, in the name of Lewis XVIII., came to receive from him.

The king repulsed Talleyrand because he had just taken a momentous resolution. The time had arrived which Necker had waited for, the time to interpose with a Constitution so largely conceived, so exactly defined, so faithfully adapted to the deliberate wishes of the people, as to supersede and overshadow the Assembly, with its perilous tumult and its prolonged sterility. He had proposed some such measure early in May, when it was rejected, and he did not insist. But now the policy unwisely postponed was clearly opportune. Secret advice came from liberal public men, urging the danger of the crisis, and the certainty that the Assembly would soon hurry to extremes. Mirabeau himself deplored its action, and Malouet had reason to expect a stouter resistance to the revolutionary argument and the sudden ascendency of Sieyès. The queen in person, and influential men at court, entreated Necker to modify his constitutional scheme; but he was unshaken, and the king stood by him. It was decided that the comprehensive measure intended to distance and annul the Assembly should be proclaimed from the throne on the following Monday.

This was the rock that wrecked the Talleyrand ministry, and it destroyed more solid structures than that unsubstantial phantom. The plan was statesmanlike, and it marks the summit of Necker's career. But he neglected to communicate with men whom he might well have trusted, and the secret was fatal, for it was kept twelve hours too long. As the princes had refused the use of their riding-school, there were only three buildings dedicated to the States-General, instead of four, and the Commons, by reason of their numbers, occupied the great hall where the opening ceremony was held, and which had now to be made ready for the royal sitting.

Very early in the morning of Saturday, June 20, the president of the Assembly, the astronomer Bailly, received notice from the master of ceremonies that the hall was wanted, in order to be prepared for Monday, and that the meetings of the Commons were meanwhile suspended for that day. Bailly was not taken by surprise, for a friend, who went about with his eyes open, had warned him of what was going on. But the Assembly had formally adjourned to that day, the members were expecting the appointed meeting, and the message came too late. Bailly deemed that it was a studied insult, the angry retort of Government, and the penalty of the recent vote, and he inferred, most erroneously as we know, that the coming speech from the throne would be hostile. Therefore he gave all the solemnity he could to the famous scene that ensued. Appearing at the head of the indignant deputies, he was denied admission. The door was only opened that he might fetch his papers, and the National Assembly that represented France found itself, by royal command, standing outside on the pavement, at the hour fixed for its deliberations.

At that instant the doubts and divisions provoked by the overriding logic of Sieyès disappeared. Moderate and Revolutionist felt the same resentment, and had the same sense of being opposed by a power that was insane. There were some, and Sieyès among them, who proposed that they should adjourn to Paris. But a home was found in the empty Tennis Court hard by. There, with a view to baffle dangerous designs, and also to retrieve his own waning influence, Mounier assumed the lead. He moved that they should bind themselves by oath never to separate until they had given a Constitution to France; and all the deputies immediately swore it, save one, who added "Dissentient" to his name, and who was hustled out by a backdoor, to save him from the fury of his colleagues. This dramatic action added little to that which had been done three days earlier. The deputies understood that a Constituent Assembly must be single, that the legislative power had, for the purpose, been transferred to them, and could not be restrained or recalled. Their authority was not to be limited by an upper house, for both upper houses were absorbed; nor by the king, for they regarded neither his sanction nor his veto; nor by the nation itself, for they refused, by their oath, to be dissolved.

The real event of the Tennis Court was to unite all parties against the crown, and to make them adopt the new policy of radical and indefinite change, outdoing what Sieyès himself had done. The mismanagement of the court drove its friends into the van of the movement. The last Royalist defender of safe measures had vanished through the backdoor.

Malouet had tendered a clause saving the royal power; but it was decided not to put it, lest it should be refused. Mirabeau, in whose eyes the decree of the 17th portended civil war, now voted, reluctantly, with the rest.

Whilst the Assembly held its improvised and informal meeting at Versailles, the king sat in council at Marly on Necker's magnanimous proposal. After a struggle, and with some damaging concessions, the minister carried his main points. They were gathering their papers, and making ready to disperse, when a private message was brought to the king. He went out, desiring them to wait his return. Montmorin turned to Necker and said, "It is the queen, and all is over." The king came back, and adjourned the council to Monday at Versailles. And it was in this way that the report of what had happened that morning told upon the Government, and the enthusiasm of the Tennis Court frustrated the pondered measures of the most liberal minister in Europe. For it was, in truth, the queen, and in that brief interval it was decreed that France, so near the goal in that month of June, should wade to it through streams of blood during the twenty-five most terrible years in the history of Christian nations.

The council of ministers, which was adjourned in consequence of the meeting in the Tennis Court, went over to the *noblesse*, and restored in their interest the principles of the old régime. It resolved that the king should rescind the recent acts of the Assembly; should maintain inviolate the division of orders, allowing the option of debate in common only in cases where neither privilege nor the Constitution were affected; that he should confirm feudal rights and even fiscal immunities, unless voluntarily abandoned, and should deny admission to public employment irrespective of class. Necker's adversaries prevailed, and the ancient bulwarks were set up again, in favour of the aristocracy.

Still, a portion of the great scheme was preserved, and the concessions on the part of the crown were such that some weeks earlier they would have been hailed with enthusiasm, and the consistent logic of free institutions exercises a coercive virtue that made many think that the King's Speech of June 23 ought to have been accepted as the greater charter of France. That was the opinion of Arthur Young; of Gouverneur Morris, who had given the final touches to the American Constitution; of Jefferson, the author of the *Declaration of Independence*; and afterwards even of Sieyès himself.

On this account, Necker wavered to the last moment, and on the Tuesday morning prepared to attend the king. His friends, his family, his daughter, the wonder of the age, made him understand that he could not sanction by his presence, at a solemn crisis, an act which reversed one essential half of his policy. He dismissed his carriage, took off his court suit, and left the vacant place to proclaim his fall. That evening he sent in his resignation. His significant absence; the peremptory language of the king; the abrogation of their decrees, which was effectual and immediate, while the compensating promises were eventual, and not yet equivalent to laws; the avowed resolve to identify the Crown with the nobles, struck the Assembly with consternation. The removal of the constitutional question to the list of matters to be debated separately was, in the existing conditions of antagonism, the end of free government. And indeed the position occupied by the king was untenable, because the division of orders into three Houses had already come to an end. For on Monday the 22nd, in the Church of St. Lewis, 149 ecclesiastical deputies, the Archbishops of Bordeaux and Vienne at their head, had joined the Commons. It was a step which they were legally authorised and competent to take, and the Revolution now had a majority not only of individual votes, but of orders. It was a forlorn hope, therefore, to separate them by compulsion.

Lewis XVI. ended by declaring that he was determined to accomplish the happiness of his people, and that if the deputies refused to co-operate he would accomplish it alone; and he charged them to withdraw. The Commons were in their own House, and, with the majority of the clergy, they resumed their seats, uncertain of the future. Their uncertainty was all at once auspiciously relieved. Dreux Brézé, the master of ceremonies, reappeared, and as he brought a message from the king he wore his plumed hat upon his head. With clamorous outcries he was told to uncover, and he uttered a reply so insolent that his son, describing the scene in public after many years, declined to repeat his words. Therefore, when he asked whether they had heard the king's order to depart, he received a memorable lesson. Mirabeau exclaimed, "Yes, but if we are to be expelled, we shall yield only to force." Brézé answered, correctly, that he did not recognise Mirabeau as the organ of the Assembly, and he turned to the president. But Bailly rose above Mirabeau, and said, "The nation is assembled here, and receives no orders." At these words the master of ceremonies, as if suddenly aware of the presence of majesty, retired, walking backwards to the door. It was at that moment that the old order changed and made place for the new. For Sieyès, who possessed the good gift of putting a keen edge to his thoughts, who had begun his career in Parliament ten days before by saying, "It is time to cut the cables," now spoke, and with superb simplicity thus defined the position: "What you were yesterday you are now. Let us pass to the order of the day." In this way the monarchy, as a force distinct from a form, was not assailed, or abolished, or condemned, but passed over. Assault, abolition, condemnation were to follow, and already there were penetrating eyes that caught, in the distance, the first gleam of the axe. "The king," said Mirabeau, "has taken the road to the scaffold."

The abdication of prerogative, which the king offered on June 23, went far; but the people demanded surrender in regard to privilege. The Assembly, submitting to the geometrical reasoning of Sieyès and to the surprise of the Tennis Court, had frightened him into an alliance with the nobles, and he linked his cause to theirs. He elected to stand or fall with interests not his own, with an order which was powerless to help him, which could make no return for his sacrifice in their behalf, which was unable for one hour to defend itself, and was about to perish by its own hand. The failure of June 23 was immediately apparent. The Assembly, having dismissed Dreux Brézé, was not molested further. Necker consented to resume office, with greatly increased popularity. Under the influence of the royal declaration forty-seven nobles, being a portion only of the Liberal minority, went over to the Commons, and Talleyrand followed at the head of twenty-five prelates. Then the king gave way. He instructed the resisting magnates to join the National Assembly. In very sincere and solemn terms they warned him that by such a surrender he was putting off his crown. The Count d'Artois rejoined that the king's life would be in danger if they persisted. There was one young nobleman rising rapidly to fame as a gracious and impressive speaker, whom even this appeal to loyal hearts failed to move. "Perish the monarch," cried Cazalès, "but not the monarchy!"

Lewis underwent the humiliation of revoking, on June 27, what he had ceremoniously promulgated on the 23rd, because there was a fatal secret. Paris was agitated, and the people promised the deputies to stand by them at their need. But what could they effect at Versailles against the master of so many legions? Just then a mutiny broke out in the French guards, the most disciplined body of troops in the capital, and betrayed the key to the hollow and unstable counsels of the Government. The army could not be trusted. Necker suspected it as early as February. In the last week of June, the English, Prussian, and Venetian envoys report that the crown was disabled because it was disarmed. The regiments at hand would not serve against the national representatives. It was resolved to collect faithful bands of Swiss, Alsatians, and Walloons. Ten foreign regiments, near 30,000 men in all, were hurried to the scene. They were the last hope of royalism. Trusty friends were informed that the surrender was only to last until the frontier garrisons could be brought to Versailles. D'Artois confided to one of them that many heads must fall. And he uttered the sinister proverb which became historic in another tragedy: If you want an omelette you must not be afraid of breaking eggs.

VI
THE FALL OF THE BASTILLE

After the dramatic intervention of the Marquis de Brézé, the king's speech of June 23 was never seriously considered by the Assembly. Yet the concessions, which it made to the spirit of political progress, satisfied philosophic observers, and there had been no time in English history where changes so extensive, proceeding from the Crown, would have failed to conciliate the people. It was a common belief in those days, expressly sanctioned by the Economists, that secondary liberties, carried far enough, are worth more than formal securities for the principle of self-government. One is of daily use and practical advantage; the other is of the domain of theory, dubiously beneficial, and without assurance of enlightenment and justice. A wise, honest, and intelligent administration gives more to men than the established reign of uncertain opinion. These arguments had more weight with philosophers than with the deputies, for it was already decided that they must make the Constitution. All the king offered, and a great deal more, they intended to take. Much that he insisted on preserving they were resolved to destroy. The offer, at its best, was vitiated by the alloy: for the most offensive privileges, immunities, and emoluments of rank were to be perpetuated, and it was against these that the fiercest force of the revolutionary movement was beating. In order that they might be abolished, the nation tendered its indefeasible support, its unconquerable power, to its representatives.

If the Assembly, content with the advantage gained over the king, had surrendered unconditionally to the nobles, and assented, for a few political reforms, to the social degradation of the democracy, they would have betrayed their constituents. On that consideration they were compelled to act. They acted also on the principle, which was not new, which came down indeed from mediæval divines, but which was newly invested with universal authority, that the law is not the will of the sovereign that commands, but of the nation that obeys. It was the very marrow of the doctrine that obstruction of liberty is crime, that absolute authority is not a thing to be consulted, but a thing to be removed, and that resistance to it is no affair of interest or convenience, but of sacred obligation. Every drop of blood shed in the American conflict was shed in a cause immeasurably inferior to theirs, against a system more legitimate by far than that of June 23. Unless Washington was an assassin, it was their duty to oppose, if it might be, by policy, if it must be, by force, the mongrel measure of concession and obstinacy which the Court had carried against the proposals of Necker. That victory was reversed, and the success of the Commons was complete. They had brought the three orders into one; they had compelled the king to retract his declaration and to restore his disgraced minister; they had exposed the weakness of their oppressors, and they had the nation at their back.

On June 27, in the united Assembly, Mirabeau delivered an address of mingled triumph and conciliation, which was his first act of statesmanship. He said that the speech from the throne contained large and generous views that proved the genuine liberality of the king. He desired to receive them gratefully without the drawbacks imposed by unthinking advisers, and to respect the just rights of the *noblesse*. He took the good without the evil, extricating Lewis from his entanglement, and tracing the line by which he might have advanced to great results. "The past," he said, "has been the history of wild beasts. We are inaugurating the history of men; for we have no weapon but discussion, and no adversary but prejudice."

Their victory brought loss as well as gain to the Commons, and there was reason to think that the counsel of Sieyès, to let the other orders take their own separate course, was founded on wisdom. Their opponents, joining under compulsion, had the means as well as the will of doing them injury.

For the clergy there was a brief season of popular favour. The country priests, sprung from the peasantry, and poorly off, shared many of their feelings. The patronage of the State went to men of birth; and one of these, the Archbishop of Aix, had proclaimed his belief that, if anybody was to be exempt from taxation, it ought to be the impoverished layman, not the wealthy ecclesiastic. When it chanced that the Committee of Constitution was elected without any member of the clergy upon it, the Commons raised a cry that they should be introduced in their proportion. They, in a fraternal spirit, refused. And the second Committee, the one that actually drew up the scheme, was composed of three churchmen to five laymen. The nobles were not reconciled, and refused to unite with men of English views in a Tory party. To them, the separation of orders was a fundamental maxim of security, which they had inherited, which they were bound to hand down.

They looked on debate in common as provisional, as an exception, to be rectified as soon as might be. They kept up the practice of also meeting separately. On July 3 there were one hundred and thirty-eight present; and on the 11th there still were eighty. They refused to vote in the divisions of the joint Assembly, because their instructions forbade. The scruple was sincere, and was shared by Lafayette; but others meant it as a protest that the Assembly was not lawfully constituted. Therefore, July 7, Talleyrand moved to annul the instructions. They could not be allowed to control the Assembly; they ought not to influence individuals. The constituencies contribute to a decision; they cannot resist it. Whatever the original wish of the electors, the final act belonged to the legislature. The king himself, on June 27, had declared the imperative mandates unconstitutional. But the deputies, in declaring themselves permanent, had cut themselves adrift from their constituents. The instructions had become the sole security that the Constitution would remain within the limits laid down by the nation, the sole assurance against indefinite change. They alone determined the line of advance, and gave protection to monarchy, property, religion, against the headlong rush of opinion, and the exigencies of popular feeling.

Sieyès, who expected no good from the co-operation of the orders which he condemned, and who thought a nobleman or prelate who did not vote better than one who voted wrong, urged that the question did not affect the Assembly, but the constituencies, and might be left to them. He carried his amendment by seven hundred to twenty-eight.

Meantime the party that had prevailed on June 23 and had succumbed on the 27th was at work to recover the lost position. Lewis had retained the services of Necker, without dismissing the colleagues who baffled him. He told him that he would not accept his resignation now, but would choose the time for it. Necker had not the acuteness to understand that he would be dismissed as soon as his enemies felt strong enough to do without him. A king who deserted his friends and reversed his accepted policy because there was no force he could depend on, was a king with a short shrift before him. He became the tool of men who did not love him, and who now despised him.

The resources wanting at the critical moment were, however, within reach, and the scheme proposed to the Count d'Artois by the wily bishop a few nights before was revived by less accomplished plotters. On July 1 it became known that a camp of 25,000 men was to be formed near Versailles under Marshal de Broglie, a veteran who gathered his laurels in the Seven

Years' War, and soon the Terrace was crowded with officers from the north and east, who boasted that they had sharpened their sabres, and meant to make short work of the ambitious lawyers, the profligate noblemen, and unfrocked priests who were ruining the country.

In adopting these measures the king did not regard himself as the originator of violence. There had been disturbances in Paris, and at Versailles the archbishop of Paris had been assaulted, and compelled to promise that he would go over to the Assembly. The leader on the other side, Champion de Cicé, archbishop of Bordeaux, came to him, and entreated him not to yield to faction, not to keep a promise extorted by threats. He replied that he had given his word and meant to keep it.

Forty years later Charles X. declared that his brother had mounted the scaffold because, at this juncture, he would not mount his horse. In truth Lewis believed that the deputies, cut off from Paris by visible battalions, would be overawed, that the army of waverers would be accessible to influence, to promises, remonstrances, and rewards, that it would be safer to coerce the Assembly by intimidation than to dissolve it. He had refused to listen to Talleyrand; he still rejected the stronger part of his scheme. By judicious management he hoped that the Assembly might be brought to undo its own usurping and unwarranted work, and that he would be able to recover the position he had taken up on June 23, the last day on which his policy had been that of a free agent.

Necker knew no more than everybody else of the warlike array. On July 7 thirty regiments were concentrated; more were within a few days' march, and the marshal, surrounded by an eager and hurried staff, surveyed his maps of suburban Paris at his headquarters at Versailles.

The peril grew day by day, and it was time for the Assembly to act. They were defenceless, but they relied on the people of Paris and on the demoralisation of the army. Their friends had the command of money, and large sums were spent in preparing the citizens for an armed conflict. For the capitalists were on their side, looking to them to prevent the national bankruptcy which the Court and the nobles were bringing on. And the Palais Royal, the residence of the Duke of Orleans, was the centre of an active organisation. Since the king had proved himself incompetent, helpless, and insincere, men had looked to the Duke as a popular prince of the Blood, who was also wealthy and ambitious, and might avail to save the principle of monarchy, which Lewis had discredited. His friends clung to the idea, and continued to conspire in his interest after the rest of the world had been repelled by the defects of his character. For a moment they thought of his son, who was gifted for that dangerous part as perfectly as the father was unfit, but his time was to be in a later generation.

The leading men in the Assembly knew their position with accuracy, and did not exaggerate the danger they were in. On July 10 their shrewd American adviser, Morris, wrote: "I think the crisis is past without having been perceived; and now a free Constitution will be the certain result." And yet there were 30,000 men, commanded by a marshal of France, ready for action; and several regiments of Swiss, famed for fidelity and valour, and destined, in the same cause, to become still more famous, were massed in Paris itself under Besenval, the trusted soldier of the Court.

On July 8, breaking through the order of debate, Mirabeau rose and the action began—the action which changed the face of the world, and the imperishable effects of which will be felt by every one of us, to the last day of his life. He moved an address to the king, warning him that, if he did not withdraw his troops, the streets of Paris would run blood; and proposing that the preservation of order should be committed to a civic guard. On the following day the Assembly voted the address, and on the 10th the Count de Clermont Tonnerre, at the head of a deputation, read it to the king. On the morning of Saturday, 11th, his reply was communicated to the Assembly. He had had three days to hasten his military preparations. At Paris, the agitators and organisers employed the time in arranging their counter measures.

The king refused to send away troops which there had been good reason to collect, but he was ready to move, with the Assembly, to some town at a distance from the turbid capital. The royal message was tipped with irony, and the deputies, in spite of Mirabeau, resolved not to discuss it. After this first thrust Lewis flung away the scabbard. That day, at council, it was noticed that he was nervous and uneasy, and disguised his restlessness by feigning sleep. At the end, taking one of the ministers aside, he gave him a letter for Necker, who was absent. The letter contained his dismissal, with an order for banishment.

Necker, who for some days had known that it must come, was at dinner. He said nothing to his company, and went out, as usual, for a drive. Then he made for the frontier, and never stopped till he reached Brussels. Two horsemen who had followed, keeping out of sight, had orders to arrest him if he changed his course. He travelled up the Rhine to his own country, on the way to his home by the lake of Geneva. At the first Swiss hotel he found the Duchess de Polignac. He had left her at Versailles, the Queen's best friend and the heart of the intrigue against him; and she was now ruined and an exile, and the forerunner of the emigration. From her, and from the letters that quickly followed, forwarded by the Assembly, he learned the events that had happened since his fall, learned that he was, for one delirious moment, master of the king, of his enemies, and of the country.

The astounding news that Necker heard at "The Three Kings" at Bâle was this. His friends had been disgraced with him, and the chief of the new ministry was Breteuil, who had been the colleague of Calonne and Vergennes, and had managed the affair of the Diamond Necklace. He had directed the policy of those who opposed the National Assembly, holding himself in the twilight, until strong measures and a strong man were called for. He now came forward, and proposed that the nobles should depart in a body, protesting against the methods by which the States-General had been sunk in the National Assembly. In one day he brought round twenty-six of the minority to his views. A few remained, who would make a light day's work for a man of conviction and resource. But resolute as Breteuil was, the Parisian democracy acted with still greater quickness and decision, and with a not less certain aim. On the 12th it became known that Necker had been sent out of the country, and that the armaments were in the hands of men who meant to employ them against the people. Paris was in disorder, but the middle class provided a civic guard for its protection. There were encounters with the troops, and some blood was shed.

New men began to appear who represented the rising classes: Camille Desmoulins, a rhetorical journalist, with literary but not political talent, harangued the people in the garden of the Palais Royal; and one of the strong men of history, Danton, showed that he knew how to manage and to direct the masses.

The 13th was a day wasted by Government, spent by Paris in busy preparation. Men talked wildly of destroying the Bastille, as a sign that would be understood. Early on July 14 a body of men made their way to the Invalides, and seized 28,000 stand of arms and some cannon. At the other extremity of Paris the ancient fortress of the Bastille towered over the workmen's quarter and commanded the city. Whenever the guns thundered from its lofty battlements, resistance would be over, and the conquered arms would be unavailing.

The Bastille not only overshadowed the capital, but it darkened the hearts of men, for it had been notorious for centuries as the instrument and the emblem of tyranny. The captives behind its bars were few and uninteresting; but the wide world knew the horror of its history, the blighted lives, the ruined families, the three thousand dishonoured graves within the precincts, and the common voice called for its destruction as the sign of deliverance. At the elections both nobles and commons demanded that it should be levelled with the ground.

As early as the 4th of July Besenval received notice that it would be attacked. He sent a detachment of Swiss, that raised the garrison to one hundred and thirty-eight, and he did no more. During the morning hours, while the invaders of the Invalides were distributing the plundered arms and ammunition, emissaries penetrated into the Bastille, under various pretexts, to observe the defences. One fair-spoken visitor was taken to the top of the dreaded towers, where he saw that the guns with which the embrasures had bristled, which were beyond the range of marksmen, and had Paris at their mercy, were dismantled and could not be fired.

About the middle of the day, when this was known, the attack began. It was directed by the *Gardes Françaises*, who had been the first to mutiny, and had been disbanded, and were now the backbone of the people's army. The siege consisted in efforts to lower the drawbridge. After several hours the massive walls were unshaken, and the place was as safe as before the first discharge. But the defenders knew that they were lost. Besenval was not the man to rescue them by fighting his way through several miles of streets. They were not provisioned, and the men urged the governor to make terms before he was compelled. They had brought down above a hundred of their assailants, without losing a man. But it was plain that the loss neither of a hundred nor of a thousand would affect the stern determination of the crowd, whilst it might increase their fury. Delauney, in his despair, seized a match, and wanted to fire the magazine. His men remonstrated and spoke of the dreadful devastation that must follow the explosion. The man who stayed the hand of the despairing commander, and whose name was Bécard, deserved a better fate than he met that day, for he was one of the four or five that were butchered. The men beat a parley, hoisted the white flag, and obtained, on the honour of a French officer, a verbal promise of safety.

Then the victors came pouring over the bridge, triumphant over a handful of Swiss and invalids—triumphant too over thirteen centuries of monarchy and the longest line of kings. Those who had served in the regular army took charge of as many prisoners as they could rescue, carried them to their quarters, and gave them their own beds to sleep in. The officers who had conducted the unreal attack, and received the piteous surrender, brought the governor to the Hôtel de Ville, fighting their way through a murderous crowd. For it was long believed that Delauney had admitted the people into the first court, and then had perfidiously shot them down. In his struggles he hurt a bystander, who chanced to be a cook. The man, prompted, it seems, less by animosity than by the pride of professional skill, drew a knife and cut off his head. Flesselles, the chief of the old municipality, appointed by the Crown, was shot soon after, under suspicion of having encouraged Delauney to resist.

Dr. Rigby, an Englishman who was at the Palais Royal, has described what he saw. First came an enormous multitude bearing aloft the keys of the conquered citadel, with the inscription, "The Bastille is taken." The joy was indescribable, and strangers shook his hand, saying, "We too are free men, and there will never more be war between our countries." Then came another procession, also shouting and rejoicing; but the bystanders looked on with horror, for the trophies carried by were the heads of murdered men. For the nation had become sovereign, and the soldiers who fired upon it were reckoned rebels and traitors. The foreign envoys were all impressed with the idea that the vengeance wrought was out of all proportion with the immensity of the thing achieved. At nightfall the marshal gave orders to evacuate Paris. Besenval was already in full retreat, and the capital was no longer in the possession of the king of France.

Meanwhile the National Assembly, aware of the strength of popular feeling around them, were calm in the midst of danger. Theirs was a diminished part, while, almost within sight and hearing, history was being unmade and made by a power superior to their own. On the morning of the 14th they elected the Committee of Eight who were to draw up the Constitution. Mounier and the friends of the English model still prevailed. By evening their chance had vanished, for the English model includes a king.

Late in the day Noailles brought authentic news of what he had witnessed; and the Assembly learned, in agitated silence, that the head of the governor of the impregnable Bastille had been displayed on a pike about the streets of Paris. Lafayette took the chair, while the President hurried with Noailles to the palace. They made no impression there. Lewis informed them that he had recalled his troops, and then he went to bed, tranquil, and persistently ignoring what it was that had been done, and what it was that had passed away.

But in the morning, when the Assembly met in disorder, and were about to send one more deputation, it was found that a change had taken place in the brief hours of that memorable night. At two o'clock the king was roused from sleep by one of the great officers of the household. The intruder, La Rochefoucauld, Duke de Liancourt, was not a man of talent, but he was universally known as the most benevolent and the most beneficent of the titled nobles of the realm. He made his master understand the truth and its significance, and how, in the capital that day, in every province on the morrow, the authority of government was at an end. And when Lewis, gradually awaking, exclaimed, "But this is a great revolt!" Liancourt replied, "No, sir, it is a great Revolution!" With those historic words the faithful courtier detached the monarch from his ministers, and obtained control over him in the deciding days that were to follow. Guided by the duke, and attended by his brothers, but without the ceremonious glories of regality, Lewis XVI. went down to the Assembly and made his submission. In the pathetic solemnity of the scene, the deputies forgot for a moment their righteous anger and their more righteous scorn, and the king returned to the palace on foot, in a sudden procession of triumph, amnestied and escorted by the entire body.

The struggle was over, and the spell was broken; and the Assembly had to govern France. To establish order a vast deputation repaired to the Hôtel de Ville, where Lally Tollendal delivered an oration thrilling with brotherhood and gladness, and appeared, crowned with flowers, before the people.

To cement the compact between Paris and Versailles, Bailly, the first president, was placed at the head of the new elective municipality, and the vice-president, Lafayette, became commander of the National Guard. This was the first step towards that Commune which was to exercise so vast an influence over the fortunes of France. It came into existence of necessity, when the action of Government was paralysed, and the space which it occupied was untenanted.

The National Guard was an invention of great import, for it was the army of society distinct from the army of the state, opinion in arms apart from authority. It was the middle class organised as a force, against the force above and the force below; and it protected liberty against the Crown, and property against the poor. It has been ever since the defence of order and the ruin of governments; for, as it was the nation itself, nobody was bold enough to fight it. Before the altar of Notre Dame Lafayette took the oath of fidelity to the people, and not to the king. He never displayed real capacity for peace or war; but in the changes of a long life he was true to the early convictions imbibed in Washington's camp.

On their return from Paris the great deputation reported that the people demanded the recall of Necker. At last the king dismissed Breteuil, and charged the Assembly to take charge of a letter to the banished statesman. His banishment had lasted five days; it was now the turn of his enemies. On the same night, July 16, the baffled intriguers went into exile. Lewis himself sent his brother away, for the safety of himself and of the dynasty. The others followed. The queen was compelled to dismiss Madame de Polignac, whom she had too confidently trusted, and she was left alone amongst her enemies. This was the first emigration. The remaining nobles announced that they abandoned resistance, and the Assembly was at last united. The fight was lost and won, and the victor claimed the spoils.

But the Assembly was not the victor, and had contributed little to the portentous change between the dismissal of Necker and the despatch of the fleet messenger with his recall. Whilst the deputies served the national cause by talking, there were plainer men at Paris who had died for it. The force that risked life and conquered was not at Versailles. It was Paris that held the fallen power, the power of governing itself, the Assembly, and France. The predominance of the capital was the new feature that enabled the monarchy to pass into a Republic.

The king had become a servant of two masters. Having recanted before his master at Versailles, it became necessary that he should submit himself to the new and mysterious authority at the Hôtel de Ville. He had yielded to representative democracy. He had to pay the same recognition to direct democracy. It was not safe to leave the Orleans stronghold entirely in their hands. Between the ministry that was gone and the ministry to come, Lewis acted by the advice of Liancourt.

Early on July 17 he made his will, heard mass, received communion, and set out to visit his good city. The queen remained behind, with all her carriages ready, in order that, at the first signal, she might fly for her life. At the barrier the king's eye fell, for the first time, on innumerable armed men, who lined the streets for miles, and wore strange colours, and did not own him as their chief. Neither the National Guard, nor the dense crowd behind them, uttered a sound of welcome. Not a voice was raised, except for the nation and its deputies.

The peace made between the king and the Assembly did not count here. All men had to know that there was a distinct authority, to which a further homage was due, even from the sovereign. At the Hôtel de Ville the homage was paid. There the king confirmed the new mayor, and approved what had been done, and he showed himself to the people with the new cockade, devised by Lafayette, to proclaim that the royal power which had ruled France since the conversion of Clovis ruled France no more. He made his way home amid acclamations, regulated by the commander of the National Guard, like the gloomy and menacing silence in which he had been received.

A new reign commenced. The head of the great house of Bourbon, the heir of so much power and glory, on whom rested the tradition of Lewis XIV., was unfit to exert, under jealous control, the narrow measure of authority that remained. For the moment there was none. Anarchy in the capital gave the signal for anarchy in the provinces, and anarchy at that moment had a terrible meaning.

The deputies who came to Paris, to share the enthusiasm of the moment, failed to notice the fact that the victorious army which gave liberty to France and power to the Assembly was largely composed of assassins. Their crimes disappeared in the blaze of their achievements. Their support was still needed. It seemed too soon to insult the patriot and the hero by telling him that he was also a ruffian. The mixed multitude was thereby encouraged to believe that the slaughter of the obnoxious was a necessity of critical times. The Russian envoy wrote on the 19th that the French people displayed the same ferocity as two centuries before.

On the 22nd, Foulon, one of the colleagues of Breteuil, and his son-in-law Berthier, also a high official, were massacred by premeditation in the streets. Neither Bailly, nor Lafayette with all his cohorts, could protect the life of a doomed man; but a dragoon who had paraded with the heart of Berthier was challenged, when he came home to barracks, and cut down by a comrade.

Lally Tollendal brought the matter before the Assembly. His father inherited the feelings of an exiled Jacobite against Hanoverian England. He was at Falkirk with Charles Edward, and charged with the Irish Brigade that broke the English column at Fontenoy. During the Seven Years' War he commanded in India, and held Pondicherry for ten months against Coote. Brought home a prisoner, he was released on parole, that he might stand his trial. He was condemned to death; and his son, who did not know who he was, was brought to the place of execution, that they might meet once on earth. But Lally stabbed himself, and lest justice should be defrauded, he was brought out to die, with a gag in his mouth to silence protest, some hours before the time.

The death of Lally is part of the long indictment against the French judiciary, and his son strove for years to have the sentence reversed. He came over to England, and understood our system better than any of his countrymen. Therefore, when Mounier, who was no orator, brought forward his Constitution, it was Lally who expounded it. By his emotional and emphatic eloquence he earned a brief celebrity; and in the Waterloo year he was a Minister of State, *in partibus*, at Ghent. He became a peer of France, and when he died, in 1830, the name disappeared. Not many years ago a miserable man, whom nobody knew and who asked help from nobody, died of want in a London cellar. He was the son of Lally Tollendal.

It is said that when, on July 22, he denounced the atrocities in Paris, he overdid the occasion, speaking of himself, of his father, of his feelings. Barnave, who was a man of honour, and already conspicuous, was irritated to such a pitch that he exclaimed: "Was this blood, that they have shed, so pure?"

Long before Barnave expiated his sin upon the scaffold he felt and acknowledged its enormity. But it is by him and men like him, and not by the scourings of the galleys, that we can get to understand the spirit of the time. Two men, more eminent than Barnave, show it still more clearly. The great chemist Lavoisier wrote to Priestley that if there had been some excesses, they were committed for the love of liberty, philosophy, and toleration, and that there was no danger of such things being done in France for an inferior motive. And this is the view of Jefferson on the massacres of September: "Many guilty persons fell without the forms of trial, and with them some innocent. These I deplore as much as anybody. But—it was necessary to use the arm of the people, a machine not quite so blind as balls and bombs, but blind to a certain degree—was ever such a prize won with so little innocent blood?" There is a work in twelve stout volumes, written to prove that it was all the outcome of the Classics, and due to Harmodius, and Brutus, and Timoleon.

But you will find that murder, approved and acknowledged, is not an epidemic peculiar to any time, or any country, or any opinion. We need not include hot-blooded nations of the South in order to define it as one characteristic of modern Monarchy. You may trace it in the Kings of France, Francis I., Charles IX., Henry III., Lewis XIII., Lewis XIV., in the Emperors Ferdinand I. and II., in Elizabeth Tudor and Mary Stuart, in James and William. Still more if you consider a class of men, not much worse, according to general estimate, than their neighbours, that is, the historians. They have praise and hero-worship for nearly every one of these anointed culprits. The strong man with the dagger is followed by the weaker man with the sponge. First, the criminal who slays; then the sophist who defends the slayer.

The royalists pursued the same tradition through the revolutionary times. Cérutti advised that Mirabeau and Target should be removed by poison; Chateaubriand wished to poniard Condorcet, and Malesherbes admired him for it; the name of Georges Cadoudal was held in honour, because his intended victim was Napoleon; La Rochejaquelein entertained the same scheme, and made no secret of it to the general, Ségur. Adair found them indignant at Vienna because Fox had refused to have the Emperor murdered, and warned him of the plot.

Those who judge morality by the intention have been less shocked at the crimes of power, where the temptation is so strong and the danger so slight, than at those committed by men resisting oppression. Assuredly, the best things that are loved and sought by man are religion and liberty— they, I mean, and not pleasure or prosperity, not knowledge or power. Yet the paths of both are stained with infinite blood; both have been often a plea for assassination, and the worst of men have been among those who claimed to promote each sacred cause.

Do not open your minds to the filtering of the fallacious doctrine that it is less infamous to murder men for their politics than for their religion or their money, or that the courage to execute the deed is worse than the cowardice to excuse it. Let us not flinch from condemning without respite or remission, not only Marat and Carrier, but also Barnave. Because there may be hanging matter in the lives of illustrious men, of William the Silent and Farnese, of Cromwell and Napoleon, we are not to be turned from justice towards the actions, and still more the thoughts, of those whom we are about to study.

Having said this, I shall endeavour, in that which is before us, to spare you the spectacles that degrade, and the plaintive severity that agitates and wearies. The judgment I call for is in the conscience, not upon the lips, for ourselves, and not for display. "Man," says Taine, "is a wild beast, carnivorous by nature, and delighting in blood." That cruel speech is as much confirmed by the events that are crowding upon us as it has ever been in royal or Christian history.

The Revolution will never be intelligibly known to us until we discover its conformity to the common law, and recognise that it is not utterly singular and exceptional, that other scenes have been as horrible as these, and many men as bad.

VII
THE FOURTH OF AUGUST

We come to-day to the most decisive date in the Revolution, the fall of the social system of historic France, and the substitution of the Rights of Man.

When the Assembly was fully constituted, it had to regulate its procedure. Sir Samuel Romilly, a friend of Dumont, and occasionally of Mirabeau, sent over an account of the practice of the British Parliament, with the cumbrous forms, the obstacles to prompt action, the contrivances to favour a minority, and to make opposition nearly equal to government. The French required more expeditious methods. They had a single Assembly with a known and well-defined commission, and the gravest danger of the hour was obstruction and delay. Every member obtained the right of initiative, and could submit a motion in writing. The Assembly might, after debate, refuse to consider it; but if not arrested on the threshold, it might be discussed and voted and passed in twenty-four hours. The security for deliberation was in the Bureaux. The Assembly was divided into thirty groups or committees, of nearly forty members each, who met separately, the Assembly in the morning, the Bureaux in the evening. This plan ensured thorough and sincere discussion, for men spoke their genuine thoughts, where there was no formality, no reporter, no stranger in the gallery. The Bureaux were disliked and suspected by the excluded public. The electorate, experiencing for the first time the sensation of having deputies at work to do their will, desired to watch them, and insisted on the master's right to look after his man. Representation was new; and to every reader of Rousseau, of Turgot, or of Mably, it was an object of profound distrust. The desire to uphold the supremacy of the deputing power over the deputed, of the constituent over his member, was distinctly part of the great literary inheritance common to them all. As the mandate was originally imperative, the giver of the mandate claimed the right of seeing to its execution. The exercise of powers that were defined and limited, that were temporary and revocable, called for scrutiny and direct control.

The Bureaux did not last, and their disappearance was a disaster. Party, as the term is used in the constitutional vocabulary, was not yet developed; and no organisation possessed the alternate power of presenting ministers to the Crown. The main lines that divided opinion came to light in the debates of September, and the Assembly fell into factions that were managed by their clubs. The President held office for a fortnight, and each new election indicated the movement of opinion, the position of parties, the rise of reputations. The united Assembly did honour to the acceding orders. The first presidents were prelates and men of rank. Out of six elections only one fell to a commoner, until the end of September, when the leader of the Liberal Conservatives, Mounier, was chosen, at what proved a moment of danger. In the same way, the thirty chairmen of the Bureaux were, with scarcely an exception, always taken from the clergy or the nobles.

As Mounier, with his friends, had dominated in the constitutional committee of thirty, and was now paramount in the new committee of eight, there was some prospect of a coalition, by which, in return for their aid in carrying the English model, the nobles would obtain easy terms in the liquidation of privilege. That is the parliamentary situation. That is the starting-point of the transactions that we have now to follow.

During the days spent in making terms between the king, the Assembly, and the capital, the provinces were depending on Paris for news, for opinions, and direction. They were informed that the Parisians had made themselves masters of the royal fortress, and had expelled the royal authority; that the king and the Assembly had accepted and approved the action; that there was no executive ministry, either old or new; and that the capital was providing for its own security and administration. The towns soon had imitations of the disorders that had been so successful, and quickly repressed them; for the towns were the seat of the middle class, the natural protectors of acquired property, and defenders of order and safety. In country districts the process of disintegration was immediate, the spontaneous recovery was slow. For the country was divided between the nobles who were rich, and their dependents who were poor. And the poverty of one class was ultimately due to innumerable devices for increasing the wealth of the other. And now there was nobody in authority over them, nobody to keep peace between them.

The first effect of the taking of the Bastille, the effacement of royalty, the suspension of the ministerial office, was the rising of the cottage against the castle, of the injured peasant against the privileged landlord, who, apart from any fault of his own, by immemorial process of history and by the actual letter of the law, was his perpetual and inevitable enemy. The events of the week between July 11 and 17 proclaimed that the authorised way to obtain what you wanted was to employ the necessary violence. If it was thorough and quick enough, there would be no present resistance, and no subsequent complaint. And if there was some excess in the way of cruelty and retribution, it was sure of amnesty on the ground of intolerable provocation and of suffering endured too long. The king had accepted his own humiliation as if it had been as good as due to him. He could not do more for others than for himself. His brief alliance with the aristocracy was dissolved. He was powerless for their defence, as they were for their own. By their formal act of submission to the Assembly on July 16, they acknowledged that their cause was lost with the Bastille. They neglected to make terms with the enemy at their homes.

The appalling thing in the French Revolution is not the tumult but the design. Through all the fire and smoke we perceive the evidence of calculating organisation. The managers remain studiously concealed and masked; but there is no doubt about their presence from the first. They had been active in the riots of Paris, and they were again active in the provincial rising. The remnant of the upper classes formed a powerful minority at Versailles; and if they acted as powerful minorities do, if they entered into compacts and combinations, they could compound for the loss of fiscal immunity by the salvation of social privilege. The people would continue to have masters—masters, that is, not of their own making. They would be subject to powers instituted formerly, whilst the Government itself obtained its credentials for the day, and there would still be an intermediate body between the nation and the sovereign. Wealth artificially constituted, by means of laws favouring its accumulation in a class, and discouraging its dispersion among all, would continue to predominate.

France might be transformed after the likeness of England; but the very essence of the English system was liberty founded on inequality. The essence of the French ideal was democracy, that is, as in America, liberty founded on equality. Therefore it was the interest of the democratic or revolutionary party that the next step should be taken after the manner of the last, that compulsion, which had answered so well with the king, should be tried on the nobles, that the methods applied at Paris should be extended to the Provinces, for there the nobles predominated. A well-directed blow struck at that favoured and excepted moment, when the country was ungoverned, might alter for ever, and from its foundation, the entire structure of society.

Liberty had been secured; equality was within reach. The political revolution ensured the prompt success of the social revolution. Such an opportunity of suppressing compromise, and sweeping the historical ruin away, had never been known in Europe.

While the local powers were painfully constituting themselves, there was a priceless interval for action. The king had given way to the middle class; the nobles would succumb to the lower, and the rural democracy would be emancipated like the urban. This is the second phase of that reign of terror which, as Malouet says, began with the Bastille. Experience had shown the efficacy of attacking castles instead of persons, and the strongholds of feudalism were assailed when the stronghold of absolutism had fallen.

It is said that one deputy, Duport, a magistrate of the parliament of Paris, had 400,000 francs to spend in raising the country against the nobles at the precise moment of their weakness. The money was scarcely needed, for the rioters were made to believe that they were acting in obedience to the law. One of their victims wrote, August 3, to Clermont Tonnerre that they were really sorry to behave in that way against good masters, but they were compelled by imperative commands from the king. He adds that seven or eight castles in his neighbourhood were attacked by their vassals, all believing that the king desired it. The charters and muniments were the main object of pillage and destruction, for it was believed that claims which could not be authenticated could not be enforced. Often the castle itself was burnt with the parchments it contained, and some of the owners perished.

The disorders raged in many parts of France. A district east and southeast of the centre suffered most. Those provinces had continued long to be parts of the Empire; and we shall see hereafter what that implies. The peasants of Eastern France rose up in arms to overthrow the ancient institutions of society, which the peasants of the West gave their lives to restore.

Rumours of all this desolation soon penetrated to the Assembly, and on August 3 it was officially reported that property was at the mercy of gangs of brigands, that no castle, no convent, no farm-house was safe. A committee moved to declare that no pretext could justify the refusal to pay the same feudal dues as before. Duport proposed that the motion be sent back to the Bureaux. The Assembly came to no conclusion. In truth, the thing proposed was impossible. The Commons, who now prevailed, could not, after sitting three months, re-impose, even provisionally, burdens which were odious, which their Instructions condemned, and which they all knew to be incapable of defence. There had been time to provide: the crisis now found them unprepared. The Court advised the nobles that nothing could save them but a speedy surrender. They also were informed, by Barère; that some of his friends intended to move the abolition of fiscal and feudal privilege. They replied that they would do it themselves. Virieu, who afterwards disappeared in a sortie, during the siege of Lyons, said to a friend: "There are only two means of calming an excited populace, kindness and force. We have no force; we hope to succeed by kindness." They knew that precious time had been lost, and they resolved that the surrender should be so ample as to be meritorious. It was to be not the redress of practical grievances, but the complete establishment of the new principle, equality.

At a conference held on the evening of August 3 it was agreed that the self-sacrifice of the ancient aristocracy of France, and the institution in its place of a society absolutely democratic, should be made by the Duke d'Aiguillon, the owner of vast domains, who was about to forfeit several thousands a year. But on August 4 the first to speak was Noailles; then d'Aiguillon, followed by a deputy from Brittany. You cannot repress violence, said the Breton, unless you remove the injustice which is the cause of it. If you mean to proclaim the Rights of Man, begin with those which are most flagrantly violated. They proposed that rights abandoned to the State should be ceded unconditionally, and that rights abandoned to the people should be given up in return for compensation. They imagined that the distinction was founded on principle; but nobody ever ascertained the dividing line between that which was property and that which was abuse. The want of definiteness enabled the landlords afterwards to attempt the recovery of much debatable ground, and involved, after long contention, the ultimate loss of all.

The programme was excessively complicated, and required years to be carried out. The nobles won the day with their demand to be compensated; but Duport already spoke the menacing words: "Injustice has no right to subsist, and the price of injustice has no right to subsist." The immensity of the revolution, which these changes implied, was at once apparent. For it signified that liberty, which had been known only in the form of privilege, was henceforward identified with equality. The nobles lost their jurisdiction; the corporation of judges lost their right of holding office by purchase. All classes alike were admitted to all employments. When privilege fell, provinces lost it as well as orders. One after the other, Dauphiné, Provence, Brittany, Languedoc, declared that they renounced their historic rights, and shared none but those which were common to all Frenchmen. Servitude was abolished; and on the same principle, that all might stand on the same level before the law, justice was declared gratuitous.

Lubersac, bishop of Chartres, the friend and patron of Sieyès, moved the abolition of the game laws, which meant the right of preserving on another man's land. It was a right which necessarily followed the movement of that night; but it led men to say that the clergy gave away generously what belonged to somebody else. It was then proposed that the tithe should be commuted; and the clergy showed themselves as zealous as the laity to carry out to their own detriment the doctrine that imposed so many sacrifices.

The France of history vanished on August 4, and the France of the new democracy took its place. The transfer of property from the upper class to the lower was considerable. The peasants' income was increased by about 60 per cent. Nobody objected to the tremendous loss, or argued to diminish it. Each class, recognising what was inevitable, and reconciled to it, desired that it should be seen how willingly and how sincerely it yielded. None wished to give time for others to remind them of inconsistency, or reserve, or omission, in the clean sweep they had undertaken to make. In their competition there was hurry and disorder. One characteristic of the time was to be unintelligent in matters relating to the Church, and they did not know how far the clergy was affected by the levelling principle, or that in touching tithe they were setting an avalanche in motion. At one moment, Lally, much alarmed, had passed a note to the President begging him to adjourn, as the deputies were losing their heads. The danger arose, as was afterwards seen, when the Duke du Chatelet proposed the redemption of tithe.

The nobles awoke next day with some misgiving that they had gone too far, and with some jealousy of the clergy, who had lost less, and who had contributed to their losses. On August 7 Necker appeared before the Assembly and exposed the want of money, and the need of a loan, for the redistribution of property on August 4 did nothing to the immediate profit of the Exchequer. But the clergy, vying with their rivals in generosity, had admitted the right of the nation to apply Church property to State uses.

On the following day the Marquis de Lacoste proposed that the new debt should be paid out of the funds of the clergy, and that tithe should be simply abolished. He expressed a wish that no ecclesiastic should be a loser, and that the parish clergy should receive an accession of income. The clergy offered no resistance, and made it impossible for others to resist.

They offered to raise a loan in behalf of the State; but it was considered that this would give them a position of undue influence, and it would not have satisfied the nobles, who saw the way to recover from the clergy the loss they had sustained. In this debate the Abbé Sieyès delivered his most famous speech. He had no fellow-feeling with his brethren, but he intended that the tithe should enrich the State. Instead of that it was about to be given back to the land, and the landowners would receive a sum of nearly three millions a year, divided in such a way that the richest would receive in proportion to his wealth. It would indemnify the laity. Not they, but the clergy, were now to bear the charge of August 4. There was one deputy who would be richer by 30,000 francs a year upon the whole transaction. The landlords who had bought their estates subject to the tithe had no claim to receive it. As all this argument was heard with impatience, Sieyès uttered words that have added no little to his moral stature: "They fancy that they can be free and yet not be just!" He had been, for three months, the foremost personage in the nation. He was destined in after years, and under conditions strangely altered, to be once more the dictator of France. More than once, without public favour, but by mere power of political thinking, he governed the fortunes of the State. He never again possessed the heart of the people.

The Assembly deemed it a good bargain to restore the tithe to the land; and the clergy knew so well that they had no friends that, on August 11, they solemnly renounced their claim. In this way the Assembly began the disendowment of the Church, which was the primitive cause of the Reign of Terror and the Civil War.

All these things are an episode. The business of the Assembly, from the end of July, was the Constitution. The first step towards it was to define the rights for which it exists. Such a declaration, suggested by America, had been demanded by the electors in several of the instructions, and had been faithfully reproduced by Mounier, July 9. It appeared, on the following day, that Lafayette had already got the required document in his pocket. Another text was produced, ten days later, by Sieyès, and another by Mounier, which was a revision of Lafayette's. Several more came out soon after.

On July 27 the archbishop of Bordeaux, in laying down the outline of the new institutions, observed that it was necessary to found them on principles defined and fixed. On the same day Clermont Tonnerre brought forward his analysis of the available ideas contained in the instructions. He went at once to the heart of the matter. Some instructions, he said, contemplated no more than the reform of existing institutions, with the maintenance of controlling tradition and the historic chain. Others conceived an entirely new system of laws and government. The distinction between the two was this, that some required a code of principles which must be the guide in preparing the Constitution; the others wished for no such assistance, but thought it possible to bind past and future together. The main conflict was between the authority of history and the Rights of Man. The Declaration was the signal of those who meant to rescue France from the ancestors who had given it tyranny and slavery as an inheritance. Its opponents were men who would be satisfied with good government, in the spirit of Turgot and the enlightened reformers of his time, who could be happy if they were prosperous, and would never risk prosperity and peace in the pursuit of freedom.

Those who imagined that France possessed a submerged Constitution that might be extracted from her annals had a difficult task. Lanjuinais desired to sail by a beacon and to direct the politics of 1789 by a charter of 864. There was a special reason, less grotesque than the archæology of Lanjuinais, which made men averse to the Declaration. Liberty, it was said, consists in the reign of the national will, and the national will is known by national custom. Law ought to spring from custom, and to be governed by it, not by independent, individual theory that defies custom. You have to declare the law, not to make it, and you can only declare what experience gives you. The best government devised by reason is less free than a worse government bequeathed by time. Very dimly, ideas which rose to power in other days and evolved the great force of nationality, were at work against a system which was to be new and universal, renouncing the influence both of time and place. The battle was fought against the men of the past, against a history which was an unbroken record of the defeat and frustration of freedom. But the declaration of rights was more needful still against dangers on the opposite side, those that were coming more than those that were going out. People were quite resolved to be oppressed no more by monarchy or aristocracy, but they had no experience or warning of oppression by democracy. The classes were to be harmless; but there was the new enemy, the State.

No European knew what security could be needed or provided for the individual from the collected will of the people. They were protected from government by authority or by minority; but they made the majority irresistible, and the *plébiscite* a tyranny.

The Americans were aware that democracy might be weak and unintelligent, but also that it might be despotic and oppressive. And they found out the way to limit it, by the federal system, which suffers it to exist nowhere in its plenitude. They deprived their state governments of the powers that were enumerated, and the central government of the powers that were reserved. As the Romans knew how monarchy would become innocuous, by being divided, the Americans solved the more artful problem of dividing democracy into two.

Many Frenchmen were convinced that Federalism would be the really liberal policy for them. But the notion was at once pushed aside by Mounier, and obtained no hearing. And the division of powers, which he substituted, was rejected in its turn. They would not admit that one force should be checked and balanced by another. They had no resource but general principles, to abolish the Past and secure the Future. By declaring them, they raised up an ideal authority over the government and the nation, and established a security against the defects of the Constitution and the power of future rulers. The opponents of the Declaration fought it on the proposal to add a declaration of duties. The idea was put forward by the most learned of the deputies, the Jansenist Camus, and the clergy supported him with energy. The Assembly decided that a system of rights belonged to politics, and a system of duties to ethics, and rejected the motion, on the morning of the 4th of August, by 570 to 433.

This was the deciding division on the question of the Rights of Man. After some days, absorbed by the crisis of aristocracy, the distracted and wearied Assembly turned again from the excitement of facts and interests to the discussion of theory. A new committee of five was appointed to revise the work of the committee of eight, which dealt with the entire Constitution.

On August 17 Mirabeau reported their scheme. His heart was not in it; and he resented the intrusion of hampering generalities and moralities into the difficult experimental science of government. He advised that the Constitution should be settled first, that the guide should follow instead of preceding. The Assembly rejected the proposals of its committees, and all the plans which were submitted by the celebrities. The most remarkable of these was by Sieyès, and it met with favour; but the final vote was taken on a less illustrious composition, which bore no author's name. The selected text was less philosophical and profound, and it roused less distant echoes than its rival; but it was shorter, and more tame, and it was thought to involve fewer doubtful postulates, and fewer formidable consequences. Between the 20th and 26th of August it was still further abridged, and reduced from twenty-four propositions to the moderate dimension of seventeen. These omissions from a document which had been preferred to very remarkable competitors are the key to the intentions of the National Assembly, and our basis of interpretation.

The original scheme included a State Church. This was not adopted. It distinguished the inequality of men from the equality of rights. This was deemed self-evident and superfluous. It derived the mutual rights of men from their mutual duties—and this terrestrial definition also disappeared, leaving the way open to a higher cause. The adopted code was meagre and ill-composed, and Bentham found a malignant pleasure in tearing it to pieces. It is, on the whole, more spiritual than the one on which it was founded, and which it generally follows; and it insists with greater energy on primitive rights, anterior to the State and aloof from it, which no human authority can either confer or refuse. It is the triumphant proclamation of the doctrine that human obligations are not all assignable to contract, or to interest, or to force.

The Declaration of the Rights of Man begins with an appeal to heaven, and defines them in the presence, and under the auspices, of Almighty God. The Preamble implies that our duties towards Him constitute our rights towards mankind, and indicates the divine origin of Law, without affirming it. The Declaration enumerates those rights which are universal, which come from nature, not from men. They are four: Liberty, Property, Security, and Self-defence. Authorities are constituted, and laws are made, in order that these original, essential, and supreme possessions of all mankind may be preserved.

The system of guarantees is as sacred as the rights which they protect. Such are the right of contributing by representatives to legislation and taxation, religious toleration, the liberty of the press. As the rights are equal, the power of ensuring them must be equal. All men alike have a share in representation, all alike are admissible to office, all must be taxed in the same proportion. The law is the same for all. The principle of equality is the idea on which the Declaration most earnestly insists. Privilege had just been overthrown, and the duty of providing against indirect means for its recovery was the occupation of the hour. That this may be secured, all powers must be granted by the people, and none must be exercised by the people. They act only through their agents. The agent who exercises power is responsible, and is controlled by the sovereign authority that delegates it.

Certain corollaries seem to follow: restricted suffrage, progressive taxation, an established church, are difficult to reconcile with equality so profoundly conceived. But this is not explicit. Questions regarding education, poverty, revision, are not admitted among the fundamentals and are left to future legislation. The most singular passage is that which ordains that no man may be molested for his opinions, even religious. It would appear that Toleration was that part of the liberal dogma for which the deputies were least prepared.

The Declaration passed, by August 26, after a hurried debate, and with no further resistance. The Assembly, which had abolished the past at the beginning of the month, attempted, at the end, to institute and regulate the future. These are its abiding works, and the perpetual heritage of the Revolution. With them a new era dawned upon mankind.

And yet this single page of print, which outweighs libraries, and is stronger than all the armies of Napoleon, is not the work of superior minds, and bears no mark of the lion's claw. The stamp of Cartesian clearness is upon it, but without the logic, the precision, the thoroughness of French thought. There is no indication in it that Liberty is the goal, and not the starting-point, that it is a faculty to be acquired, not a capital to invest, or that it depends on the union of innumerable conditions, which embrace the entire life of man. Therefore it is justly arraigned by those who say that it is defective, and that its defects have been a peril and a snare.

It was right that the attempt should be made; for the extinction of privilege involved a declaration of rights. When those that were exclusive and unequal were abandoned, it was necessary to define and to insist on those that were equal and the property of all. After destroying, the French had to rebuild, and to base their new structure upon principles unknown to the law, unfamiliar to the people, absolutely opposed to the lesson of their history and to all the experience of the ages in which France had been so great. It could not rest on traditions, or interests, or any persistent force of gravitation. Unless the idea that was to govern the future was impressed with an extreme distinctness upon the minds of all, they would not understand the consequences of so much ruin, and such irrevocable change, and would drift without a compass. The country that had been so proud of its kings, of its nobles, and of its chains, could not learn without teaching that popular power may be tainted with the same poison as personal power.

VIII
THE CONSTITUTIONAL DEBATES

When the Assembly passed the Rights of Man, they acted in harmony for the last time. Agreement on first principles did not involve agreement in policy, and in applying them to the Constitution, a week later, the division of parties appeared.

From the tennis court to the great constitutional debate, the Moderates, who may be called the Liberals, were predominant. Mounier was their tactician, Clermont Tonnerre and Lally Tollendal were their orators, Malouet was their discreet adviser. They hoped, by the division of powers and the multiplication of checks, to make their country as free as England or America. They desired to control the Representatives in three ways: by a Second Chamber, the royal veto, and the right of dissolution. Their success depended on the support of Ministers and of reconciled Conservatives. Whilst the Constitution for them was a means of regulating and restraining the national will, it was an instrument for accomplishing the popular will for their rivals rising to power on the crest of the wave.

The Democrats refused to resist the people, legitimately governing itself, either by the English or the American division of power. There was little concentration yet of the working class in towns, for the industrial age had hardly dawned, and it was hard to understand that the Third Estate contained divergent interests and the material of a coming conflict. The managers of the democratic party were Duport, Lameth, and Barnave, aided sometimes by Sieyès, sometimes by Talleyrand, and by their sworn enemy Mirabeau.

The nobles, weak in statesmanship, possessed two powerful debaters: Cazalès, who reminded men of Fox, but who, when not on his legs, had little in him; and Maury, afterwards Cardinal and Archbishop of Paris, a man whose character was below his talents. Numbering nearly a third of the Assembly, and holding the balance, it was in their power to make a Constitution like that of 1814.

How these three parties acted in that eventful September, and what in consequence befell, we have now to consider.

The five weeks from August 27 to October 1 were occupied with the constitutional debates. They were kept within narrow limits by the Rights of Man, which declared that the nation transmits all powers and exercises none. On both sides there were men who were impatient of this restriction, and by whom it was interpreted in contrary ways. Some wished for security that the national will should always prevail, through its agents; the others, that they should be able to obstruct it. They struggled for an enlarged construction, and strove to break the barrier, in the republican or the royalist direction.

The discussion opened by a skirmish with the clergy. They observed the significant omission of a State church in the Declaration of Rights, and feared that they would be despoiled and the Church disestablished. The enthusiasm of the first hour had cooled. One after another, ecclesiastics attempted to obtain the recognition of Catholicism. Each time the attempt was repulsed. The clergy drifted fast into the temper which was confessed by Maury when he said, "The proposed measure would enable the Constitution to live: we vote against it."

The scheme of the Committee was produced on August 31, and was explained by Lally in a speech which is among the finest compositions of the time. He insisted on the division of the legislative, and the unity of the executive, as the essentials of a free government. On the following day Mirabeau spoke on the same side. He said that the danger was not from the Crown, but from the representatives; for they may exclude strangers and debate in secret, as the English law allows, and these may declare themselves permanent, and escape all control. Through the king, the public possesses the means of holding them in check. He is their natural ally against usurping deputies, and the possible formation of a new aristocracy. The legislature enjoys a temporary mandate only. The perpetual representative of the people is the king. It is wrong to deny him powers necessary for the public interest. It is the partial appearance of a view that was expanded by Napoleon.

Mounier defended his plan on September 4. On several points there was no large variety of opinion. It was practically admitted that there could be no governing without Parliament, that it must meet annually, that its acts require the royal assent, that it shall be elected indirectly, by equal districts, and a moderate property franchise. Mounier further conceded that the

Constitution was not subject to the royal veto, that Ministers should not be members of the Assembly, that the Assembly, and not the king, should have the initiative of proposing laws, and that it should have the right of refusing supplies. The real question at issue was whether the representatives of the people should be checked by an Upper House, by the king's power of dissolution, and by an absolute or a temporary veto.

Mounier had private friends among his opponents, and they opened a negotiation with him. They were prepared to accept his two Houses and his absolute veto. They demanded in return that the Senate should have only a suspensive veto on the acts of the representatives, that there should be no right of Dissolution, that Conventions should be held periodically, to revise the Constitution. These offers were a sign of weakness. The Constitutional party was still in the ascendant, and on August 31 the Bishop of Langres, the chief advocate of a House of Lords, was chosen President by 499 to 328. If the division of the legislature into two was sure of a majority, then the proposed bargain was one-sided, and the Democrats would have taken much more than they gave. Mounier, counting on the support of those whose interest was that he should succeed, rejected the offer. He had already been forced, by the defection of friends, to abandon much that he would have wished to keep; and the plan which he brought forward closely resembled that under which France afterwards prospered.

Nevertheless, the failure of that negotiation is a fatal date in constitutional history. With more address, and a better knowledge of the situation, Mounier might have saved half of the securities he depended on. He lost the whole. The things he refused to surrender at the conference were rejected by the Assembly; and the offers he had rejected were not made again. When the legislature was limited to two years, the right of dissolution lost its value. The right of revision would have caused no more rapid changes than actually ensued; for there were fourteen Constitutions in eighty-six years, or a fundamental revision every six or seven years. Lastly, the veto of the Senate had no basis of argument, until it was decided how the Senate should be composed.

The disastrous ruin of the cause was brought on by want of management, and not by excess of conservatism. Mounier inclined to an hereditary House of Peers; and that, after August 4, was not to be thought of. But he knew the difficulty, and, however reluctantly, gave way. And he attached undue importance to the absolute veto; but that was not the point on which the conference broke up. He was supported by Lafayette, who dreaded as much as he did the extinction of the royal power; at times by Mirabeau, whom he detested. Even Sieyès was willing to have two Houses, and even three, provided they were, in reality, one House, deliberating in three divisions, but counting all the votes in common. He also proposed that there should be a renewal of one-third at a time; so that there would be three degrees of the popular infusion and of proximity to Mother Earth.

Mounier, with some of his friends, deserves to be remembered among the men, not so common as they say, who loved liberty sincerely; I mean, who desired it, not for any good it might do them, but for itself, however arduous, or costly, or perilous its approach might be. They subordinated the means to the end, and never regarded conditional forms as an emanation of eternal principles. Having secured the Rights of Man, they looked with alarm at future legislation, that could not improve, and might endanger them. They wished the Constituent Assembly to bind and bar its successors as far as possible; for none would ever speak with so much authority as the genuine voice of the entire people.

By an extraordinary fortune, the nation, this time, had responded wisely. It was certain that it would not always do so well. It had passions; it had prejudices; it was grossly ignorant; it was not disinterested; and it was demoralised by an evil tradition. The French were accustomed to irresponsible power. They were not likely to consent that the power in their hands should be inferior to that which had been exercised over them, or to admit that an entire people is not above the law which it obeys. It was to be expected that they would endeavour by legislation to diminish those securities for the minority and the weaker cause which were appointed by the Rights of Man. Opinion was changing rapidly, and had become more favourable to violence, more indulgent to crime. A draft project of the Rights of Man had appeared, in which the writer avowed that, by the law of nature, a man may do what he likes in the pursuit of happiness, and, to elude oppression, may oppress, imprison, and destroy.

The man who wrote thus quickly acquired a dread ascendancy over the people, and was able to defy police and governments and assemblies, for it was the beginning of Marat. Lists of proscription were circulated; threatening letters poured in on the deputies; and Paris, at the end of August, was preparing to march upon Versailles, to expel obnoxious members, and, when they ceased to be inviolable, to put them on their trial. These were first-fruits of liberty, and the meed and reward of Liberals. No man can tell in what country such things would remain without effect. In

France it was believed that civic courage was often wanting. De Serre, the great orator of the Restoration, once affirmed, from the tribune, that the bulk of the representatives had always been sound. He was interrupted by a furious outcry, and challenged by his legitimist audience to say whether he included the Convention, which, by a majority, condemned the king to death. His answer, very famous in parliamentary history, was, "Yes, even the Convention. And if it had not deliberated under poniards, we should have been spared the most terrible of crimes."

The opposition presented a united front, but was rent by many stages of gravitation towards Democracy. They also were generally anxious to establish political freedom, even by the greatest sacrifices. By freedom they meant, first, deliverance from known and habitual causes of oppression. True, there might be others; but they were less clear and less certain. All European experience proclaimed that the executive constantly masters the legislative, even in England. It was absurd to suppose that every force that, for centuries, had helped to build up absolutism, had been destroyed in two months. They would rise again from the roots, and the conflict would be constantly renewed.

The salvation seemed to lie in the principle that all power is derived from the people, and that none can exist against the people. The popular will may be expressed by certain forms; it cannot be arrested by obstacles. Its action may be delayed; it cannot be stopped. It is the ultimate master of all, without responsibility or exemption, and with no limit that is not laid down in the Rights of Man. The limits there defined are sufficient, and individual liberty needs no further protection. Distrust of the nation was not justified by the manner in which it had chosen and instructed its deputies.

In studying this group of public men, men to whom the future belonged, we are forced to admit the element of national character. No philosophy is cheaper or more vulgar than that which traces all history to diversities of ethnological type and blend, and is ever presenting the venal Greek, the perfidious Sicilian, the proud and indolent Spaniard, the economical Swiss, the vain and vivacious Frenchman. But it is certainly true that in France the liberty of the press represents a power that is not familiar to those who know its weakness and its strength, who have had experience of Swift and Bolingbroke and Junius. Maury once said, "We have a free press: we have everything." In 1812, when Napoleon watched the grand army crossing the Niemen to invade Russia, and whistled the tune of Malbrook, he interrupted his tune to exclaim, "And yet all that is not equal to the songs of Paris!" Chateaubriand afterwards said that, with the liberty of the press, there was no abuse he would not undertake to destroy. For he wrote French as it had never been written, and the magnificent roll of his sentences caught the ear of his countrymen with convincing force. When, in 1824, he was dismissed from the Foreign Office, his friend, the editor of the *Journal des Débats*, called on the Prime Minister Villèle and warned him, "We have overthrown your predecessor, and we shall be strong enough to overthrow you." Villèle replied, "You succeeded against him by aid of royalism: you cannot succeed against me but by aid of revolution." Both prophecies came true. The alliance of Chateaubriand with the newspaper turned out the Ministry in 1827, and the Monarchy in 1830.

In September 1789, the liberty of the press was only four months old, and the reign of opinion was beginning on the Continent. They fancied that it was an invincible force, and a complete security for human rights. It was invaluable if it secured right without weakening power, like the other contrivances of Liberalism. They thought that when men were safe from the force above them, they required no saving from the influence around them. Opinion finds its own level, and a man yields easily and not unkindly to what surrounds him daily. Pressure from equals is not to be confounded with persecution by superiors. It is right that the majority, by degrees, should absorb the minority. The work of limiting authority had been accomplished by the Rights of Man. The work of creating authority was left to the Constitution. In this way men of varying opinions were united in the conclusion that the powers emanating from the people ought not to be needlessly divided.

Besides Sieyès, who found ideas, and Talleyrand, who found expedients, several groups were, for the time, associated with the party which was managed by Duport. There were some of the most eminent jurists, eager to reform the many systems of law and custom that prevailed in France, who became the lawgivers of successive Assemblies, until they completed their code under Napoleon. Of all the enemies of the old monarchical *régime*, they were the most methodical and consistent. The leader of the Paris Bar, Target, was their most active politician. When he heard of a plan for setting the finances in order he said, "If anybody has such a plan, let him at once be smothered. It is the disorder of the finances that puts the king in our power." The Economists were as systematic and definite as the lawyers, and they too had much to destroy. Through Dupont de Nemours their theories obtained enduring influence.

There were two or three of the future Girondins who taught that the people may be better trusted than representatives, and who were ready to ratify the Constitution, and even to decide upon the adoption of laws, by the popular vote. And there were two men, not yet distinctly divided from these their future victims, who went farther in opposition to the Rights of Man, and towards the confusion of powers. In their eyes, representation and delegation were treason to true democracy. As the people could not directly govern itself, the principle exacted that it should do so as nearly as possible, by means of a perpetual control over the delegates. The parliamentary vote ought to be constantly brought into harmony with the wish of the constituency, by the press, the galleries and the mob. To act consciously in opposition to the delegating power was a breach of trust. The population of Paris, being the largest collected portion of sovereign power, expresses its will more surely than deputies at second hand. Barère, who was one of these, proposed an ingenious plan by which every law that passed remained suspended until after the next elections, when the country pronounced upon it by imperative mandate. Thus he disposed of royal veto and dissolution.

Robespierre would not suspend the law, but left it to the next legislature to rectify or revoke the errors of the last. He argued that powers require to be checked in proportion to the danger they present. Now the danger from a power not representative exceeds that from a power that represents, and is better acquainted with the needs and wishes of the mass. A nation governs itself, and has a single will, not two. If the whole does not govern the part, the part will govern the whole. Robespierre conceived that it was time to constitute powers sufficient to conquer the outward foe, and also the inward; one for national safety, and one for national progress, and the elevation of the poor at the expense of the minorities that have oppressed them. He stands at the end of the scale, and the idea of liberty, as it runs through the various sets of thought, is transformed into the idea of force. From Sieyès to Barnave, from Barnave to Camus, from Camus to Buzot, and from Buzot the Girondin to Robespierre the Jacobin who killed the Girondins, we traverse the long line of possible politics; but the transitions are finely shaded, and the logic is continuous.

In the second week of September the Constitution of Mounier was defeated by the union of these forces. The main question, the institution of a Senate, was not seriously debated. It was feared as the refuge of the defeated classes, and was not defended by those classes themselves. They were not willing that a new aristocracy should be raised upon their ruins; and they suspected that Government would give the preference to that minority of the nobles who went over in time, and who were renegades in the eyes of the rest. It was felt that a single Chamber is stronger in resistance to the executive than two, and that the time might come for a senate when the fallen aristocracy had ceased to struggle, and the Crown was reconciled to its reduced condition.

On September 9 the President of the Assembly, La Luzerne, bishop of Langres, was driven by insult to resign. The next day the Assembly adopted the single Chamber by 499 to 89, the nobles abstaining.

On September 11 the decisive division took place. Mounier had insisted on the unlimited right of veto. The debate went against him. It was admitted on his own side that the king would, sooner or later, have to yield. The others agreed that the king might resist until two elections had decided in favour of the vetoed measure. He might reject the wish of one legislature, and even of two; he would give way to the third. The Ministers themselves were unable to insist on the absolute veto in preference to the suspensive thus defined. A letter from the king was sent to the Assembly, to inform them that he was content with the temporary veto. Mounier did not allow the letter to be read, that it might not influence votes. He was defeated by 673 to 325. The Conservatives had deserted him when he defended the Upper House; and now the king deserted him when he defended the rights of the Crown. It was a crushing and final disaster. For he fell, maintaining the cause of aristocracy against the nobles, and the cause of prerogative against the monarch. The Democrats triumphed by 410 votes one day, and 350 the next. The battle for the Constitution on the English model was fought and lost.

On September 12 Mounier and his friends retired from the Committee. A new one was at once elected from the victorious majority. At this critical point a secret Council was held, at which the royalists advised the king to take refuge in the provinces. Lewis refused to listen to them. The majority, elated with success, now called on him to sanction the decrees of August 4. His reply, dated September 18, is drawn up with unusual ability. He adopted the argument of Sieyès on the suppression of tithe. He said that a large income would be granted to the land, and that the rich, who ought to contribute most, would, on the contrary, receive most. Small holders would profit little, while those who possessed no land at all would now be mulcted for payment of the clergy. Instead of relieving the nation, it would relieve one class at the expense of another, and the rich at the expense of the poor.

The Assembly insisted that the abolition of feudalism was part of the Constitution, and ought to receive an unconditional sanction. But they promised to give most respectful attention to the remarks of the king, whenever the decrees came to be completed by legislation. The royal sanction was accordingly given on the following day. Thereupon the Assembly made a considerable concession. They resolved, on September 21, that the suspensive veto should extend over two legislatures. The numbers were 728 to 224.

The new Committee, appointed on the 15th, took a fortnight to complete their scheme, on the adopted principles that there should be one Chamber, no dissolution, and a power of retarding legislation without preventing it. On the 29th it was laid before the Assembly by their reporter, Thouret. The voice was the voice of Thouret, but the hand was the hand of Sieyès. At that juncture he augured ill of the Revolution, and repented of his share in it. His Declaration of Rights had been passed over. His proposal to restore the national credit by the surrender of tithe had been rejected. His partition of the Assembly, together with partial renewal, which is favourable to the executive, by never allowing the new parliament to rise, like a giant refreshed, from a general election, had encountered no support. It remained that he should compose the working machinery for his essential doctrine, that the law is the will of him that obeys, not of him that commands. To do this, the Abbé Sieyès abolished the historic Provinces, and divided France into departments. There were to be eighty, besides Paris; and as they were designed to be as nearly as possible equal to a square of about forty-five miles, they differed widely in population and property. They were to have an average of nine deputies each: three for the superficial area, which was invariable; three, more or less, for population; and again three, more or less, according to the amount which the department contributed to the national income. In this way territory, numbers and wealth were represented equally.

Deputies were to be elected in three degrees. The taxpayers, in their primary assemblies, chose electors for the Commune, which was the political unit, and a square of about fifteen miles; the communal electors sent their representatives to the department, and these elected the deputy. Those who paid no taxes were not recognized as shareholders in the national concern. Like women and minors, they enjoyed the benefit of government; but as they were not independent, they possessed no power as active citizens. By a parallel process, assemblies were formed for local administration, on the principle that the right of exercising power proceeds from below, and the actual exercise of power from above.

This is mainly the measure which has made the France of to-day; and when it became law, in December, the chief part of the new Constitution was completed. It had been the work of these two months, from August 4 to September 29. The final promulgation came two years later. No legislative instrument ever failed more helplessly than this product of the wisdom of France in its first parliamentary Assembly, for it lasted only a single year.

Many things had meanwhile occurred which made the constructive design of 1789 unfit to meet the storms of 1792. The finances of the State were ruined; the clergy and the clerical party had been driven into violent opposition; the army was almost dissolved, and war broke out when there was not a disciplined force at the command of Government. After Varennes, the king was practically useless in peace, and impossible in times of danger and invasion; not only because of the degradation of his capture and of his imprisonment on the throne, but because, at the moment of his flight, he had avowed his hostility to the institutions he administered.

The central idea in the plan of September 29, the idea of small provinces and large municipalities, was never appreciated and never adopted. Sieyès placed the unit in the Commune, which was the name he gave to each of the nine divisions of a department. He intended that there should be only 720 of these self-governing districts in France. Instead of 720, the Assembly created 44,000, making the Commune no larger than the parish, and breaking up the administrative system into dust. The political wisdom of the village was substituted for that of a town or district of 35,000 inhabitants.

The explanation of the disastrous result is as much in the Court as in the Legislature, and as much in the legislation that followed as in the policy of the moment in which the great issues were determined, and with which we are dealing. No monarchical constitution could succeed, after Varennes; and the one of which we are speaking, the object of the memorable conflict between Mounier and Sieyès, is not identical with the one that failed. The repudiation of the English model did not cause the quick passage from the Constitution of 1791 to the Republic. Yet the scheme that prevailed shows defects which must bear their portion of blame. Political science imperatively demands that powers shall be regulated by multiplication and division. The Assembly preferred ideas of unity and simplicity.

The old policy of French parliaments nearly suggested a court of revision; but that notion, not yet visible in the Supreme Court of the United States, occurred to Sieyès long after. An effective Senate might have been founded on the provincial assemblies; but the ancient provinces were doomed, and the new divisions did not yet exist, or were hidden in the maps of freemasonry.

Power was not really divided between the legislative and the executive, for the king possessed no resource against the majority of the Assembly. There was no Senate, no initiative, no dissolution, no effective veto, no reliance on the judicial or the Federal element. These are not defects of equal importance; but taken together, they subverted that principle of division which is useful for stability, and for liberty is essential.

The reproach falls not only on those who carried the various measures, but also on the minority that opposed them. Mounier encouraged the suspicion and jealousy of Ministers by separating them from the Assembly, and denying to the king, that is to them, the prerogative of proposing laws. He attributed to the absolute veto an importance which it does not possess; and he frustrated all chance of a Second Chamber by allowing it to be known that he would have liked to make it hereditary. This was too much for men who had just rejoiced over the fall of the aristocracy. In order to exclude the intervention of the king in favour of a suspensive veto, he accepted the argument that the Constitution was in the hands of the Assembly alone. When Lewis raised a just objection to the decrees of August 4, this argument was turned against him, and the Crown suffered a serious repulse.

The intellectual error of the Democrats vanishes before the moral error of the Conservatives. They refused a Second Chamber because they feared that it would be used as a reward for those among them to whose defection they partly owed their defeat. And as they did not wish the Constitution to be firmly established, they would not vote for measures likely to save it. The revolutionists were able to count on their aid against the Liberals.

The watchword came from the Palace, and the shame of their policy recoils upon the king. Late in September one of his nobles told him that he was weary of what he saw, and was going to his own country. "Yes," said the king, taking him aside; "things are going badly, and nothing can improve our position but the excess of evil." On this account Royer Collard, the famous *Doctrinaire*, said, in later times, that all parties in the Revolution were honest, except the Conservatives.

From the end of August the Paris agitators, who managed the mob in the interest of a dynastic change directed a sustained pressure against Versailles. Thouret, one of the foremost lawyers in the Assembly, who was elected President on August 1, refused the honour. He had been warned of his unpopularity, and gave way to threats. Yielding to the current which, as

Mirabeau said, submerges those who resist it, he went over to the other side, and soon became one of their leaders. The experience of this considerable man is an instance of the change that set in, and that was frequent among men without individual conviction or the strength of character that belongs to it.

The downward tendency was so clearly manifest, the lesson taught by successful violence against the king and the aristocracy was so resolutely applied to the Assembly, that very serious politicians sought the means of arresting the movement. Volney, who was no orator, but who was the most eminent of the deputies in the department of letters, made the attempt on September 18. He proposed that there should be new elections for a parliament that should not consist of heterogeneous ingredients, but in which class interests should be disregarded and unknown. He moved that it should represent equality. They reminded him of the oath not to separate until France was a constitutional State, and the protest was ineffectual. But in intellectual France there was no man more perfectly identified with the reigning philosophy than the man who uttered this cry of alarm.

On October 2 the first chapters of the Constitution were ready for the royal assent. They consisted of the Rights of Man, and of the fundamental measures adopted in the course of September. Mounier, the new President, carried to the king the articles by which his cause had been brought to its fall. Lewis undertook to send his reply; and from Mounier came no urging word. They both fancied that delay was possible, and might yet serve. The tide had flowed so slowly in May, that they could not perceive the torrent of October. On the day of that audience of the most liberal of all the royalists, the respite before them was measured by hours.

All through September, at Paris, Lafayette at the head of the forces of order, and the forces of tumult controlled by the Palais Royal had watched each other, waiting for a deadly fight. There were frequent threats of marching on Versailles, followed by reassuring messages from the General that he had appeased the storm. As it grew louder, he made himself more and more the arbiter of the State. The Government, resenting this protectorate, judged that the danger of attack ought to be averted, not by the dubious fidelity and the more dubious capacity of the commander of the National Guard, but by the direct resources of the Crown. They summoned the Flanders regiment, which was reputed loyal, and on October 1 it marched in, a thousand strong. The officers, on their arrival, were invited by their comrades at Versailles to a festive supper in the theatre. The men were admitted, and made to drink the health of the king; and in the midst of a scene of passionate enthusiasm the king and queen appeared. The demonstration that ensued meant more than the cold and decent respect with which men regard a functionary holding delegated and not irrevocable powers. It was easy to catch the note of personal devotion and loyalty and the religion of the Cavalier, in the cries of these armed and excited royalists. The managers at Paris had their opportunity, and resolved at once to execute the plot they had long meditated.

Whilst the Executive, which alone upheld the division of powers and the principle of freedom, was daily losing ground at the hands of its enemies, of its friends, and at its own, a gleam of hope visited the forlorn precincts of the Court. Necker had informed the Assembly that he could not obtain a loan, and he asked for a very large increase of direct taxation. He was heard with impatience, and Mirabeau, who spoke for him, made no impression. On September 26 he made another effort, and gained the supreme triumph of his career. In a speech that was evidently unprepared, he drew an appalling picture of the coming bankruptcy; and as he ended with the words "These dangers are before you, and you deliberate!" the Assembly, convulsed with emotion, passed the vote unanimously, and Necker was saved. None knew that there could be such power in man.

In the eighteen months of life that remained to him, Mirabeau underwent many vicissitudes of influence and favour; but he was able, in an emergency, to dominate parties. From that day the Court knew what he was, and what he could do; and they knew how his imperious spirit longed to serve the royal cause, and we shall presently see who it was that attempted to flatter and to win him when it was too late, and who had repelled him when it might yet have been time.

We have reached the point at which the first part of the Revolution terminates, and the captivity of the monarch is about to begin. The events of the next two days, October 5 and 6, form a complete and coherent drama, that will not bear partition, and must occupy the whole of our attention next week.

IX
THE MARCH TO VERSAILLES

The French Revolution was approved at first by the common judgment of mankind. Kaunitz, the most experienced statesman in Europe, declared that it would last for long, and perhaps for ever. Speaking less cautiously, Klopstock said: "I see generations crushed in the struggle; I see perhaps centuries of war and desolation; but at last, in the remote horizon, I see the victory of liberty." Even at St. Petersburg the fall of the Bastille was hailed with frantic joy. Burke began by applauding. He would not listen to Tom Paine, who had been the inspirer of a revolution himself, and who assured him that the States-General would lead to another. He said, afterwards, that the Rights of Man had opened his eyes; but at Holland House they believed that the change came a few days earlier, when the Church was attacked. The Americans were not far from the opinion of Burke. By the middle of the summer Jefferson thought that all that was needful had been obtained. Franklin took alarm at the events of July. Washington and Hamilton became suspicious soon after.

For the September decrees were directed not only against the English model, but still more against the American. The Convention of 1787 had constructed a system of securities that were intended to save the Union from the power of unchecked democracy. The National Assembly resolutely swept every security away. Nothing but the Crown was left that could impede the direct operation of the popular will, or that could make the division of powers a reality. Therefore the Liberal party looked to the king as much as the Conservative, and wished as much as they, and even more than they, to strengthen his hands. Their theory demanded a divided legislature. Having lost that, they fell back on Montesquieu, and accepted the division of legislative, executive, and judicial powers. These theoretic subtleties were unintelligible to the people of France. Men who were as vehement for the king in October as they had been vehement against him in June appeared to them to be traitors. They could not conceive that the authority which had so long oppressed them, and which it had required such an effort to vanquish, ought now to be trusted and increased. They could not convince themselves that their true friends were those who had suddenly gone over to the ancient enemy and oppressor, whose own customary adherents seemed no longer to support him.

Public opinion was brought to bear on the Assembly, to keep up the repression of monarchy which began on June 23. As the Crown passed under the control of the Assembly, the Assembly became more dependent on the constituencies, especially on that constituency which had the making of French opinion, and in which the democratic spirit was concentrated. After the month of August the dominant fact is the growing pressure of Paris on Versailles. In October Paris laid its hand on its prey. For some weeks the idea of escaping had been entertained. Thirty-two of the principal royalists in the Assembly were consulted, and advised that the king should leave Versailles and take refuge in the provinces. The late minister, Breteuil, the Austrian ambassador, Mercy, were of the same opinion, and they carried the queen with them. But Necker was on the other side.

Instead of flight they resolved upon defence, and brought up the Flanders regiment, whose Colonel was a deputy of the Left. In the morning the Count d'Estaing, who held command at Versailles, learnt with alarm that it had been decided to omit the health of the nation. The Prussian envoy writes that the officers of the Guards, who had not yet adopted the Tricolor, displayed the utmost contempt for it. It required no exaggeration to represent the scene in a light odious to the public. When Madame Campan came home and described with admiration what she had just beheld, Beaumetz, a deputy, and friend of Talleyrand, became very grave, and took his leave, that he might make up his mind whether he should not emigrate at once. Hostile witnesses reported the particulars to the press next day, and it was stated, figuratively or literally, that the Royal Guards had trampled the national colours under foot. Marat came over to inquire, and Camille Desmoulins says that he hurried back to Paris making as much noise as all the trumpets of the Last Day.

The feast had been held on a Thursday. On the Sunday, October 4, Paris was in a ferment. The insult to the nation, the summoning of troops, the projected flight, as was now supposed, to the fortress of Metz, were taken to mean civil war, for the restoration of despotism. At the Palais Royal the agitators talked of going out to Versailles, to punish the insolent guards. On the evening of Sunday, one district of the city, the Cordeliers, who were governed by Danton, were ready to march. The men of other districts were not so ready for action, or so zealous to avenge the new cockade. To carry the entire population more was required than the vague rumour of Metz, or even than the symbolical outrage.

There was hunger among the 800,000 inhabitants of Paris, between last year's corn that was exhausted, and the new harvest that was not yet ground. Nobody, says Dumont, could wonder if so much suffering led to tumult. The suffering was due to poverty more than to scarcity; but Lafayette asserted that above £2000 a week were paid to bakers, or to millers, to create discontent by shortening supplies. There were people who thought that money spent in this way would rouse indignation against the incompetent and inactive Assembly. Upon sixteen days in the course of September the bakers' shops had to be guarded by troops. The reduced noble families were putting down their establishments; and 200,000 passports were issued to intending *émigrés* in the two months following the fall of the Bastille.

The primary offender, responsible for subsistence, was the municipality of the capital; and their seat of office was the first object of attack. Early on the Monday morning a multitude of excited women made their way into the Hôtel de Ville. They wanted to destroy the heaps of papers, as all that writing did them no good. They seized a priest, and set about hanging him. They rang the tocsin, bringing all the trained battalions and all the ragged bands of the city to the Place de Grève. They carried away several hundreds of muskets, and some useless cannon; and they fetched torches, that they might burn the building to the ground. It was the headquarters of the elected municipality; but the masses were becoming conscious that they were not the Third Estate, that there was a conflict of interest between property and labour, and they began to vent their yet inarticulate rage upon the middle class above them. It presently appeared that these revolutionary heroines, knitting companions of the future guillotine, were not all infuriated or implacable. Parcels of banknotes that they took away were brought back; the priest was left unhung; the torches that were to have lighted the conflagration were extinguished without difficulty. They were easily persuaded that their proper sphere of action was Versailles, with its Assembly, that was able to do everything, and did nothing for the poor. They played the genuine part of mothers whose children were starving in their squalid homes, and they thereby afforded to motives which they neither shared nor understood the aid of a diamond point that nothing could withstand. It was this first detachment of invading women that allowed Stanislas Maillard to lead them away.

Maillard was known to all the town as a conqueror of the Bastille. Later, he acquired a more sinister celebrity. But on that 5th of October, as the calculating controller of dishevelled tumult, he left on those who saw him an impression of unusual force. Whilst he mustered his army in the Champs Elysées, and recruiting parties were sent through the streets, an emissary from the Hôtel de Ville hastened to warn the Government at Versailles. He was able to announce that the National Guard were coming.

Lafayette appeared late upon the scene, and did nothing to hinder the expedition of Maillard. He thought the danger contemptible, and believed that there were resources at Versailles enough to stop it, although there were seven or eight thousand women and some hundreds of men among them. Both Necker and Mounier, the President of the Assembly, confirm the fact.

When the news of what they must be prepared for reached ministers, the king was out shooting, some miles away, and nothing could be done without him. The queen was found at the Trianon, which she never saw again. An officer who came on foot from Paris told the king of his danger. He refused his name, but stated that there was no man in the service who had greater reason to complain. A mounted messenger arrived from the Minister of the Interior, and Lewis took horse and galloped to Versailles. The streets were already crowded with disorderly people, and shots were fired as he rode by.

The roads from Paris to Versailles cross the Seine at three points, and the general officers who were in the ministry declared that they might be defended with the troops that were at hand. St. Priest, the Minister of the Interior, advised the king to meet the army of Paris at Sèvres, and order it to retire. If they refused, he thought that they could be beaten.

Necker was against giving battle, and two important colleagues were with him. He was ready to take the king to Paris, seeing the objections, as he always did to every proposal, but hoping that public opinion, stimulated by the presence of the Court, which had not been seen there for generations, would sustain the Crown against the Assembly. He had held that opinion from the first, and he refused to be answerable for civil war. Lewis, unable to decide, went to consult the queen. She would be sent away, with her children, if there was a fight. She declared that she would remain if the king remained, and would not allow him to incur dangers which she did not share. This resolution made it impossible for him to adopt a manly or spirited course. The Council broke up without deciding anything.

Whilst this was going on, between three and four in the afternoon Maillard reached Versailles with his column of women. Their quality had deteriorated by the recruits made on the way, and there had been a large accession of ferocity. Besides the women who followed Maillard from the Hôtel de Ville, some of whom believed that hunger is caused by bad government, and can be appeased by good, others displayed the aprons in which they meant to carry the queen to Paris, bit by bit. And there was a group, more significant than either, who were well supplied with money, to be distributed among the soldiers of the Flemish regiment, and who effectually performed their office.

Maillard, who had prevented depredation by the way, made straight for the Assembly, and was admitted with a deputation of his followers. They arrived at a moment of excitement. The king had accepted the nineteen paragraphs of the Constitution, with the proviso that he retained the executive power undiminished. He had put off the Rights of Man until it should be seen how they were affected by the portions of the constitution yet to pass. The reply was not countersigned by a minister; and the deputies saw in it an attempt to claim the right of modifying the fundamental laws. They brought up the imprudences of the dinner of welcome, and argued that there must be a plot.

Mirabeau had never stood in a more difficult position. He clung to the monarchy, but not to the king. He was ready to serve the Count of Provence, or even the Duke of Orleans, but not a feeble executive; and he judged that, as things were going, there would soon be no king to serve. Through his friend La Marck he had attempted to terrify the Court, and to induce them to accept his services. La Marck had represented to the queen the immense value of the aid of such a man; and the queen had replied, decisively, that she hoped they would never fall so low as to need help from Mirabeau.

He defended the king's answer on the ground he had held before, that the Declaration ought to follow the Constitution, and ought not to precede it. Speaking of the scene at the officers' dinner, he said that the king was inviolable—the king, and no other person. The allusion was so clear that the royalists were reduced to silence. The Assembly resolved that the king should be requested to give his assent, unconditionally. Before the deputation had left, Maillard entered the Assembly.

Mirabeau had received early notice of the intended attack by a large body of Parisians, and had advised Mounier to adjourn in time. Mounier fancied that Mirabeau was afraid, and said that every man must die at his post. When Maillard appeared with a few women, he allowed him to speak. As the orator of the women whom he had brought from the Hôtel de Ville, Maillard asked for cheap bread, denounced the artificial famine and the Royal Guards. When rebuked by Mounier for using the term "citizens," he made a very effective point by saying that any man who was not proud to be a citizen ought at once to be expelled. But he admitted that he did not believe all the imputations that were made by his followers; and he obtained a cheer for the Royal Guard by exhibiting a regimental cocked hat with the tricolor cockade.

The Assembly gave way, and sent Mounier at the head of a deputation to invite the king's attention to the demands of his afflicted subjects. Whilst the deputies, with some of the women, stood in the rain, waiting for the gates to be opened, a voice in the crowd exclaimed that there was no want of bread in the days when they had a king, but now that they had twelve hundred they were starving. So that there were some whose animosity was not against the king, but against the elect of the people.

The king at once conceded all that Mounier asked for his strange companions, and they went away contented. Then their friends outside fell upon them, and accused them of having taken bribes; and again it became apparent that two currents had joined, and that some had honestly come for bread, and some had not. Those who had obtained the king's order for provisioning Paris, and were satisfied, went back to bring it to the Hôtel de Ville. They were sent home in a royal carriage. Maillard went with them. It was fully understood that with all his violence and crudity he had played a difficult part well.

Mounier remained at the Palace. He was not eager to revisit the scene of his humiliation, where vociferous women had occupied the benches, asking for supper, and bent on kissing the President. He wished the king now to accept the Rights of Man, without waiting for the appointed deputation from the Assembly. Although they were in part his work, he was no longer wedded to them as they stood, and thought, like Mirabeau, that they were an impediment. But a crisis had arrived, and this point might be surrendered, to save the very existence of monarchy. He waited during many eventful hours, and returned after ten at night to find that the bishop of Langres, disgusted with the scene before him, had adjourned the Assembly. Mounier instantly convoked them, by beat of drum. He had other things to speak of besides the Rights of Man; for he knew that an invader more formidable than Maillard with his Amazonian escort was approaching.

For the later weeks of September Lafayette had cast his influence on the side of those who designed to strengthen the executive. He had restrained his men when they threatened to come to support the National Assembly. To yield to that movement was to acknowledge defeat, and loss of available popularity and power. When he came to the Hôtel de Ville and found that his army was resolved to go, he opposed the project, and for many hours held his ground. The men whom he commanded were not interested on their own account in the daily allowance of food. Their anger was with the Royal Guards, and their purpose was to take their place. Then there would be less danger of resistance to the decrees, or of flight to the provinces.

Lafayette could not appear before the king at their head without evident hostility and revolt; for their temper was threatening, and he was rapidly losing control. By delay and postponement he gained something. Instead of arriving as an assailant, he came as a deliverer. When he remonstrated, his soldiers said that they meant no injury to the king, but that he must obey or abdicate. They would make their general Regent; but if he refused to put himself at their head, they would take his life. They told him that he had commanded long enough, and now he must follow. He did not yield until the tumult had risen high, and the strain on his authority was breaking.

Early in the afternoon the watchers who followed the march of the women from the rare church towers reported that they had crossed the Seine without opposition. It was known, therefore, that the road was open, that the approach of the army would be under cover of the contingent that had preceded, that there was no danger of collision.

About four o'clock Lafayette sent word to the Hôtel de Ville—for his men would not allow him out of sight—that it was time to give him his orders, as he could not prevent the departure. They were brought to him where he sat in the saddle in the Place de Grève, and he read them with an expression of the utmost alarm. They contained all that ambition could desire, for the four points which he was directed to insist on made him Dictator of France. But it was added that the orders were given because he demanded them. Lafayette never produced that document; and he left it to the commissaries sent with him to urge the one demand in which he was interested, the establishment of the Court at Paris.

He started about five o'clock, with nearly 20,000 men. From the barrier by which he left Paris he sent a note in pencil to reassure the Government as to his intentions. It was a march of seven hours. At the passage of the Seine, he sent on an officer with further explanations; and he declared that he was coming under compulsion, and would have gone back if the bridge had been held in force. Before Versailles he halted his men, and made them take the oath of fidelity to the king and the Assembly.

The news of his coming had been received with terror. A man, dressed like a workman, who had been on the march with him, hurried forward to the Palace, and was at once admitted. It was the future Duke de Richelieu, twice, in after years, Prime Minister. What he told of the mood of the men added to the alarm. Another Council was held, at which the majority were in favour of flight. "Sir," said St. Priest, "if you go to Paris, it may cost you your crown." "That advice," said Necker, "may cost you your head." Nobody doubted that flight signified civil war. But St. Priest carried his point, and rode off to prepare Rambouillet for the royal family. As he knew that the decision was the gravest that could be taken, and that Necker's words were probably true, he dropped into a walk, and was overtaken by his wife. From her he learnt that the hazardous decision had been reversed, and that the king would remain at Versailles. His interview with the deputation of women had had a momentary success, and provoked cries of "Vive le Roi!" Thereupon Necker recovered the lost ground, with the aid of Liancourt, who first brought the king to Paris in the summer. The carriages, which were ready, were countermanded. Later on, they were again sent for, but this time they were stopped by the people.

The confusion of counsel was such that one of the ministers afterwards declared that, if the Duke of Orleans had appeared and pressed his demands, he would have obtained everything. It is said that the managers of his party saw this, and showed him his opportunity, during the panic that preceded Lafayette. It is even stated that they brought him to the very door of the council chamber, and that he flinched, with the regency within reach of his hand. When the National Guard arrived, his chances vanished.

Lafayette never was able to prove the Duke's complicity in the crime of that night. When the Duke asked him what evidence he had, he replied that if he had had evidence he would have sent him for trial; but that he had enough reason for suspicion to require that he should leave the country. Thrice the Duke, forcibly encouraged by Mirabeau, refused to go. Thrice the general insisted, and the Duke started for England. Mirabeau exclaimed that he would not have him for a lackey. A long inquiry was held, and ended in nothing. The man who knew those times best, Roederer afterwards assured Napoleon that, if there was an Orleanist conspiracy, Orleans himself was not in it.

The women who invaded Versailles were followed by groups of men of the same description as those who committed the atrocities which followed the fall of the Bastille. As night fell they became formidable, skirmished with the guard, and tried to make their way into the Palace. At first, when his captains asked for orders to disperse the crowd, Lewis, against the advice of his sister, replied that he did not make war on women. But the men were armed, and evidently dangerous. The command, at Versailles, was in the hands of d'Estaing, the admiral of the American war, who at this critical moment showed no capacity. He refused to let his men defend themselves, and ordered them to withdraw. St. Priest grew impatient. Much depended on their having repressed the riot without waiting to be rescued by the army of Paris. He summoned the admiral to repel force by force. D'Estaing replied that he waited the king's orders. The king gave none. The minister then said: "When the king gives no orders, a general must judge and act for himself." Again the king was silent. Later, the same day, he adopted the words of St. Priest, and made them his own. He said that the Count d'Estaing ought to have acted on his own responsibility. No orders are needed by a man of spirit, who understands his duty. It was the constant wish of Lewis XVI. to be in the hands of stronger men, who would know how to save him in spite of himself.

Mounier had obtained his unqualified assent to the Rights of Man, and urged him to seize the moment to take refuge in some faithful province. It was the dangerous, but the honourable course, and there was hope that the Assembly, standing by him, would prevent an outbreak of war. He conveyed the royal message to the Assembly, at a night sitting, much hindered by the continued presence of the visitors from Paris. Just then Lafayette arrived, with his overwhelming force. He assured Mounier and his friends that the men he commanded would now be easy to satisfy. But he said nothing of the real purpose of his presence there. From the Assembly he passed on to the king. Leaving his 20,000 men behind him in the darkness, he appeared at the Palace gate, accompanied only by the commissaries from the Hôtel de Ville.

The Swiss behind the bars warned him to reflect what he was about to do. For he was entering a place crowded with men passionately excited against the revolutionary general, who, whether he came to save or to destroy, was no longer a subject, but a master. The general told them to let him in. As he passed, a voice called out, "There goes Cromwell." Lafayette stood still and answered, "Cromwell would not have come alone." Madame de Staël watched him as he entered the royal presence. His countenance, she says, was calm. Nobody ever saw it otherwise. Lewis received him with a sensation of relief, for he felt that he was safe. At that moment the sovereign indeed had perished, but the man was safe. The language of Lafayette was respectful and satisfactory. He left to his companions the disagreeable duty of imposing terms, and they exposed to the king the object of this strange interposition of the middle class in arms. He replied that he had already sanctioned the Rights of Man, that the minister would arrange with the municipality for the provisioning of Paris, that he himself would trust his person to the custody of the National Guard. The fourth, and only essential matter, the transfer of the Court to Paris, was left unsettled. That was to be the work reserved for the morrow. Word was sent to the Hôtel de Ville that all was well.

Lafayette, holding the issue in his hands, betrayed no impatience, and abstained from needless urging. His men undertook the outer line of defence, but the Palace itself was left to the Royal Guards. The king did not at once realise the position, and attempted to combine the old order with the new. For the remainder of the night there was a divided command and an uncertain responsibility. Between Lafayette outside and D'Estaing within, there was an unguarded door.

The general believed that he had done enough, and would easily gather the ripe fruit in the morning. Having informed the President of the Assembly, still ostensibly sitting, that order was restored, he went home to bed. He had had a long and trying day. His rest was destined to be short. Before daybreak a small band of ruffians, of the kind which the Revolution furnished as a proper instrument for conspirators, made their way by the garden entrance into the Palace. Those who aimed at the life of the king came upon a guard-room full of sleeping soldiers, and retired. The real object of popular hatred was the queen, and those who came for her were not so easily turned from their design. Two men on guard who fired upon them were dragged into the street and butchered, and their heads were borne as trophies to the Palais Royal. Their comrades fled for safety to the interior of the Palace. But one, who was posted at the door of Marie Antoinette, stood his ground, and his name, Miomandre de Sainte Marie, lives as a household word. One of the queen's ladies, whose sister has left a record of the scene, was awakened by the noise and opened the door. She saw the sentry, his face streaming with blood, holding a crowd at bay. He called to her to save the queen and fell, with the lock of a musket beaten into his brain. She instantly fastened the lock, roused the queen, and hurried her, without stopping to dress, to the king's apartment.

The National Guard from Paris, who were outside, had not protected the two first victims; but then they interfered, and the Gardes Françaises, who had been the first mutineers, and had become the solid nucleus of the Parisian army, poured into the Palace. As they had made their expedition of the day before for no other purpose than to drive the royal troops away and to take their place, none could tell what the meeting of the two corps would be, and the king's men barricaded themselves against the new comers. But an officer reminded the Gardes Françaises of the day when the two regiments had withstood the English, side by side, and theirs had been rescued by the Gardes du Corps. So they called out, "Remember Fontenoy"; and the others answered the challenge and unbarred the door.

By the time that Lafayette appeared, roused from untimely slumber, his men were masters of the Palace, and stood between the royal family and the raging mob of baffled murderers. He made the captured guardsmen safe; but although he was in supreme command, he did not restore order outside. The last of the four points he had been instructed to obtain, the removal of the Court to his custody at the Tuileries and his own permanent elevation to a position superior to the throne, was not yet conceded. Until that was settled, the loyalty of his forces was restrained. Nobody was arrested. Men whose hands were red with the blood of Varicourt and Miomandre were allowed to defy justice, and a furious crowd was left for hours without molestation under the windows of the king. The only cry left for them to raise was "Paris," and it was sure in time to do its work. The king could not escape, for Lafayette held every gate. He could not resist, for Lafayette commanded every soldier. The general never pressed the point. He was too cautious to attend the council where the matter was considered, as if the freedom of choice was left. This time Necker had his way, and he came forward and announced to the assembled people that the Court was about to move to Paris. Lewis, who had wandered, helpless and silent, between his chair and the balcony, spoke at last, and confirmed it.

In that moment of triumph Lafayette showed himself a man of instinct and of action. The multitude had sufficiently served his purpose; but their own passions were not appeased, and the queen personified to them all the antagonistic and unpopular forces. The submission of the king was a foregone conclusion: not so the reconciliation of the queen. He said to her, "What are your Majesty's intentions?" She answered, "I know my fate, I mean to die at the feet of the king." Then Lafayette led her forward, in the face of the storm, and, as not a word could be heard, he respectfully kissed her hand. The populace saw and cheered. Under his protectorate, peace was made between the Court and the democracy.

In all these transactions, which determined the future of France, the Assembly had no share. They had had no initiative and no counsel. Their President had not known how to prevent the irruption of the women; he had supplied them with bread, and had been unable to turn them out until the National Guard arrived. After two in the morning, when he heard that all was quiet at the Palace, he adjourned the sitting. Next day he proposed that they should attend the king in a body; but Mirabeau would not allow it to be done. One hundred deputies gave a futile escort to the royal family, and the Assembly followed soon after. The power was passing from them to the disciplined people of Paris, and beyond them and their commander to the men who managed the masses. Their reign had lasted from July 16 to October 6.

It took seven hours to bring the royal family from Versailles to Paris, at a foot pace, surrounded by the victorious women, who cried: "We bring the baker, the baker's wife, and the baker's boy." And they were right. Supplies became abundant; and the sudden change encouraged many to believe that the scarcity had not been due to economic causes.

X
MIRABEAU

The transfer of the Government to Paris, which degraded and obscured the king, at once made the queen the foremost person in the State. Those days of October are an epoch in her character as well as in her life, and we must turn our thoughts to her, who had so much influence and so much sorrow, and who beyond all women in European history, excepting one, has charmed and saddened mankind. She had proved inferior to her position during the years of her prosperity, and had disgraced herself, even in her mother's eyes, by her share in the dismissal of Turgot. The Court was filled with stories injurious to her good name, and the calumny of the diamond necklace showed so clearly what a Prince of the Church thought her capable of, staking his existence on his belief, that her own sister suspected her, and they remained long estranged. Her frivolity was unchecked by religion; but a year or two before her misfortunes began, she became more serious; and when they were about to end, a priest found his way into the prison, and she was prepared to die. At first, she was dreaded as the most illiberal influence near the throne, and the Parliament of Paris denounced her as the occult promoter of oppression. In the decisive days of June 1789 she induced Lewis to sacrifice to the cause of aristocracy the opportune reforms that might have retrieved his fortunes. The emigration left her to confront alone the vengeance of the people. The terrific experience of October, when she saw death so near, and was made to feel so keenly the hatred she inspired, sobered in a moment the levity of her life, and brought out higher qualities. It was on that day that she began to remind those around her whose daughter she was. Ignorant as she was and passionate, she could never become a safe adviser. But she acquired decision, vigour, and self-command, and was able sometimes to strengthen the wavering mind of her husband. Too brave to be easily frightened, she refused at first the proffered aid of Mirabeau; and when, too late, she bent her pride to ask for it, she acted with her eyes open, without confidence or hope. For the surging forces of the day, for the idea that might have saved her, the idea of a government uniting the best properties of a monarchy with the best properties of a republic, she had neither sympathy nor understanding. Yet she was not wedded to the maxims that had made the greatness of her race, and the enmity of the princes and the *émigrés* saved her from the passions of the old *régime*. Condé spoke of her as a democrat; and she would have been glad to exchange the institutions of 1791 for something like the British constitution as it existed in those Tory days. She perished through her insincerity more than through the traditional desire for power. When the king was beheaded, the Prince Bishop of Bamberg and Würzburg, reputed the most sagacious and enlightened among the prelates of the empire, was heard to say, "It ought to have been the queen." We who see farther may allow the retribution that befell her follies and her errors to arrest our judgment.

Marie Antoinette's negotiation with Mirabeau, and the memorable endeavour of Mirabeau to restore the constitutional throne, is the central feature in the period now before us.

By the compulsory removal to Paris the democracy became preponderant. They were strengthened by the support of organized anarchy outside, and by the disappearance of their chief opponents within. Mounier was the first to go. The outrage at Versailles had occurred while he presided, and he resigned his seat with indignation. He attempted to rouse his own province against the Assembly, which had betrayed its mandate, and renounced its constituents; but Dauphiné, the home and basis of his influence, rejected him, and he went into exile. His example was followed by Lally Tollendal and a large number of moderate men, who despaired of their country, and who, by declining further responsibility, helped to precipitate the mischief they foresaw.

The constitutional cause, already opposed by Conservatives, was now deserted by the Liberals. Malouet remained at his post. He had been less prominent and less eager than Mounier, and he was not so easily discouraged. The Left were now able to carry out in every department of the State their interpretation of the Rights of Man. They were governed mainly by two ideas. They distrusted the king as a malefactor, convicted of the unpardonable sin of absolutism, whom it was impossible to subject to too much limitation and control; and they were persuaded that the securities for individual freedom which are requisite under a personal government are superfluous in a popular community conducting its affairs by discussion and compromise and adjustment, in which the only force is public opinion.

The two views tended to the same practical result—to strengthen the legislative power, which is the nation, and weaken the executive power, which is the king. To arrest this tendency was the last effort that consumed the life of Mirabeau. The danger that he dreaded was no longer the power of the king, but the weakness of the king.

The old order of things had fallen, and the customary ways and forces were abolished. The country was about to be governed by new principles, new forms, and new men. All the assistance that order derives from habit and tradition, from local connection and personal credit, was lost. Society had to pass through a dangerous and chaotic interval, during which the supreme need was a vigorous administration. That is the statesmanlike idea which held possession of Mirabeau, and guided him consistently through the very tortuous and adventurous course of his last days. He had no jealousy of the Executive. Ministers ought to be chosen in the Assembly, ought to lead the Assembly, and to be controlled by it; and then there would be no motive to fear them and to restrict their action. That was an idea not to be learnt from Montesquieu, and generally repudiated by theorists of the separation of powers. It was familiar to Mirabeau from his experience of England, where, in 1784, he had seen the country come to the support of the king against the parliament. Thence he gathered the conception of a patriot king, of a king the true delegate and mandatory of the nation, in fact of an incipient Emperor. If his schemes had come to anything, it is likely that his democratic monarch might have become as dangerous as any arbitrary potentate could be, and that his administration would have proved as great an obstacle to parliamentary government as French administration has always been since Napoleon. But his purpose at the time was sincerely politic and legitimate, and he undertook alone the defence of constitutional principles. During the month of September Mirabeau raised the question of a parliamentary Ministry, both in the press and in the Assembly. He prepared a list of eminent men for the several offices, assigning to himself a seat in the Cabinet without a portfolio. It was a plan to make him and Talleyrand masters of the Government. The Ministers of the day did not trust him, and had no wish to make way for him, and when, on November 6, he proposed that Ministers be heard in the National Assembly, the Archbishop of Bordeaux instigated Montlosier and Lanjuinais to oppose him. Both were men of high character, and both had some attainments; and in their aversion for him, and for his evident self-seeking, they carried a motion forbidding deputies to take office. By this vote, of November 7, which permanently excluded Mirabeau from the councils of the king, the executive was deprived of authority. It is one of the decisive acts of the Constituent Assembly, for it ruined the constitutional monarchy.

Mirabeau was compelled to rely on a dissolution as the only prospect of better things. He knew that the vote was due as much to his own bad name as to a deliberate dislike of the English practice. The question for him now was whether he could accomplish through the Court what was impossible through the Assembly. He at once drew up a paper, exhorting the king to place himself at the head of the Revolution, as its moderator and guide. The Count of Provence refused to submit his plans to the king, but recommended him for the part of a secret adviser. Just then an event occurred, which is mysterious to this day, but which had the effect of bringing Mirabeau into closer relations with the king's brother. At Christmas, the Marquis de Favras was arrested, and it was discovered that he was a confidential agent of the Prince, who had employed him to raise a loan for a purpose that was never divulged—some said, to carry off the king to a frontier fortress, others suspected a scheme of counter-revolution. For the electoral law excluded the ignorant and the indigent from the franchise, limiting the rights of active citizenship to those who paid a very moderate sum in taxes. It was obvious that this exclusion, by confining power to property, created the raw material for Socialism in the future. Some day a dexterous hand might be laid on the excluded multitude congregated at Paris, to overthrow the government of the middle class. The Constituent Assembly was in danger of being overtrumped, and was necessarily suspicious.

By Mirabeau's advice, the Count of Provence at once made a public declaration of sound revolutionary sentiments, and disavowed Favras. His speech, delivered at the Hôtel de Ville, was well received and he rose in popular favour. Meantime, his unhappy confederate was tried for treason against the nation, and found guilty. Favras asked whether, on a full and explicit confession, his life would be spared. He was told that nothing could save him. The judge exhorted him to die in silence, like a brave man. The priest who assisted him afterwards professed that he had saved the life of the Count of Provence. Favras underwent his fate with fortitude, keeping his secret to the end. The evidence which would have compromised the prince was taken away, and no historian has seen it. The fatal documents were restored to him when he became king by the daughter of the man who had concealed them.

For some weeks the Count of Provence was ambitious of power, and allowed Mirabeau to put him forward as a kind of Prime Minister, or for a position analogous to that of the Cardinal-nephew in seventeenth-century Rome. He had ability, caution, and, for the moment, popularity; but he was irresolute, indolent, and vain. If anything could be made of him, it was clear that the active partner would be Mirabeau. He was neither loved nor trusted by the king and queen, and with such a confederate at his elbow he might become formidable. Necker devised a plan by which his scheming was easily frustrated. The king appeared before the Assembly, without preliminaries, and delivered an unexpected statement of policy, adopting the entire work of the Revolution, as far as it had gone, and praising in particular the recent division of Provinces into departments.

Every step, until that day, had been taken reluctantly, feebly, under compulsion. Every concession had been a defeat and a surrender. On February 4, under no immediate pressure, Lewis deliberately took the lead of the movement. It was an act, not of weakness, but of policy, not a wound received and acquiesced in, but a stroke delivered. The Assembly responded by at once taking the civic oath to maintain the Constitution. As that instrument did not yet exist, none could say what the demonstration would involve. It was adopted for the sake of committing the remnant of the privileged orders who yielded under protest.

Mirabeau's aristocratic brother threw away his sword, saying that there was nothing else for a gentleman to do, when the king abandoned his sceptre. Mirabeau himself was indignant with what he called a pantomime; for he said that Ministers had no right to screen their own responsibility behind the inviolate throne. He saw that his patron was ingeniously set aside and stranded, and he conceived that his own profound calculations were baffled. Yet the perspicacity that he seldom wanted failed him at that moment. For the reconciliation of the people with the king, the executive triumphing in its popularity, guiding the Revolution to its goal, was the exact reproduction of his proposals, and was borrowed from his manifestoes.

The significance of this was at once felt by the foreign advisers of the queen. Mercy Argenteau, who had been Austrian ambassador throughout the reign, and who was a faithful and intelligent friend, suggested that if they sincerely accepted the policy, they would do well to take the politician with it, that the Count of Provence could be best disabled by depriving him of his prompter, that the magic is not in the wand but in the hand that waves it. The queen hesitated, for Mirabeau had threatened her in the last days at Versailles, and it was not yet proved that he was not concerned in the attempt to murder her. She declared that nothing would induce her to see him, and she wished for somebody who could undertake to manage him, and who would be responsible for his conduct. Mercy, regardless of her scruples, sent for La Marck, who was at his Belgian home, opposing the Emperor, and fostering a Federal republic, and who in consequence was not in favour with Marie Antoinette. La Marck was intimate with Mirabeau, and kept him in pocket money. He undertook the negotiation, with little hope of a profitable result; and at his house Mercy and Mirabeau had a secret meeting. They parted, well pleased with each other. Mirabeau advised that the king should leave Paris, and the advice bore fruit. Mercy did not declare the intentions of the Court, and Mirabeau continued to act in his own way, treating with Lafayette for money or an embassy, and attacking the clergy, with whose cause Lewis was more and more identified. To this interval belongs the famous scene where he exclaimed that from the place where he stood he could see the window from which a king of France fired on his Protestant subjects. Maury, not perceiving the snare, bounded from his seat, and cried out, "Nonsense! it is not visible from here."

When he made that speech it is clear that Mirabeau was not exerting himself to secure confidence at Court; and for some weeks in spring the negotiation hung fire. At length, La Marck convinced the queen that his friend had been falsely accused of the crime of October, and the king proposed that he should be asked to write down his views. He peremptorily rejected La Marck's advice that the Ministers should be admitted to the secret. He avowed to Mercy that he intended soon to change them for men who could co-operate with Mirabeau; but he was resolved not to place himself at once irrevocably in the power of a man in whom he had no confidence, and who was only the subject of an experiment. Consequently, Mirabeau's first object of attack was the Ministry, and the king's forces were divided. The position was a false one from end to end; but this hostility to Necker served to disguise the reality. On the 10th of May, 1790, he drew up a paper which La Marck carried to the queen, and which at once had the effect of making the Court zealous to complete the bargain. La Marck asked Mirabeau what were his conditions. He replied that he would be happy on £1000 a year, if his debts could be paid; but he feared that they were too heavy for him to expect it. On inquiry, it turned out that they were a little over £8000. Lewis

XVI. offered to clear them off, to give him £3000 a year while the Assembly lasted, and a million francs down whenever it came to an end.

In this way both parties were secure. Mirabeau could not play false, without losing, not only his income, but an eventual sum of £40,000. The king could not cast him off without wasting the considerable sum paid to his creditors. The Archbishop of Toulouse undertook the delicate task of dealing with them; and meeting his debtor constantly, a strange intimacy arose between the two men.

Mirabeau, wild with the joy of his deliverance, forgot all prudence and precaution. He took a town house and a country house; he bought books and pictures, carriages and horses, and gave dinner-parties at which six servants waited on his guests. After a few months he wanted money, and more was given without question. The Government proposed at last to buy him an annuity, with one-fourth of the capital which was to fall due at the dissolution; but the intention was not carried out. The entire sum that Mirabeau received, up to his death, from the king amounted to about £12,000. In return, between June 1 and February 16 he wrote fifty-one notes for the Court discussing the events of the day, and exposing by degrees vast schemes of policy. When they came to be known, half a century ago, they added immeasurably to his fame, and there are people who compare his precepts and prescriptions with the last ten years of Mazarin and the beginning of the Consulate, with the first six years of Metternich or the first eight of Bismarck, or, on a different plane, with the early administration of Chatham.

Mirabeau himself was proud of his new position, and relied on this correspondence to redeem his good name. He was paid to be of his own opinion. The king had gone over to him; he had changed nothing in his views to meet the wishes of the king. His purpose throughout had been the consolidation of representative monarchy on the ruins of absolutism. To the king in league with privilege he was implacably opposed. To the king divested of that complicity he was a convinced and ardent friend.

The opportunity of proving his faith was supplied by Captain Cook. In his last voyage the navigator visited the island since named after his lieutenant Vancouver, and sailed into Nootka Sound, to which, in his report, he drew the attention of the Government. Three or four years before, the Spaniards had been there, and had taken formal possession; and the Russians, spreading southward along the coast, acknowledged their right, and withdrew. But the place was far north of the regions they actually occupied; and English adventurers, with the sanction of the Government, settled there, and opened a trade in peltry with China. After a year or two, the Spaniards came in force, and carried them off, with their ships and their cargoes; and claiming the entire Pacific seaboard from Cape Horn to Alaska, they called on the English Ministers to punish their intruding countrymen. They also equipped a fleet of forty sail of the line, assuring the British *chargé d'affaires* that it was only to protect themselves against the Revolution. Pitt was not lulled by these assurances, or by the delivery of the confiscated ships. He had authorised the proceedings of the traders with the intention of resisting the Spanish claim beyond the limits of effective occupation. He now demanded reparation, and fitted out a fleet superior to that with which Nelson crushed the combined navies of France and Spain. Under the treaty of 1761 Spain demanded the support of France. If the French armed, as the Spaniards were arming, there was reason to hope that England, in so very dubious a question, would listen to terms; and if France refused to stand by a manifest engagement, Spain would be free to seek new friends. The Emperor sustained the appeal. It would be well for him if England was diverted from the concerns of Eastern Europe, and if France was occupied in the West. The French Ministers admitted their obligation and began to arm.

On May 14, just after the first negotiation between Mirabeau and the Court, the matter came before the Assembly. It was a common belief that war would strengthen the executive. The democratic leaders repudiated the Family Compact, and resented an alliance which was not national but dynastic and of the essence of those things which they were sweeping away. They sent pacific messages to the British embassy, and claimed for the representative assembly the right of pronouncing on peace and war.

Mirabeau, unlike many others, regarded a European war as a danger to the throne. But he was preparing for civil war, and meant to secure the army and navy on the royal side. He demanded for the king the exclusive right of declaring war and making peace. That is the principle under a constitution where the deputies make the Ministers. In France, Ministers were excluded from parliament and the principle did not apply. Barnave answered Mirabeau, and defeated him. On May 22, in the most powerful constitutional argument he ever delivered, Mirabeau insisted that, if the ultimate decision rested with the Assembly, it could act only on the proposition of the Crown. In legislation, the king had no initiative. Mirabeau established the royal initiative in peace and war. It was the first-fruit of the secret compact. The new ally had proved not only that he was capable and strong, but that he was faithful. For by asking more than he could obtain he had incurred, for the moment, a great loss of credit. The excess of his unwonted royalism made him an object of suspicion from that day. To recover the ground, he issued an amended version of his first speech; but others printed the two texts in parallel columns, and exposed the fraud. He had rendered an important service, and it was done at serious cost to himself. The event cemented the alliance, and secured his position with the king.

The Assembly voted a solemn declaration, that France would never make war for conquest, or against freedom. After that, Spain had little to hope for, and Pitt became defiant. Negotiations lasted till October. The Assembly appointed a Committee on Foreign Affairs, in which Mirabeau predominated, casting all his influence on the side of peace, and earning the gratitude and the gold of England. At last, the mutinous temper of the Brest fleet settled the question.

The great Bourbon alliance was dissolved, and Pitt owed a signal triumph to the revolutionary spirit and the moderating influence of Mirabeau. His defence of the prerogative deserved a reward, and he was received in a secret audience by Marie Antoinette. The interview took place at St. Cloud, July 3. The statesman did not trust his new friends, and he instructed the nephew who drove him, in disguise, to the back door, to fetch the police if he did not reappear in three-quarters of an hour. The conversation was satisfactory, and Mirabeau, as he kissed the queen's hand, declared with chivalrous fervour that the monarchy was saved. He spoke sincerely. The comedian and deceiver was not the wily and unscrupulous intriguer, but the inexperienced daughter of the Empress-queen. She never believed in his truth. When he continued to thunder against the Right, the king and queen shook their heads, and repeated that he was incorrigible. The last decision they came to in his lifetime was to reject his plans in favour of that which brought them to Varennes. But as the year wore on, they could not help seeing that the sophistical free-lance and giver of despised advice was the most prodigious individual force in the world, and that France had never seen his like. Everybody now perceived it, for his talent and resource increased rapidly, since he was steadied by a definite purpose, and a contract he could never afford to break. The hostile press knew of his visit to St. Cloud three days after it occurred, and pretended to know for how many millions he had sold himself. They were too reckless to obtain belief, but they were very near the truth; and the secret of his correspondence was known or guessed by at least twenty persons.

With this sword hanging over him, with this rope round his neck, in the autumn and winter of 1790, Mirabeau rose to an ascendancy in which he outweighed all parties. He began his notes by an attempt to undermine the two men who stood in his way. Lafayette was too strong for him. On the first anniversary of the Bastille he received an ovation. Forty thousand National Guards assembled from all parts of France for the feast of Federation. At an altar erected in the Champ de Mars, Talleyrand celebrated his last Mass, and France sanctioned the doings of Paris. The king was present, but all the demonstration was for the hero of two hemispheres, on his white charger. In November a new Ministry took office, composed of his partisans. Mirabeau attempted a coalition, but Lafayette did not feel the need of his friendship. He said, "I have resisted the king of England in his power, the king of France in his authority, the people in its rage; I am not going to yield to Mirabeau."

Necker was less tenacious of office, and rather than consent to an increased issue of *assignats*, resigned, much to his honour, and retired obscurely. Mirabeau triumphed. He had opposed the *assignats* at first, although Clavière defended them in his newspaper. He now changed his attitude. He not only affirmed that the Church lands would be adequate security for paper, making it equivalent to gold, but he was willing that the purchase money should be paid in *assignats*, doing away with bullion altogether. But the cloven hoof appeared when he assured the king that the plan which he defended would fail, and would involve France in ruin. He meant that it would ruin the Assembly, and would enable the king to dissolve. The same Machiavellian purpose guided him in Church questions. He was at heart a Liberal in matters of conscience, and thought toleration too weak a term for the rights inseparable from religion. But he wished the constitutional oath to be imposed with rigour, and that the priests should be encouraged to refuse it. He declined to give a pledge that the Assembly would not interfere with doctrine, and he prepared to raise the questions of celibacy and of divorce in order to aggravate the irritation. He proposed to restore authority by civil war; and the road to civil war was bankruptcy and persecution. Meantime, the court of inquiry vindicated him from aspersions connected with the attack on Versailles; as chairman of the Diplomatic Committee, he was the arbiter of foreign policy. Necker and all his colleagues save one had gone down before him; he was elected President of the Jacobins in November, and when he asked for leave of absence, the Assembly, on the motion of Barnave, requested him not to absent himself. Montmorin, the only member of Necker's Ministry who remained at his post, made overtures to him, and they came to an understanding. The most remarkable of all the notes to the king is the one that records their conversation. They agreed on a plan of united action. Mirabeau thereupon drew up the 47th note, which is a treatise of constitutional management and intrigue, and discloses his designs in their last phase but one, at Christmas 1790.

Mirabeau never swerved from the fundamental convictions of 1789, and he would have become a republican if Lewis had gone over to the reactionary *émigrés*. But he wished him to retire to some provincial town, that he might not be in the power of the Assembly, and might be able to disperse it, backed by the growing anger of the country. Meantime, opinion was to be worked and roused by every device. He set himself strenuously to form a central party out of the various groups of deputies. Montmorin was in friendly touch with some of them, and he had the command of money. Mirabeau laboured to gain over others. Late one night he had a long conference with Malouet, whom he dazzled, and who influenced a certain number of votes.

On the other hand, the action of Montmorin extended to Barnave. It seemed reasonable to suppose that a combination which reached from Barnave on the Left to Malouet on the Right would be strong enough either to retrieve its errors, or to break it up, in conjunction with the Court.

At the end of January, 1791, Mirabeau became President for the first time, and he occupied the chair with unforeseen dignity and distinction. He had attained the summit of his career. Just then, the king's aunts announced their departure for Rome. There was much discontent, because, if they could be detained, it would be more easy to keep the king at Paris. Mirabeau made the Assembly feel that interference with the princesses would be contemptible. Twice they were stopped on their way, and twice released. Everybody saw what this implied, and Paris was agitated. A tumult broke out in the Tuileries garden, which Mirabeau, summoned from table, at once appeased. He was confident in his strength, and when the Assembly discussed measures against emigration, he swore that he would never obey a body guilty of inquisitorial dictation. He quelled the murmurs of the Left by exclaiming, "*Silence aux trente voix!*" This was the date of his breach with the Democrats. It was February 28, and he was to dine with the Duke d'Aiguillon. When he came, the door was shut in his face. By La Marck's advice, he went that night to the Jacobins, hoping to detach the club from the leaders. But he had shown his hand, and his enemies knew how to employ their opportunity. Duport and Lameth attacked him with extreme violence, aiming at his expulsion. The discussion is not reported. But three of those who were present agree that Mirabeau seemed to be disconcerted and appalled by the strength of the case against him, and sat with the perspiration streaming down his face. His reply was, as usual, an oratorical success; but he did not carry his audience with him, and he went home disheartened. The Jacobin array stood unbroken.

On March 4, Lord Gower wrote that the governing power was passing to Mirabeau. But on the same day he himself avowed to La Marck that he had miscalculated, and was losing courage. On the 25th there was a debate on the Regency, in which he spoke with caution, and dissembled. That day the ambassador again wrote that Mirabeau had shown that he alone was fit for power. Then the end came. Tissot, meeting him soon after the scene at the Jacobins, thought that he looked like a dying man. He was sinking under excess of work combined with excess of dissipation. When he remonstrated with his brother for getting drunk, the other replied, "Why grudge me the only vice you have not appropriated?" It was remembered afterwards, when suspicion arose, that he had several attacks of illness during that month of March. On the 26th he was brought in to Paris from his villa in an alarming condition. La Marck's interests were concerned in a debate on mineral property which was fixed for the following day. Fortified with a good deal of Tokay, Mirabeau spoke repeatedly. It was the last time. He came back to his friend and said, "Your cause is won, but I am lost." When his danger became known, it seemed that nothing had occurred to diminish public confidence, or tarnish the lustre of his fame. The crowd that gathered in the street made it almost impossible to approach his door. He was gratified to know that Barnave had called, and liked to hear how much feeling was shown by the people of Paris. After a consultation, which was held on April 1, he made up his mind to die, and signed his will. Talleyrand paid him a long visit, and took away a discourse on the law of Inheritance, which he read in the Assembly before the remains of his friend were cold, but which did not deserve the honour, being, like about thirty of his speeches, the work of a stranger. The presence of Talleyrand, with whom he had quarrelled, was welcome to Mirabeau, who, though not a believer, did not wish it to be thought that he had rejected the consolations of religion. The parish priest came, but, being told of the prelate's presence, went away; and a report spread that the dying sinner had received the ministrations of a more spiritual ecclesiastic than the Bishop of Autun.

Mirabeau never knew how little the royal personages whom he served esteemed his counsels; and he died believing that he alone could have saved the monarchy, and that it would perish with him. If he had lived, he said that he would have given Pitt trouble, for there was a change in his foreign policy. On January 28 he still spoke of the eternal fraternity of England; but in March he was ready to call out the fleet, in the interest of Russia, and was only prevented by the attack of which he died. Whether he supported England against Spain, or Russia against England, his support was paid for in gold. To his confederates, his illness was a season of terror. If an enemy disguised as a creditor caused seals to be set upon his papers, a discovery must have ensued that would ruin many reputations and imperil many lives. He clung to the secret documents on which he intended that his fame should rest. On the day of his death, when they were deposited with La Marck, the secretary who had transcribed them stabbed himself. On the morning of Saturday, April 2, there was no hope, and Mirabeau asked for opium. He died before the prescription was made up. Several doctors who made the post-mortem examination believed that there were marks of poison; but when they were warned that they would be torn to pieces, and the king also, they held their peace.

Odious as he was, and foredoomed to fail, he was yet the supreme figure of the time. Tocqueville, who wrote the best book, or one of the two best books, on the subject, looking to the permanent result, describes the Revolution as having continued and completed the work of the monarchy by intensifying the unity of power. It is more true to say that the original and essential spirit of the movement was decentralisation—to take away from the executive government, and to give to local authorities. The executive could not govern, because it was obliged to transmit orders to agents not its own, whom it neither appointed nor dismissed nor controlled. The king was deprived of administrative power, as he had been deprived of legislative power. That distrust, reasonable in the old régime, ought to have ceased, when the Ministers appointed by the king were deputies presented by the Assembly. That was the idea by which Mirabeau would have preserved the Revolution from degenerating through excess of decentralisation into tyranny. As a Minister, he might have saved the Constitution. It is not to the discredit of the Assembly that the horror which his life inspired made his genius inefficient, and that their labours failed because they deemed him too bad for power.

If Mirabeau is tried by the test of public morals, the only standard of political conduct on which men may be expected to agree, the verdict cannot be doubtful. His ultimate policy was one vast intrigue, and he avowedly strove to do evil that good might come. The thing is hardly less infamous in the founder of the Left Centre than in Maury and his unscrupulous colleagues of the Right. There was at no time a prospect of success, for he never had the king or the queen for one moment with him.

The answer is different if we try him by a purely political test, and ask whether he desired power for the whole or freedom for the parts. Mirabeau was not only a friend of freedom, which is a term to be defined, but a friend of federalism, which both Montesquieu and Rousseau regarded as the condition of freedom. When he spoke confidentially, he said that there was no other way in which a great country like France could be free. If in this he was sincere, and I believe that he was sincere, he deserves the great place he holds in the memory of his countrymen.

XI
SIEYÈS AND THE CONSTITUTION CIVILE

Before coming to the conflict between Church and State, with which the legislation of 1790 closes, I must speak of a man memorable far beyond Mirabeau in the history of political thought and political action, who is the most perfect representative of the Revolution. I mean the Abbé Sieyès. As a priest without a vocation, he employed himself with secular studies, and mastered and meditated the French and the English writers of the age, politicians, economists, and philosophers. Learning from many, he became the disciple of none, and was thoroughly independent, looking beyond the horizon of his century, and farther than his own favourites, Rousseau, Adam Smith, and Turgot. He understood politics as the science of the State as it ought to be, and he repudiated the product of history, which is things as they are. No American ever grasped more firmly the principle that experience is an incompetent teacher of the governing art. He turned resolutely from the Past, and refused to be bound by the precepts of men who believed in slavery and sorcery, in torture and persecution. He deemed history a misleading and useless study, and knew little of its examples and its warnings. But he was sure that the Future must be different, and might be better. In the same disdainful spirit he rejected Religion as the accumulated legacy of childhood, and believed that it arrested progress by depreciating terrestrial objects. Nevertheless he had the confidence of Lubersac, Bishop of Tréguier, and afterwards of Chartres, who recommended him to the clergy of Montfort as their deputy.

Sieyès preferred to stand for the Third Estate at Paris, where he was elected last of all the candidates. One of his preliminary tracts circulated in 30,000 copies, and had promptly made him famous, for it was as rich in consequences as the ninety-five theses of Wittenberg. His philosophy of history consisted in one idea. Barbarians had come down from Germany on the people of civilised and imperial Gaul, and had subjugated and robbed them, and the descendants of the invading race were now the feudal nobles, who still held power and profit, and continued to oppress the natives. This identification of privileged noble with conquering Frank was of older date;

and in this century it has been made the master-key to modern history. When Thierry discovered the secret of our national development in the remarks of Wamba the Witless to Gurth, under the Sherwood oaks, he applied to us a formula familiar to his countrymen; and Guizot always defined French history as a perpetual struggle between hostile nations until the eighteenth century made good the wrong that was done in the fifth.

Right or wrong, the theory of Sieyès was adopted by his most learned successors, and must not be imputed to ignorance. His argument is that the real nation consisted of the mass of men enjoying no privilege, and that they had a claim for compensation and reprisal against those who had been privileged to oppress and to despoil them. The Third Estate was equal to the three Estates together, for the others had no right to be represented. As power exercised otherwise than by consent, power that does not emanate from those for whose use it exists, is a usurpation, the two first orders must be regarded as wrongdoers. They ought to be repressed, and the means of doing harm taken from them.

Although Sieyès neither wrote well nor spoke well, yet within a fortnight of his maiden speech he had vanquished the ancient order of things in France. The Court, the Church and the *Noblesse* had gone down before the imposing coherence of his ideas. He soon lost confidence in the Assembly, as it fell under the control of intruding forces, and he drew back into an attitude of reserve and distrust. Many of his measures were adopted, but he deemed that they were spoilt in the process, and that men who sought popular applause were averse from instruction.

Sieyès was essentially a revolutionist, because he held that political oppression can never be right, and that resistance to oppression can never be wrong. And he was a royalist, not as believing in the proprietary right of dynasties, but because monarchy, justly limited and controlled, is one of many forces that secure the liberty which is given by society and not by nature. He was a Liberal, for he thought liberty the end of government, and defined it as that which makes men most completely masters of their faculties, in the largest sphere of independent action. He was also a democrat, for he would revise the constitution once in a generation; and he described the law as the settled will of those who are governed, which those who govern have no share in making. But he was less a democrat than a Liberal, and he contrived scientific provision against the errors of the sovereign nation. He sacrificed equality by refusing the vote to those who paid no taxes, and he preferred an elaborate system of indirect and filtered election. He broke the direct tide of opinion by successive renewals, avoiding dissolution. According to his doctrine, the genuine national will proceeds from debate, not from election, and is ascertained by a refined intellectual operation, not by coarse and obvious arithmetic. The object is to learn not what the country thinks, but what it would think if it was present at the discussion carried on by men whom it trusted. Therefore there is no imperative mandate, and the deputy governs the constituent. He mitigated democracy by another remarkable device. The Americans have made the guardians of the law into watchers on the lawgiver, giving to the judiciary power to preserve the Constitution against the legislature. Sieyès invented a special body of men for the purpose, calling them the constitutional jury, and including not judges, for he suspected those who had administered the ancient law of France, but the *élite* of veteran politicians.

Thus, although all power emanates from the nation alone, and very little can be delegated to an hereditary and irresponsible monarch, he intended to restrict its exercise at every point, and to make sure that it would never be hasty, or violent, and that minorities should be heard. In his sustained power of consistent thinking, Sieyès resembles Bentham and Hegel. His flight is low, and he lacks grace and distinction. He seems to have borrowed his departments from Harrington, the distilled unity of power from Turgot, the rule of the mass of taxpayers over the unproductive class above them, from the notion that labour is the only source of wealth, which was common to Franklin and Adam Smith. But he is profoundly original, and though many modern writers on politics exceed him in genius and eloquence and knowledge, none equal him in invention and resource. When he was out of public life, during the Legislative Assembly, he acted as adviser to the Girondins. Therefore he became odious to Robespierre who, after the fall of Danton, turned against him, and required Barère to see what he could be charged with. For, he said, Sieyès has more to answer for as an enemy to freedom than any who have fallen beneath the law.

The Abbé's nerves never quite recovered from the impressions of that time. When he fell ill, forty years later, and became feverish, he sent down to tell the porter that he was not at home, if Robespierre should call. He offered some ideas for the Constitution of 1795, which found no support. He patiently waited till his time came, and refused a seat on the Directory. In 1799, when things were at the worst, he came back from the embassy at Berlin, took the command, and rendered eminent service. He had no desire for power. "What I want," he said, "is a sword." For a moment he had thought of the Duke of Brunswick and the Archduke Charles; at last he fixed on Joubert, and sent him to fight Suworow in Italy. If he had come home crowned with victory, the remnant of the National Assembly was to have been convoked, to place the daughter of Lewis on her father's throne.

At Novi, in the first action, Joubert fell, and Moreau commanded the retreat. Sieyès now applied to him. Moreau was not yet the victor of Hohenlinden. His ascendancy was doubtful, and he hesitated. They were conferring together when news came that Bonaparte had escaped from Egypt, and would soon be at Paris. Sieyès exclaimed, rather impudently, "Then France is saved!" Moreau retorted, "I am not wanted. That is the man for you." At first Bonaparte was reserved, and took so much time to feel his way that Sieyès, who was the head of the government, called him an insolent fellow who deserved to be shot. Talleyrand brought them together, and they soon came to an understanding. The conspiracy of Brumaire would have failed at the deciding moment but for the Abbé. For Bonaparte, when threatened with outlawry, lost his head, and Sieyès quietly told him to drive out the hostile deputies. Thereupon the soldier, obeying the man of peace, drew his sword and expelled them.

Everybody now turned to the great legislator of 1789 for the Constitution of the hour. With incomparable opportunities for observation, he had maturely revolved schemes for the government of France on the lines of that which was rejected in 1795. He refused to write anything; but he consented to dictate, and his words were taken down by Boulay de la Meurthe, and were published long after, in a volume of which there is no copy at Paris or in London.

What I have just said will give you a more favourable view of Sieyès than you may find in books. The Abbé was not a high-minded man, and he has no friends in his own country. Some dislike him because he was a priest, some because he was an unfrocked priest. He is odious to royalists as a revolutionist, and to republicans as a renegade. I have spoken of him as a political thinker, not as a writer, an orator, or an administrator. Mr. Wentworth Dilke and Mr. Buckle[1] have pointed out something more than specks in the character of Burke. Even if much of what they say is true, I should not hesitate to acknowledge him as the first political intellect of his age. Since I first spoke of Sieyès, certain papers have come to light tending to show that he was as wicked as the rest of them. They would not affect my judgment on his merit as a thinker.

[1] Dilke, *Papers of a Critic*, vol. ii. pp. 309-384; Buckle, *History of Civilisation*, ed. J. M. Robertson, pp. 258-269.

In this oracular manner the Constitution of 1799 came into existence, and it was not his fault that it degenerated in the strong hands of Napoleon. He named the three Consuls, refusing to be one himself, and he passed into ceremonious obscurity as president of the Senate.

When the Emperor had quarrelled with his ablest advisers he regretted that he had renounced the aid of such an auxiliary. He thought him unfit to govern, for that requires sword and spurs; but he admitted that Sieyès often had new and luminous ideas, and might have been useful to him beyond all the ministers of the Empire. Talleyrand, who disliked Sieyès, and ungenerously reproached him with cupidity, spoke of him to Lord Brougham as the one statesman of the time. The best of the political legacy of the Revolution has been his work. Others pulled down, but he was a builder, and he closed in 1799 the era which he had opened ten years before. In the history of political doctrine, where almost every chapter has yet to be written, none will be more valuable than the one that will show what is permanent and progressive in the ideas that he originated.

It was the function of the constituent Assembly to recast the laws in conformity with the Rights of Man, to abolish every survival of absolutism, every heirloom of inorganic tradition, that was inconsistent with them. In every department of State they were obliged to make ruins, to remove them, and to raise a new structure from the foundation. The transition from the reign of force to the reign of opinion, from custom to principle, led to a new order through confusion, uncertainty, and suspense. The efficacy of the coming system was nowhere felt at first. The soldiers, who were so soon to form the finest army ever known, ran away as soon as they saw a shot fired. The prosperous finances of modern France began with bankruptcy. But in one division of public life the Revolution not only made a bad beginning, but went on, step by step, to a bad end, until, by civil war and anarchy and tyranny, it had ruined its cause. The majority of the clergy were true to the new ideas, and on some decisive occasions, June 19 and August 4, promoted their victory. Many prelates were enlightened reformers, and even Robespierre believed that the inferior clergy were, in the bulk, democratic. Nevertheless the Assembly, by a series of hostile measures, carefully studied, and long pursued, turned them into implacable enemies, and thereby made the Revolution odious to a large part of the French people.

This gradual but determined change of front, improbable at first, and evidently impolitic, is the true cause of the disastrous conflict in which the movement of 1789 came to ruin. Had there been no ecclesiastical establishment to deal with, it may be that the development of Jacobin theory, or the logic of socialism, would have led to the same result. As it was, they were secondary causes of the catastrophe that was to follow. That there was a fund of active animosity for the church, in a generation tutored by Voltaire, Diderot, Helvétius, Holbach, Rousseau and Raynal, none could doubt. But in the men of more immediate influence, such as Turgot, Mirabeau and Sieyès, contempt was more visible than resentment; and it was by slow degrees that the full force of aversion predominated over liberal feeling and tolerant profession. But if the liberal tendency had been stronger, and tolerant convictions more distinct, there were many reasons which made a collision inevitable between the Church and the prevailing ideas. The Gallican Church had been closely associated with the entire order of things which the Assembly, at all costs, was resolved to destroy. For three centuries from the time when they became absolute the French kings had enjoyed all the higher patronage. No such prerogative could be left to the Crown when it became constitutional, and it was apparent that new methods for the appointment of priest and prelate, that a penetrating change in the system of ecclesiastical law, would be devised.

Two things, chiefly, made the memory of monarchy odious: dynastic war and religious persecution. But the wars had ended in the conquest of Alsace, and in the establishment of French kings in Spain and Naples. The odium of persecution remained; and if it was not always assignable to the influence of the clergy, it was largely due to them, and they had attempted to renew it down to the eve of the Revolution. The reduction of the royal power was sure to modify seriously the position of men upon whom the royal power, in its excess, had so much relied, and who had done so much to raise up and to sustain it. People had come to believe that the cause of liberty demanded, not the emancipation, but the repression of the priesthood. These were underlying motives; but the signal was given by financial interests. The clergy, being a privileged order, like the nobles, were involved in the same fate. With the nobles, at the same night sitting of August 4, they surrendered the right of taxing, and of not being taxed.

When the principle of exemption was rejected, the economists computed that the clergy owed 100 millions of arrears. Their tithes were abolished, with a promise of redemption. But this the landowners would not suffer, and they gained largely by the transaction. It followed that the clergy, instead of a powerful and wealthy order, had to become salaried functionaries. Their income was made a charge on the State; and as the surplice fees went with the abolished tithe, the services of the parish priest to his parishioners were gratuitous. It was not intended that the priests should be losers, and the bargain was a bad one for the public. It involved an expenditure of at least two millions a year, at a time when means were wanting to pay the national creditor. The consequences were obvious. The State, having undertaken to remunerate the inferior clergy out of a falling revenue, had a powerful motive to appropriate what remained of the Church property when the tithes were lost. That resource was abundant for the purpose. But it was concentrated in the hands of the higher clergy and of religious orders—both under the ban of opinion, as nobles or as corporations. Their wealth would clear off the debts of the clergy, would pay all their salaries and annuities, and would strengthen the public credit. After the first spoliation, in the month of August, these consequences became clear to all, and the secularisation of Church property was a foregone conclusion.

On October 10 Talleyrand moved that it be appropriated by the State. He computed that after ample endowment of the clergy, there would be a present and increasing surplus of £2,000,000 a year. It was difficult for the clergy to resist the motion, after the agreement of August, that the State should make provision for them. The Archbishop of Paris had surrendered the tithe to be disposed of by the nation; and he afterwards added the gold and silver vessels and ornaments, to the value of several millions. Béthizy, Bishop of Usez, had declared the Church property a gift of the nation, which the nation alone could recall. Maury, loosely arguing, admitted that property is the product of law; from which it followed that it was subject to modification by law. It was urged in reply that corporate property is created by law, but not private, as the individual has his rights from nature. The clergy complained that the concessions of August were applied to their destruction in November, but they suffered by their change of front. Boisgelin, Archbishop of Aix, proposed a practical and statesmanlike arrangement. As the credit of the Church stood better than the credit of the State, he offered to advance £16,000,000 as a loan to the Government on the security of Church property, which it would thus become impossible for the Assembly to tamper with. The State would be rescued from its present difficulties; the Church would secure the enjoyment of its wealth for the future.

By restoring the finances, and the authority of government, it was believed that this plan would ensure the success of the Revolution, and would prevent the collapse that was already threatening. Necker, for a moment, was fascinated. But his wife reminded him that this compact would establish Catholicism for ever as the State Church in France, and he broke off the conference. Talleyrand's motion was altered and reproduced in a mitigated form; and on November 26, 1789, 568 votes to 346 decided that the possessions of the clergy were at the disposal of the nation. On December 19 it was resolved that the sum of 16 millions should be raised by the sale of the new national property, to be the basis for an issue of paper money. That was the beginning of the *assignats* that rendered signal service at first, and fell rapidly after two years. It was made apparent that more was at work below the surface than the financial purpose. There was the desire to break up a powerful organisation, to disarm the aristocratic episcopate, and to bind the individual priest to the Revolution. Therefore Malouet made no impression when he urged that they were taking on themselves the maintenance not only of the priesthood, but of the poor; and that no surplus would be available as long as there was a Frenchman starving.

In August, 1789, a committee on Church questions had been appointed, and in February, as it did not agree, its numbers were increased, and the minority was swamped. Thereupon they reported against the religious orders. Monasticism for some time had been declining, and the monks fell, in a few years, from 26,000 to 17,000. Nine religious orders disappeared in the course of twelve years. On February 13, 1790, the principle that the civil law supported the rule against the monk was abandoned. Members of monastic orders were to depart freely if they liked, and to remain if they liked. Those who elected to leave were to receive a pension. The position of those who remained was regulated in a series of decrees, adverse to the system, but favourable to the inmate. It was not until after the fall of the throne that all monastic orders were dissolved, and all their buildings were seized.

When the property of the Church became the property of the State, the committee drew up a scheme of distribution. They called it the Civil Constitution of the Clergy, meaning the regulation of relations between Church and State under the new Constitution.

The debate began on May 29, and the final vote was taken on July 12. The first object was to save money. The bishops were rich, they were numerous, and they were not popular. Those among them who had been chosen by the Church itself for its supreme reward, the Cardinal's hat—Rohan, Loménie de Brienne, Bernis, Montmorency and Talleyrand—were men notoriously of evil repute. Here then the Committee proposed to economise, reducing the number by fifty, and their income to a thousand a year. Each of the departments, just created, was to become a diocese. There were no archbishops. This was not economy, but theory. By putting all bishops on the same level, they lowered the papacy. For the Jansenists influenced the Assembly, and the Jansenists had, for a century, borne persecution, and had learnt to look with aversion both on papacy and prelacy, under which they had suffered, and they had grown less averse to presbyterianism. As they took away the patronage from the king, and did not transfer it to the Pope who was a more absolute sovereign than the king, and besides was a foreigner, they met the difficulty by the principle of election, which had been upheld by high authorities, and had played a great part in earlier times. The bishop was to be chosen by the departmental electors, the parish priest by the district electors; and this was to be done in the Church after Mass. It was assumed, but not ordained, that electors of other denominations would thereby be excluded. But at Strasburg a bishop was elected by a Protestant majority. In conformity with the opinion of Bossuet, the right of institution was taken away from Rome.

It was the office of the king to negotiate with the Pope, and he might have saved the Revolution, the limited monarchy, and his own life, if he had negotiated wisely. The new dioceses, the new revenues, were afterwards accepted. The denial of papal institution was in the spirit of Gallicanism; and the principle of election had a great tradition in its favour, and needed safeguards. Several bishops favoured conciliation, and wished the measure to be discussed in a National Council. Others exhorted the Pope to make no concession. Lewis barely requested him to yield something; and when it became clear that Rome wished to gain time, on August 24 he gave his sanction. At the same time he resolved on flight, relying on provincial discontent and clerical agitation to restore his throne.

On November 27 the Assembly determined to enforce acceptance of the Civil Constitution. Every ecclesiastic holding preferment or exercising public functions was required to take an oath of fidelity to the Constitution of France, sanctioned by the king. The terms implicitly included the measure regarding the Church, which was now part of the Constitution, and which a large majority of the bishops had rejected, but Rome had not. Letters had come from Rome which were suppressed; and after the decree of November and its sanction by the king on December 26, the Pope remained officially silent.

On the 4th of January 1791 the ecclesiastical deputies were summoned to take the prescribed oath. No conditions or limitations were allowed, Mirabeau specially urging rigour, in the hope of reaction. When the Assembly refused to make a formal declaration that it meant no interference with the exclusive domain of religion, the great majority of clerical deputies declined the oath. About sixty took it unconditionally, and the proportion out of doors was nearly the same. In forty-five departments we know that there were 13,426 conforming clergy. It would follow that there were about 23,000 in the whole of France, or about one-third of the whole, and not enough for the service of all the churches. The question now was whether the Church of France was to be an episcopal or a presbyterian Church. Four bishops took the prescribed oath; but only one of them continued to act as the bishop of one of the new sees. Talleyrand refused his election at Paris, and laid down his mitre and the ecclesiastical habit. Before retiring, he consecrated two constitutional bishops, and instituted Gobel at Paris. He said, afterwards, that but for him the French constitutional Church would have become presbyterian, and consequently democratic, and hostile to the monarchy.

Nobody could be more violently opposed to royalism than some of the elected prelates, such as Fauchet, Bishop of Calvados, who acted with the Girondins and perished with them, or Grégoire, the Bishop of Blois, Grégoire was the most conspicuous, and is still the best known of the constitutional clergy. He was a man of serious convictions, and as much sincerity as is compatible with violence. With much general information, he was an inaccurate writer, and in spite of the courage which he manifested throughout the Reign of Terror, an unimpressive speaker. He held fast to the doctrines of an elementary liberalism, and after the fall of the Terrorists he was active in the restoration of religion and the establishment of toleration. He was absent on a mission, and did not vote for the death of the king; but he expressed his approval, and dishonoured his later years by dissembling and denying it. Gobel, the Bishop of Paris, was far inferior to Grégoire. Hoping to save his life, he renounced his office under the Convention, after having offered his retractation to the Pope for £12,000. For a time it was believed that the clergy of the two churches could co-exist amicably, and a moderate pension was granted to the nonjurors. But there was disorder and bloodshed at Nîmes, and in other parts of France, and it was seen that the

Assembly, by its ecclesiastical legislation, had created the motive and the machinery for civil war. The nonjuring clergy came to be regarded as traitors and rebels, and the mob would not suffer them to celebrate mass in the only church that remained to them at Paris. Bailly said that when the law has spoken conscience must be silent. But Talleyrand and Sieyès insisted on the principle of toleration, and succeeded in causing the formula to be adopted by the Assembly. It was not observed, and was entirely disregarded by the second legislature.

The Civil Constitution injured the Revolution not only by creating a strong current of hostile feeling in the country, but by driving the king to seek protection from Europe against his people. The scheme of negotiation which led to the general war in 1792, having been delayed by disunion among the powers and the extreme caution of the Emperor Leopold, began in the midst of the religious crisis in the autumn of 1790. The problem for us is to discover why the National Assembly, and the committee that guided it, did not recognise that its laws were making a breach in the established system of the Church, whether Gallican or Roman, that they were in flagrant contradiction with the first principles of the Revolution; and why, in that immense explosion of liberal sentiment, there was no room for religious freedom. They believed that there was nothing in the scheme to which the Pope would not be able to consent, to avoid greater evils, if the diplomacy of the king was conducted wisely. What was conceded by Pius VII. to Bonaparte might have been conceded by Pius VI. to Lewis XVI. The judgment of Italian divines was in many instances favourable to the decree of the National Assembly, and the College of Cardinals was not unanimous against it. Their opinions found their way to Paris, and were bought up by Roman agents. When the Concordat of 1801 was concluded, Consalvi rejoiced that he had done so well, for he was empowered, if necessary, to make still greater concessions. The revolutionary canonists were persuaded that the Pope, if he rejected the king's overtures, would be acting as the instrument of the aristocratic party, and would be governed by calculated advantage, not by conscience. Chénier's tragedy of Charles IX. was being played, and revived the worst scenes of fanatical intolerance. The hatred it roused was not allayed by the language of Pius VI. in the spring of 1791, when, too late to influence events, he condemned the Civil Constitution. For he condemned liberty and toleration; and the revolutionists were able to say that there could be no peace between them, and that Rome was the irreconcilable adversary of the first principles on which they stood. The annexation of the papal dominions in France was proposed, in May 1791, when the rejection of the Civil Constitution became known. It was thrown out at first, and adopted September 14. We shall see, later on, that the conflict thus instituted between the Revolution and the Church hastened the fall of the throne, and persecution, and civil war.

I have repeatedly pointed to the jealousy of the executive as a source of fatal mischief. This is the greatest instance of the harm it did. That the patronage could not be left in the hands of the king absolutely, as it was by the Concordat of Leo X., was obvious; but if it had been given to the king acting through responsible ministers, then much of the difficulty and the danger would have been overcome, and the arrangement that grew out of the Concordat of Napoleon would have been anticipated. That idea was consistently rejected, and, stranger still, the idea of disestablishment and separation was almost unperceived. A whole generation later, under the influence of American and Irish examples, a school of Liberals arose among French Catholics who were as distinct from the Gallicans as from the Ultramontanes, and possessed the solution for the perpetual rivalry of Church and State. For us, the great fact is that the Revolution produced nothing of the sort, and went to ruin by its failure in dealing with the problem.

XII
THE FLIGHT TO VARENNES

The direct consequence of the ecclesiastical laws was the flight of the king. From the time of his removal to Paris, in October 1789, men began to study the means by which he might be rescued, and his ministers were ready with the necessary passports. During the summer of 1790, which he spent at St. Cloud, various plans were proposed, and constantly rejected. The queen was opposed to them, for she said: "What can the king do, away from Paris, without insight, or spirit, or ascendancy? Say no more about it." But a change came over them on August 24, when the Civil Constitution was sanctioned. As soon as it was voted in July, Mirabeau informed Lewis that he undertook to convey him, publicly, to Rouen, or Beauvais, or Compiègne, where he would be out of reach, and could dissolve the Assembly and proclaim a better system of constitutional laws. Civil war would inevitably follow; but Mirabeau believed that civil war would lead to the restoration of authority, if the king put himself in the hands of the Marquis de Bouillé, the general commanding at Metz. Bouillé had acquired a high reputation by his success against the English in the West Indies, and he increased it at this moment by the energy with which he suppressed a mutiny in the garrison of Nancy. *For* the service thereby rendered to the State and the cause of order, he received, under pressure from Mirabeau, the thanks of the Assembly. The king begged him to nurse his popularity as he was reserved for greater things. This is the first intimation of the secret; and it is confirmed by the Princess Elizabeth, within a week of the sanction given to the Civil Constitution. But although, in that month of September, Lewis began to meditate departure from Paris, and accepted the general proposed to him, he did not adopt the rest of the scheme which would have made him dependent on Mirabeau. At that moment his strongest motive was the desire to be released from the religious entanglement; and he hoped to restore the Church to its lost position on condition of buying up the *assignats* with the property of the suppressed orders. It had been computed that the Church would be able to save the public credit by a sacrifice of forty millions, or to ruin the revolutionary investor by refusing it. Therefore the king would not entertain the proposals of Mirabeau, who was not the man to execute a policy favourable to the influence of the priesthood. It was committed to a different politician.

Breteuil, the rival of Necker, was the man preferred to Mirabeau. He was living at Soleure as the acknowledged head of the Royalists who served the king, and who declined to follow the princes and the *émigrés* and their chief intriguer Calonne. Breteuil was now consulted. He advised the king to depart in secret and to take refuge in a frontier fortress among faithful regiments, within reach of Austrian supports. In this way Breteuil, not Mirabeau, would be master, and the restoration would have been in favour of the old *régime*, not of the constitutional monarchy. On one point only the two advisers agreed: Breteuil, like Mirabeau, recommended Bouillé as the man of action. His reply was brought by the Bishop of Pamiers, an eighteenth-century prelate of the worldly sort, who was afterwards selected to be the minister of finance if Brunswick had conquered. On October 23 the bishop was sent to Metz to initiate Bouillé.

In point both of talent and renown, Bouillé was the first man in the army as the emigration had left it. He served reluctantly under the new order, and thought of making himself a new career in Russia. But he was ambitious, for he had been always successful, and the emissary from the king and from Breteuil opened a tempting future. He proposed three alternatives. The king was to choose between Valenciennes, which would be the safest and swiftest journey; Besançon, within reach of the friendly Swiss who were under agreement to supply a large force on demand; and Montmédy, a small fortified town close to the frontier, and not far from Luxemburg which was the strongest of the imperial fortresses. All this meant plainly Montmédy. Besançon was so far that there was time to be overtaken, and Valenciennes was not in Bouillé's territory. Nothing could be done before the spring, for the emperor was not yet master of his revolted provinces; and a long correspondence was carried on between the general at Metz, and Count Fersen at Paris, who acted for Lewis XVI. and controlled the whole. At Christmas, Bouillé sent his eldest son to Paris to arrange details with him.

During the first months of 1791, which were the last of his life, the ascendancy of Mirabeau rose so rapidly that the king wavered between him and Breteuil. In February, La Marck appeared at Metz, to lay Mirabeau's bolder plan before the soldier on whose sword its execution was to depend. Bouillé at once preferred it to Breteuil's and was ready to carry it out. But Fersen was so confident in pledging himself to contrive the departure from

Paris at night and in secret, he was so resolute and cool, that he dispelled all doubts, and early in March he announced that the king had finally decided for Montmédy. His hesitation was over, and Mirabeau was rejected. Lewis could not have taken his advice without surrendering his own main object, the restoration of the Gallican Church. It was the essence of Mirabeau's policy to sacrifice the priesthood. His last counsels were given on February 23, five weeks before he died. He advised that the king, when driving out, should be forced by the people to go home; or better still, that a mob should be gathered in the court of the Tuileries to prevent him from going out. He hoped that such an outrage would cause the Assembly to secure greater liberty of movement, which would serve his purpose at the proper time.

The opportunity was found on April 18, when it became known that the royal family were moving to St. Cloud. Easter was at hand; and at Easter, the king of France used to receive communion in public. But Lewis could not receive communion. He was responsible for the Civil Constitution which he had sanctioned, and for the schism that was beginning. With that on his conscience he was required to abstain, as people would otherwise infer that neither he nor the priest who absolved him saw anything to regret in the rising storm. Therefore to avoid scandal it was well to be out of the way at the time. The royal family were stopped at their very door, as Mirabeau had desired. For more than an hour they sat in the carriage, hooted and insulted by the mob, Lafayette vainly striving to clear the way. As they returned to the palace, the queen indiscreetly said to those about them: "You must admit now, gentlemen, that we are not free." The case for flight was strengthened by the events of that day, except in the eyes of some who, knowing the suggestion of Mirabeau, suspected a comedy, and wondered how much the king had paid that a howling mob might call him a fat pig to his face.

The emperor could no longer refuse aid to his sister without the reproach of cruelty. He was now requested to move troops near enough to the frontier to justify Bouillé in forming a camp in front of Montmédy, and collecting supplies sufficient for the nucleus of a royal army. He was also asked to advance a sum of money for first expenses. Leopold, who scarcely knew Marie Antoinette, showed extreme reserve. His hands were not free in the East. He sympathised with much of the work of the Revolution; and he was not sorry to see France weakened, even by measures which he disapproved. His language was discouraging throughout. He would promise nothing until they succeeded in escaping; and he believed they could not escape. The queen resolved to discover whether the gross indignity to which she had been subjected had made some softening impression on her brother; and the Count de Durfort was sent to seek him in his Italian dominions, with ample credentials. The agent was not wisely chosen. He found Leopold at Mantua, conferring with the Count d'Artois, and he fell into the hands of Calonne. On his return he produced a paper in twenty-one paragraphs, drawn up by Calonne, with the emperor's replies, showing that Leopold would invade France in the summer, with 100,000 men, that the royal family were to await his coming, and that, in effect, he had accepted the programme of the *émigrés*.

The queen was persuaded that she would be murdered if she remained at Paris while her brother's forces entered France. She believed that the *émigrés* detested her; that they were prepared to sacrifice her husband and herself to their own cause; and that if their policy triumphed, the new masters would be worse than the old. She wrote to Mercy that it would become an intolerable slavery. She resolved to incur the utmost risk rather than owe her deliverance to d'Artois and his followers. Marie Antoinette was right in her estimate of feeling in the *émigré* camp. Gustavus III. spoke for many when he said, "The king and queen, personally, may be in danger; but that is nothing to a danger that threatens all crowned heads."

After their arrest at Varennes, Fersen was amazed at the indecent joy of the French in Brussels, of whom many avowed their satisfaction that the king and queen were captured. For the plan concerted with Bouillé was to serve monarchy, not aristocracy. In her passionate resistance to the party of d'Artois, Condé, and Calonne, the queen felt herself the champion of popular royalism. In the language of the day, she was for a counter-constitution, they for a counter-revolution. There was a personal question also. The queen relied on Breteuil to save her from Calonne, whom she suspected of having tampered with the king's confessor to learn Court secrets. When she saw the answer from Mantua, she at once knew his hand. If that was her brother's policy, it was time to make a rush for freedom. The Jacobin yoke could be borne, not the yoke of the *émigrés*. Breteuil warned them to lose no time, if they would escape from thraldom to their friends. When Marie Antoinette resolved that flight with the risk of capture would be better than rescue by such hands, she knew but half the truth. The document brought back from Mantua by Durfort was a forgery. It governed history for 100 years; and the genuine text was not published until 1894. And we know now that Calonne, behind the back of the Count d'Artois, fabricated the reply which lured the king and queen to their fate. On June 9 Mercy wrote that they were deceived. In their terror and uncertainty, they fled. The first motive of Lewis had been the horror of injuring a religion which was his own. When he signed the decree imposing the oath on the clergy, which began the persecution, he said, "At least, it is not for long."

The elections to the next Assembly were appointed for July 5. If the first Assembly was allowed to accomplish its work, all that had been done to discredit one party and to conciliate another, all the fruit of Mirabeau's expensive intrigues, would be lost. The final determination that sent them along the road to Varennes was the treason hatched at Mantua. They ran the gauntlet to the Argonne in the cause of limited monarchy, to evade revolution and reaction. That was the spirit in which Mirabeau urged departure, and in which Bouillé came to the rescue; and it is that which made the queen odious to the expatriated nobles. But it was not the policy of Breteuil. He refused to contemplate anything but the restoration of the unbroken crown. The position was ambiguous. Contrary forces were acting for the moment in combination. Between the reactionary statesman and the constitutional general, there was no security in the character of the king.

The calculation on which the flight to Montmédy was undertaken was not, in itself, unreasonable. There was a strong party in the Assembly with which it was possible to negotiate. In the Rhone district, along the Loire, in parts of western and southern France, hundreds of thousands of the most intrepid men on earth were ready to die for the altar and the throne. But they were not willing to expose themselves for a prince in whose hands the best cause was doomed to fail, and whose last act as king was to betray his faithful defenders. Instigated by Bouillé, the queen asked her brother to lend some regiments to act with the royal forces as auxiliaries in case of resistance. She wished for 30,000 men. That is the significant fact that justifies the postmaster of St. Ménehould and the patriots of Varennes. The expedition to Montmédy was a first step towards civil war and foreign invasion. That is what these men vaguely understood when they stopped the fugitives.

For the management of the journey the best advice was not always taken. Instead of two light carriages, the royal party insisted on travelling in one large one, which Fersen accordingly ordered. The route by Rheims would have been better, because Varennes was off the post road. But Varennes was preferred on the ground that Rheims was the coronation city, and the king might be recognised. The shortest way to Montmédy passed through Belgian territory; but it was thought dangerous to cross the frontier. It was urged that a military display on the road would lead to trouble, but it was decided that it was necessary beyond Châlons. Bouillé's advice was not always sound, but there was one point on which it proved fatal to reject it. He wished the travellers to be accompanied by an experienced officer, whom he knew to be masterful, energetic, and quick in an emergency. The king thought of several, but the queen was disinclined to have a stranger in the carriage. But she asked for three able-bodied officers, to be employed as couriers, adding that they need not be unusually intelligent. In those words the coming story is told. The three couriers answered too faithfully the specified qualification.

The departure had been fixed for the second week of June. Bouillé still hoped for a movement among the imperialists, and he requested a delay. On the 16th he was informed that the royal family would start at midnight on the 20th. He had sent one of his colonels, the Duke de Choiseul, to Paris for the last instructions. Choiseul's horses were to fetch the king at Varennes, and he was to entertain him in his house at Montmédy. He had the command of the farthest detachment of cavalry on the road from Montmédy to Châlons, and it was his duty to close up behind the royal carriage, to prevent pursuit, and to gather all the detachments on the road, as the king passed along. He would have arrived at the journey's end with at least 400 men. His last orders were to convey the king across the frontier, if Bouillé should fall. The great abbey of Orval was only a few miles away, and it was thought that, at the last moment, it might be found safer than the hostile soil of France.

Choiseul was not equal to the difficult part he had to perform. He set out for his post on the Monday afternoon, carrying with him a marshal's baton, which had belonged to his uncle, and the queen's hairdresser, Léonard. For Thursday was the solemn festival of Corpus Christi, when a military mass would be celebrated in the camp, and, in the presence of the assembled army, Bouillé was to be made a marshal of France. The queen could not be allowed to appear at such a function without the artist's help, and he was hurried away, much against his will, without a word of explanation. The king's sister learned the same day what was before her. There had been an idea of sending her on with the children, or with the Countess of Provence. The Princess, who was eminently good, and not always gracious, did not enjoy the confidence of the queen. She was one of those who regarded concession as surrender of principle, and in the rift between the Princes and Marie Antoinette she was not on the side of compromise. Provence came to supper, and the brothers met for the last time. That night their ways parted, leading the one to the guillotine, and the other to the throne which had been raised by Napoleon above every throne on earth. The Count and Countess of Provence both started at the same time as the rest, and reached Belgium in safety.

Fersen, directing matters with skill and forethought, made one mistake. Two attendants on the royal children were taken, in a hired carriage, to Claye, the second stage on the eastern road; and it was their driver who made known, on his return, which way the fugitives had taken.

When everybody was in bed, and the lights were out, the royal family went out by a door that was not in use, and got into a hackney coach. The last to come was the queen, who had been frightened by meeting Lafayette. Afterwards she asked him whether he had recognised her. He replied that if he had met her not once but thrice, he could never have recognised her, after what she had told him the day before; for she had said that they were not going away. Bailly, who was at home, ill, had taken alarm at the persistent rumours of departure, and urged Lafayette to redouble his precautions. After a last inspection the general assured the mayor that Gouvion was on guard, and not a mouse could escape. The journalists, Marat and Fréron, had also been warned. Fréron went to the Tuileries late at night, and satisfied himself that all was quiet. Nobody took notice of a coachman, chatting and taking snuff with a comrade, or guessed that it was the colonel of Royal Swedes, who in that hour built himself an everlasting name. It was twelve when the queen arrived; and the man, who had made her heart beat in happier years, mounted the box and drove away into the darkness. Their secret was known, and their movements had been observed by watchful eyes. The keeper of the wardrobe was intimate with General Gouvion. She had warned him in good time, and had given notice to persons about the queen that she knew what was going on. The alarm was given at two in the morning, but that she might not be compromised it was given by devious ways. A traveller from Marseilles was roused at his lodgings by a friendly voice. He refused to get up, and went to sleep again. Some hours later the visitor returned, and prevailed with the sleeper. He came from the palace, and reported that the king was gone. They took the news to one of the deputies, who hastened to Lafayette, while the man from the palace disappeared. Lafayette, as soon as he was dressed, conferred with the mayor and with the president of the Assembly, Beauharnais, the first husband of the Empress Josephine, and they persuaded him that nothing could avert civil war but the capture of the king. Thereupon Lafayette wrote an order declaring that Lewis had been carried off, and calling on all good citizens to bring him back. He believed that too much time had been lost; but nothing less than this, which was a warrant for arrest, would have appeased the rage of the people at his lack of vigilance. He despatched his officers, chiefly towards Lille. One of them, Romeuf, whom he directed to follow the road to Valenciennes, was stopped by the mob, and brought before the Assembly. There he received a new commission, with authority to make the king a prisoner. As he rode out, after so much delay, he learned that the fugitives had been seen on the road to Meaux, and that they had twelve hours' start.

There is much in these transactions that is strangely suspicious. Lafayette did not make up his mind that there was anything to be done until others pressed him. He sent off all his men by the wrong roads, while Baillon, the emissary of the Commune, struck the track at once. He told Romeuf that it was too late, so that his heavy day's ride was only a formality. Romeuf, who was the son of one of his tenants, got into many difficulties, and did not give his horse the spur until the news was four hours old. At Varennes he avowed that he had never meant to overtake them, and the king's officers believed him. Gouvion, second in command of the guard, knew by which door the royal party meant to leave, and he assured the Assembly that he had kept watch over it, with several officers, all night. Lewis had even authorised Mme. de Tourzel to bring Gouvion with her, if she met him on her way to the carriage. Burke afterwards accused Lafayette of having allowed the departure, that he might profit by the arrest. Less impassioned critics have doubted whether the companion of Washington was preparing a regency, or deemed that the surest road to a republic is by a vacant throne.

The coach that was waiting beyond the gates had been ordered for a Russian lady, Madame de Korff, who was Fersen's fervent accomplice. She supplied not only the carriage, but £12,000 in money, and a passport. As she required another for her own family, the Russian minister applied to Bailly. The mayor refused, and he was obliged to ask Montmorin, pretending that the passport he had just given had been burnt by mistake. The numbers and description tallied, but the destination was Frankfort. As the travellers quitted the Frankfort road at Clermont, the last stage before Varennes, this was a transparent blunder. Half an hour had been lost, but the first stage, Bondy, was reached at half-past one. Here Fersen, who had sat by his coachman, flourishing the whip, got down, and the family he had striven so hard to save passed out of his protection. He wished to take them all the way, and had asked Gustavus for leave to travel in the uniform of the Swedish Guard. But Lewis would not allow him to remain, and underrated the value of such an escort. Fersen took the north road, and reached Belgium without difficulty. In the following winter he was again at the Tuileries. As a political adviser he was unfortunate, for he was one of those concerned in the Brunswick proclamation which cost the king his crown.

The travellers pursued their way without molestation to Châlons, and there, as they were about to meet their faithful soldiery, they fancied that the danger was over. In reality the mischief was already done, and by their own fault their fate was sealed. As they were sure to be pursued, safety depended on celerity. The point of peril was Varennes, for a good horseman at full speed might ride 146 miles in less than thirteen hours, and would arrive there about nine at night, if he started at the first alarm. It was calculated that the royal family, at 7½ miles an hour, would reach Varennes between 8 and 9. The margin was so narrow that there was no time to lose. The king thought it sufficient to reach Bouillé's outposts before he could be overtaken, and they would be met a stage beyond Châlons. To secure the meeting it was necessary to keep time. The hours were exactly determined; and as the agreement was not observed, the troopers were useless. Before Châlons four hours had been lost—not by accident, as the royalist legend tells, for Valory the outrider testifies that it took but a few minutes to repair. Bouillé knew the ignoble cause of his own ruin and of so much sorrow, but never revealed it. When he came to England he misled questioners, and he exacted an oath from his son that he would keep the miserable secret for half a century. The younger Bouillé was true to his word. In 1841 he confided to a friend that the story whispered at the time was true, and that the king stopped a couple of hours at Étoges, over an early dinner at the house of Chanilly, an officer of his household, whose name appears in his will. When people saw what came of it, there was a generous conspiracy of concealment, which bewildered posterity, until Bouillé's tale was told.

At Pont de Somme-Vesle, 8 or 9 miles beyond Châlons, Choiseul was in command. His men had been badly received at St. Ménehould, and their presence perturbed the country people. Nobody believed the pretence that so many horsemen were required to protect the passage of treasure, and they began to suspect that the treasure was the queen herself, flying to Austria. Choiseul took alarm; for if the king arrived in the midst of sedition, the worst might be expected. He had been positively instructed that the king would pass at half-past two. Fersen had said that he might rely on it, and there was to be a courier riding an hour ahead. When three o'clock came, without any sign of king or courier, Choiseul resolved to move away, hoping that his departure would allay the ferment and secure safe passage. He sent Léonard forward, with instructions to the officers in command at St. Ménehould, Clermont, and Varennes, that all seemed to be over for the day, and that he was starting to join Bouillé; and after some further watching, he withdrew with all his men. For this Bouillé afterwards demanded that he should be tried by court-martial.

It had been settled that if the king did not appear at Bondy by half-past two in the morning, the courier who had preceded him was to push on, and warn the officers that there was no more to be done. As no courier made his appearance in the afternoon, it was certain that the fugitives had got out of Paris, where the danger lay. If Choiseul found it necessary to move his men, he was to leave a staff officer, Goguelat, to wait the king's coming, and to be his guide. But Choiseul took Goguelat with him, leaving no guide; and instead of keeping on the high road, to block it at a farther point, he went off into byways, and never reappeared until all was over at Varennes. His error is flagrant, but it was due to the more tragic folly of his master. Not long after he had abandoned his post the king arrived, and passed unhindered. Again he changed horses without resistance at the next post-town, which was St. Ménehould, and went on to Clermont en Argonne. Some of the bystanders thought they had recognised him under his disguise, and the loudest of them was Drouet, who, as postmaster, had just had a quarrel with one of the officers, and was in the dangerous mood of a man who has his temper to recover. The town council assembled, and on hearing the grounds of his suspicion, commissioned him to follow the travellers and stop their flight. They did not doubt that Lewis was about to throw himself into the arms of Austria. It was not his first intention, for he hoped to make a stand at Montmédy; but the prospect of effective action on French soil had diminished.

Bouillé's command was narrowed. He could not trust his men; and Leopold did not stir. The basis of the scheme had crumbled. Whether within the frontier or beyond it, success implied an Austrian invasion. Bouillé's plan, from its inception, had no other meaning; and it was executed under conditions which placed Lewis more completely in the hands of the calculating emperor. It became more and more apparent that his destination was not the camp of Montmédy, but the abbey of Orval in Luxemburg. The men of St. Ménehould who resolved to prevent his escape acted on vague suspicion, but we cannot say that, as Frenchmen, they acted wrongly. They had no certainty, and no authority; but while they deliberated a pursuing horseman rode into the town, bringing what they wanted. An officer of the National Guard, Baillon, had got away from Paris early in the day, with orders from Bailly and Lafayette, and took the right road. He was delayed for two hours by an encounter with M. de Briges, one of the king's men, whom he succeeded in arresting. To save time he sent forward a fresh rider, on a fresh horse, to stop the fugitives; and this messenger from Châlons brought the news to St. Ménehould, not long after the coach had rolled away.

When Drouet started on the ride that made his fortune, he knew that it was the king, and that Paris did not mean him to escape. An hour had been lost, and he met his postboys returning from Clermont. From them he learnt that the courier had given the word Varennes, and not Verdun. By a short cut, through the woods, he arrived just in time. Meantime St. Ménehould was seething; the commanding officer was put under arrest, and his troops were prevented from mounting. One man, Lagache, warned by the daughter of his host that the treasure for the army chest had evaporated and the truth was out, sprung on his horse and opened a way through the crowd with a pistol in each hand.

Drouet told the story to the National Assembly more to his own advantage, claiming to have recognised the queen whom he had seen at Paris, and the king by his likeness on an *assignat*. On a later day he declined all direct responsibility, and said that he followed the coach in consequence of orders forwarded from Châlons, not on his own initiative or conjecture. When he gave the second version he was a prisoner among the Austrians, and the questioner before whom he stood was Fersen. At such a moment even a man of Drouet's fortitude might well have stretched a point in the endeavour to cast off odium. Therefore the account recorded by Fersen has not supplanted the popular tradition. But it is confirmed by Romeuf, who says, distinctly, that the postmaster of St. Ménehould was warned by the message sent on by Baillon. Romeuf's testimony, contained in the protocols of the Assembly, where I have seen it, was omitted in the *Moniteur*, in order that nothing might deface the legend of the incautious traveller, the treacherous banknote, and the vigilant provincial patriot, who was the idol of the hour as the man who had preserved his country from invasion and civil war.

Clermont, like the other post towns, was agitated by the presence of cavalry; and after the king had pursued his journey, the authorities despatched a messenger to rouse Varennes. Passing the royal party at full speed, he shouted something which they did not understand, but which made them think that they were detected. He was superseded by the superior energy and capacity of Drouet, and plays no part in the adventure. There was an officer at Clermont who knew his business; but his men deserted him, and he reached Varennes alone. At Varennes the two men in the secret, Bouillé's younger son and Raigecourt, were with the horses, at the farther end of the town, over the bridge, keeping no look-out. They relied on Goguelat, on Choiseul, on d'Andouins who commanded at St. Ménehould, on Damas at Clermont, and above all on the promised courier, who was to ride an hour ahead to warn them in time. But they expected no warning that night. If there was any watchfulness in them, it was put to sleep by Léonard, who had gone through an hour before with Choiseul's fatal letter. The king was arrested a few hundred yards from their inn, and they were aware of nothing. When they heard, they galloped away on the road to Stenay, where they knew that the general was keeping anxious vigil. Drouet passed the carriage near the entrance of the town, where the couriers were wrangling with the postilions and looking about in the dark for the relays. With the help of half a dozen men who were finishing their wine at the inn, he barricaded the bridge.

There the king's passport betrayed him, for it was made out for Frankfort, and Varennes was not on the road to Frankfort. The party were therefore detained and had to spend the night at the house of Sauce, municipal officer and grocer, while the drums beat, the tocsin rang, the town was roused with the cry of fire, and messengers were sent to bring in national guards from the country round. At first Sauce beguiled the king over a bottle of wine, and then introduced a travelled fellow-townsman who identified him. A scene of emotion followed, and loyal citizens pressed their sovereign in their arms. They talked of escorting him to Montmédy, a hundred strong, and Lewis, ready to believe them, declared he would be content with fifty. As night wore on, a number of officers collected: Choiseul and Goguelat, after their long ride from Pont de Somme-Vesle; the Count de Damas from Clermont; and at last Deslon, a captain of the German horse that Bouillé chiefly trusted. Choiseul's men, and some of those quartered at Varennes, were faithful, and it was thought possible to clear the street. Urged by the queen, Damas wished to attempt it, and long after he assured an English friend that he regretted that he did not lead the charge, in defiance of the king's optimism, and of his reluctance to be saved by the sword. He said to Deslon in German, "Mount and attack!" But Deslon saw that it was too late. Goguelat threatened to cut his way out, and was unhorsed by a pistol shot.

Drouet was master of the situation. It was he who managed the hesitating soldiers and the hesitating townsmen. At five in the morning Romeuf and Baillon arrived, with Lafayette's order, and the decree of the sovereign Assembly. There was no more illusion then about pursuing the journey, and all the king's hope was that he might gain time for Bouillé to deliver him. Bouillé was at Stenay, twenty miles off. He spent the night watching the road, with his arm through his horse's bridle. Long after every possible allowance for delay, his son came up with the tidings of Varennes. The trumpets roused the Royal Germans, but their colonel was hostile, and precious hours were lost. Bouillé gave all his money to his men, told them what manner of expedition they were on, told them that their king was a prisoner, and led them to the rescue. It was past nine when he reached the height that looks down on the valley of the Aire. The horses were tired, the bridge was barricaded, the fords were unknown. All was quiet at Varennes, and the king was already miles away on the road to Clermont. It was the end of a bright dream, and of a career which had been noted for unvarying success.

As the unhappy man, who had so narrowly missed the prize, turned his horse's head in the direction of exile, he said to his son, "Do you still praise my good fortune?" That evening he rode across the frontier with a group of officers, and his men fired on him as he passed. He issued an angry declaration, and composed a defence of his conduct, saying that nobody had remained at his post except himself. But he knew that king and constitution were lost because he was not on the spot, and had posted inexperienced men where his own presence was needed. He could not recover his balance, and became as unwise and violent as the rest. The *émigrés* did not trust him, and assigned him no active part in the invasion of the following year. His fame stood high among the English who had fought him in the West Indies, and Pitt offered him the command in San Domingo, which the Duke of Portland obliged him to relinquish.

Lewis XVI. was brought back to Paris by an insolent and ferocious crowd, and looked back with gratitude to the equivocal civilities of Sauce. The journey occupied four days, during which the queen's hair turned grey. Three deputies, sent by the Assembly, met the dolorous procession half way, and took charge of the royal family. The king at once assured them that he had intended to remain at Montmédy, and there to revise the Constitution. "With those words," said Barnave, "we shall save the monarchy." Latour Maubourg refused his turn in the royal carriage, on the plea that his legs were too long for comfort, and advised the king to employ the time in domesticating his companions. The advice partly succeeded, for Barnave was made a friend. Nothing could be made of Pétion, who states in his narrative that the princess fell in love with him. General Dumas assumed command, and, by posting cavalry on one of the bridges, managed to bring the horses to a trot, and left the crowd behind.

When they came to the forest of Bondy, the Hounslow Heath of France, a band of ruffians from the capital made a determined attack, and were with difficulty beaten off. At last, Lefebvre, the future Marshal Duke of Dantzick, met them with a company of grenadiers. As there was danger in the narrow streets of Paris, Lafayette took them round through the Champs Elysées. Word had been passed that not a sign of hatred or of honour should be given, and a horseman rode in front, commanding silence. The order was sullenly obeyed. The day before this funereal scene the Prussian envoy wrote home that the king might be spared, from motives of policy, but that nothing could save the queen. They had reached the terrace of the Tuileries when there was a rush and a struggle, in which Dumas lost his hat and his belt and his scabbard, and nearly had his clothes torn from his back. A group of deputies came to his assistance, and no blood was shed. A carriage came after, with Drouet conspicuous on high and triumphant. He received a grant of £1200, and was elected to the Convention in the following year. Taken prisoner by the Prussians, he impressed Goethe by his coolness in adversity. The Austrians took him at the siege of Maubeuge, and he was exchanged for the king's daughter. In the communistic conspiracy of Babeuf he nearly lost his life, and for a time he lived in a cavern, underground. Napoleon gave him the Legion of Honour, made him subprefect of St. Ménehould, and was his guest when he visited Valmy. In the Hundred Days Drouet was again a deputy, and then vanished from sight and changed his name. When he died, in 1824, his neighbours learned with surprise that they had lived with the sinister contriver of the tremendous tragedy.

XIII
THE FEUILLANTS AND THE WAR

Tuesday, June 21, the day on which the departure of the king became known, was the greatest day in the history of the Assembly. The deputies were so quick to meet the dangers of the situation, they were so calm, their measures were so comprehensive, that they at once restored public confidence. By the middle of the day the tumult in the streets was appeased, and the ambassadors were astonished at the tranquillity of Paris. They wrote home that all parties put aside their quarrels, and combined in a sincere endeavour to save the State. That was the appearance of things on the surface and for the moment. But the Right took no share in acts which they deemed a usurpation of powers calculated to supersede monarchy, and to make the crisis serve as the transition to a Republic. To the number of almost 300 they signed a protest, declaring that they would take no further part in the deliberations. Their leader, Cazalès, went away to Coblenz, and was coldly received as a man who had yielded too much to parliamentary opinions, whose services had been unavailing, and who repented too late.

The king's flight, while it broke up the Conservative party, called the Republican party into existence. For Lewis had left behind him a manifesto, meditated during many months, urging the defects of the Constitution, and denouncing all that had been effected since he had suffered violence at Versailles. Many others besides Lewis were aware of the defects, and desired their amendment. But the renunciation of so much that he had sanctioned, so much that he had solemnly and repeatedly approved, exposed him to the reproach of duplicity and falsehood. He not only underwent the ignominy of capture and exposure; he was regarded henceforth as a detected perjurer. If the king could never be trusted again, the prospects of monarchy were hopeless. The Orleans party offered no substitute, for their candidate was discredited. Men began to say that it was better that what was inevitable should be recognised at once than that it should be established later on by violence, after a struggle in which more than monarchy would be imperilled, and which would bring to the front the most inhuman of the populace. To us, who know what the next year was to bring, the force and genuineness of the argument is apparent; but it failed to impress the National Assembly. Scarcely thirty members shared those opinions, and neither Barère nor Robespierre was among them. The stronghold of the new movement was the Club of the Cordeliers. The great body of the constitutional party remained true to the cause, and drew closer together. Lameth and Lafayette appeared at the Jacobins arm in arm; and when the general was attacked for negligence in guarding the Tuileries, Barnave effectually defended him. This was the origin of the Feuillants, the last organisation for the maintenance of monarchy. They were resolved to save the Constitution by amending it in the direction of a strengthened executive, and for their purpose it was necessary to restore the king. If his flight had succeeded, it was proposed to open negotiations with him, for he would have it in his power to plunge France into foreign and domestic war. He was more formidable on the frontier than in the capital. Malouet, the most sensible and the most respected of the royalists, was to have been sent to treat, in the name of the Assembly, that, by moderating counsels, bloodshed might be averted, and the essentials of the Revolution assured. But, on the second evening, a tired horseman drew rein at the entrance, and the joyous uproar outside informed the deputies before he could dismount that he came with news of the king. He was the Varennes doctor, and he had been sent at daybreak to learn what the town was to do with its prisoners.

The king, ceasing to be a danger, became an embarrassment. He could not at once be replaced on the throne. Without prejudging the future, it was resolved that he be detained at the Tuileries until the Constitution, completed and revised, was submitted to him for his free assent. Thus, for ten weeks, he was suspended. The Assembly governed and legislated, without reference to his sanction; and the interregnum was so prolonged that the monarchy could never recover. When, in September, Lewis resumed his royal function, he was no longer an integral element in the State, but an innovation and an experiment. On the day when, standing uncovered before the legislators, he promised fidelity to their Constitution, it seemed natural to them, in the presence of tarnished and diminished majesty, to sit down and put their hats on. The triumvirs, who had foiled Mirabeau, began immediately after his death to sustain the royal cause in secret. Montmorin called on Lameth before he was up, and began the negotiation. Barnave frequented the house of Montmorin, but took care always to come accompanied, in order to prevent a bribe. His two days' journey in the royal company confirmed him in his design. Having reduced the prerogative when it was excessive, they revived it when it had become too weak, and the king could no longer inspire alarm. They undertook to devise props for the damaged throne. "If not Lewis XVI.," said Lafayette, "then Lewis XVII." "If not this king," said Sieyès, "find us another." This was the predominant feeling.

When an attack was made on the king at the Jacobins, all the deputies present, excepting six, seceded in a body, and founded a new club at the Feuillants. On July 15, in a speech which was considered the finest heard in France since Mirabeau, Barnave carried an overwhelming vote in favour of monarchy. He said that the revolutionary movement could go no farther without carrying away property. He dreaded the government of the poor over the rich; for Barnave's political philosophy consisted in middle-class sovereignty—government by that kind of property which depends on constant labour, integrity, foresight, and self-denial, excluding poverty and opulence. Defeated at the Jacobins and in the Assembly, the republicans prepared a demonstration on the Champ de Mars, where a petition was signed for the dethronement of the king. The Assembly, fearing a renewal of the scenes at Versailles, commissioned Bailly and Lafayette to disperse the meeting. On July 17 a collision ensued, shots were fired, and several petitioners were killed. The Jacobins, for the moment, were crushed. Robespierre, Marat, even Danton, effaced themselves, and expected that the Feuillants would follow up their victory. It seemed impossible that men who had the resolution to shoot down their masters, the people of Paris, and were able to give the law, should be so weak in spirit, or so short of sight, as to throw away their advantage, and resume a contest on equal terms with conquered and injured adversaries.

The Feuillants were thenceforward predominant and held their ground until the Girondins overthrew them on March 18. It was the rule at their club to admit none but active citizens, paying taxes and possessing the franchise. The masses were thus given over to the Jacobins. By their energy at the Champ de Mars, July 17, Lafayette and his new friends had aroused the resentment of a vindictive party; and when they took no advantage of the terror they inspired, the terror departed, and the resentment remained. It was agreed that Malouet should move amendments to the Constitution. The Feuillants were to oppose, and then to play into his hands. But Malouet was deserted by his friends, the agreement was not carried out, and the revision failed in the Assembly. The Committees proposed that the famous decree of November 7, by which no deputy could accept office, should be revoked. The exclusion was maintained, but ministers were allowed to appear and answer for their departments. No other important amendment was carried, and no serious attempt was made to adjust and harmonise the clauses voted during two hurried years. Various reforms were vainly brought forward; and they indicate, as well as the sudden understanding between Malouet and Barnave, that the deputies had little faith in the work they had accomplished. They were tired of it. They were no longer on the crest of the wave, and their power had passed to the clubs and to the press. They were about to disappear. By an unholy alliance between Robespierre and Cazalès the members of the National Assembly were ineligible to the Legislature that was to follow. None of those who drew up the Constitution were to have a share in applying it. The actual rulers of France were condemned to political extinction. Therefore the power which the Feuillants acquired by their very dexterous management of the situation produced by the king's flight could not last; their radical opponents had time on their side, and they had logic.

Lewis, after his degradation, was an impossible king. And the republicans had a future majority in reserve, whenever the excluded class was restored to the right of voting which it had enjoyed in 1789 before equality was a fundamental law, and which the Rights of Man enabled them to claim. And now the incident of Varennes supplied the enemies of the throne with a new argument. The wretched incompetence of Lewis had become evident to all, and to the queen herself. She did not hesitate to take his place, and when people spoke of the Court, it was the queen they meant. The flight, and the policy that led to it, and that was renewed by the failure, was the policy of relying on foreign aid, especially that of the emperor. The queen was the connecting link, and the chief negotiator. And the object she pursued was to constrain the French people, by means of the emperor's influence on the Powers, either by the humiliating parade of power at a congress, or by invasion. That is what she was believed to be contriving, and the sense of national independence was added to the motive of political liberty to make the Court unpopular. People denounced the Austrian cabal, and the queen as its centre. It was believed that she wished to govern not only through the royal authority restored, but through the royal authority restored by foreign oppressors. The Revolution was confronted with Europe. It had begun its work by insurrection, and it had to complete its work by war. The beginning of European complications was the flight to Varennes.

Early in September the Constitution was presented to Lewis XVI. The gates were thrown open. The guards who were his gaolers were withdrawn. He was ostensibly a free man. If he decided to accept, his acceptance would be voluntary. The Emperor, Kaunitz, Malesherbes, advised him to accept. Malouet preferred, as usual, a judicious middle course. Burke was for refusal. He said that assent meant destruction, and he thought afterwards that he was right, for the king assented and was destroyed. Burke was not listened to. He had become the adviser of Coblenz, and great as his claims were upon the gratitude of both king and queen, he was counted in the ranks of their enemies. Mercy, who transmitted his letter, still extant in the archives of France, begged that it might not influence the decision. After ten days of leisurely reflection, but without real hesitation, for everything had been arranged with Lameth and Barnave, the leaders of the majority, Lewis gave his sanction to the Constitution of 1791, which was to last until 1792, and the National Assembly was dissolved. Political delinquents, including the accomplices of Varennes, received an amnesty.

By right of the immense change they made in the world, by their energy and sincerity, their fidelity to reason and their resistance to custom, their superiority to the sordid craving for increase of national power, their idealism and their ambition to declare the eternal law, the States-General of 1789 are the most memorable of all political assemblies. They cleared away the history of France, and with 2500 decrees they laid down the plan of a new world for men who were reared in the old. Their institutions perished, but their influence has endured; and the problem of their history is to explain why so genuine a striving for the highest of earthly goods so deplorably failed. The errors that ruined their enterprise may be reduced to one. Having put the nation in the place of the Crown, they invested it with the same unlicensed power, raising no security and no remedy against oppression from below, assuming, or believing, that a government truly representing the people could do no wrong. They acted as if authority, duly constituted, requires no check, and as if no barriers are needed against the nation. The notion common among them, that liberty consists in a good civil code, a notion shared by so famous a Liberal as Madame de Staël, explains the facility with which so many revolutionists went over to the Empire. But the dreadful convulsion that ensued had a cause for which they were not responsible. In the violent contradiction between the new order of things in France and the inorganic world around it, conflict was irrepressible. Between French principles and European practice there could be neither conciliation nor confidence. Each was a constant menace to the other, and the explosion of enmity could only be restrained by unusual wisdom and policy.

The dissolution of the Whig party in England indicates what might be expected in the continental monarchies where there were no Whigs. We shall presently see that it was upon this rock, in the nature of things, that the Revolution went to pieces. The wisest of the statesmen who saw the evil days, Royer Collard, affirmed long after that all parties in the Revolution were honest, except the Royalists. He meant that the Right alone did wrong with premeditation and design. In the surprising revulsion that followed the return from Varennes, and developed the Feuillants, it was in the power of the Conservatives to give life to constitutional monarchy. That was the moment of their defection. They would have given much to save an absolute king: they deliberately abandoned the constitutional king to his fate.

The 1150 men who had been the first choice of France now pass out of our sight. The 720 deputies of the Legislative Assembly were new and generally obscure names. Nobles, clergy, conservatives did not reappear, and their place was taken by the Feuillants, who, in the former Assembly, would have belonged to the Left. The centre of gravity shifted far in the revolutionary direction. The Constitution was made. The discussion of principles was over, and the dispute was not for doctrines but for power. The speakers have not the same originality or force; they are not inventors in political science; they are not the pioneers of mankind. In literary faculty, if not in political, they surpass their predecessors, and are remembered for their eloquence if not for statecraft.

Reinhard, a German traveller who fell in with a group of the new deputies on their way to Paris, fell under their charm, and resolved to cast his lot with a country about to be governed by such men. Whilst he rose to be an ambassador and minister of foreign affairs, his friends were cut off in their prime, for they were the deputies who came from Bordeaux, and gave the name of their department to the party of the Gironde. By their parliamentary talents they quickly obtained the lead of the new Assembly; and as they had few ideas and no tactics, they allowed Sieyès to direct their course.

Robespierre, through the Jacobin Club, which now recovered much of the ground it had lost in July, became the manager of the Extreme Left, which gradually separated from Brissot and the Girondins. The ministry was in the hands of the Feuillants, who were guided by Lameth, while Barnave was the secret adviser of the queen. She followed his counsels with aversion and distrust, looking upon him as an enemy, and longing to throw off the mask, and show him how he had been deceived. As she could not understand how the same men who had depressed monarchy desired to sustain it, she played a double and ignoble part. The tactics of the Feuillant advisers brought a revival of popular feeling in favour of the Court, which seemed inconceivable at the epoch of the arrest. King and queen were applauded in the streets, and at the theatre the cry "Long live the king!" silenced the cry "Long live the nation!" This was in October 1791, before the Legislative Assembly had divided into parties, or found a policy.

When the Assembly summoned the *émigrés* to return by the month of January, the king fully agreed with the policy though not with the penalty. But when a Commission reported on the temper of the clergy, and described the mischief that was brewing in the provinces between the priests of the two sections, and severe measures of repression were decreed against nonjurors, he interposed a veto. The First Assembly had disendowed the clergy, leaving them a pension. The Second, regarding them as agitators, resolved to proceed against them as against the *émigrés*. Lewis, in resisting persecution, was supported by the Feuillants. But the Assembly was not Feuillant, and the veto began its estrangement from the king. A new minister was imposed on him. The Count Narbonne de Lara was the most brilliant figure in the *noblesse* of France, and he lived to captivate and dazzle Napoleon. Talleyrand, who thought the situation under the Constitution desperate, put forward his friend; and Madame de Staël, the queen of constitutional society, obtained for him the ministry of war. The appointment of Narbonne was a blow struck at the Feuillants, who still desired to reform the institutions, and who were resolute in favour of peace. At the same time, Lafayette laid down his command of the National Guard, and stood as a candidate to succeed Bailly in the office of mayor. But Lafayette had ordered the capture of the royal family, and could not be forgiven. The queen obtained the election of Pétion instead of Lafayette; and behind Pétion was Danton. What the Feuillants lost was added to the Girondins, not yet distinct from the Jacobins; and as the Feuillants were for two chambers, for peace, and for an executive independent of the single Assembly and vetoing its decrees, the policy of its opponents was to bring the king into subjection to the Legislature, to put down the discontented clergy, and to make the emigration a cause for war.

The new minister, Narbonne, was accepted as a war minister, while his Feuillant colleague at the Foreign Office, Delessart, was obstinately pacific. On December 14 Lewis came down to the Legislature, and announced that he would insist that the *émigrés* should receive no encouragement beyond the frontier. It was the first act of hostility and defiance, and it showed that the king was parting with his Feuillant friends. But Delessart spoilt the effect by keeping back the note to the emperor for ten days, and communicating it then with precautions.

Leopold II. was one of the shrewdest and most cautious of men. He knew how to wait, and how to give way. He had no wish that his brother-in-law should again be powerful, and he was not sorry that France should be disabled by civil dissension. But he could not abandon his sister without dishonour; and he was afraid of the contagion of French principles in Belgium, which he had reconciled and pacified with difficulty. Moreover, a common action in French affairs, action which might eventually be warlike, was a means of closing the long enmity with Prussia, and obtaining a substitute for the family alliance with France, which had become futile. Therefore he was prepared, if they had escaped, to risk war for their restoration, and induced the Prussian agent to sign an undertaking which went beyond his instructions.

When the disastrous news reached him from Varennes, Leopold appealed to the Powers, drew up an alliance with Prussia, and joined in the declaration of Pilnitz, by which France was threatened with the combined action of all Europe unless the king was restored to a position worthy of kings. The threat implied no danger, because it was made conditional on the unanimity of the Powers. There was one Power that was sure not to consent. England was waiting an opportunity to profit by French troubles. It had already been seriously proposed by Bouillé, with the approval of Lewis, to purchase aid from George III. by the surrender of all the colonies of France. Therefore Leopold thought that he risked nothing by a demonstration which the *émigrés* made the most of to alarm and irritate the French people. But when the king freely accepted the Constitution, the manifesto of Pilnitz fell to the ground. If he was content with his position, it could not be the duty of the Powers to waste blood and treasure in attempting to alter it. The best thing was that things should settle down in France. Then there would be no excitement spreading to Belgium, and no reason why other princes should be less easily satisfied than Lewis himself. "The king," said Kaunitz, "the king, good man, has helped us out of our difficulty himself." Still more, when he obtained a revival of popularity which seemed a marvel after the events of June, when he freely vetoed acts which he disapproved, and appeared to be acting in full agreement with a powerful and still dominant party, the imperial government hoped that the crisis was over. And this was the state of things in October and November.

The *émigrés*, conscious of their repulse at Pilnitz, made it their business to undeceive the emperor, and to bring him back to the scheme of intervention. The Spanish Bourbons were with them, and had recalled their ambassador, and fitted out a fleet in the Mediterranean. Gustavus of Sweden was eager to invade France with a Swedish army to be conveyed in Russian ships, and paid for in Mexican piastres, and with Bouillé by his side. Catherine II. gave every encouragement to the German Powers to embroil themselves with France, and to leave her to deal uncontrolled with Poland and Turkey. The first to emigrate had been the Comte d'Artois and his friends, who had conspired against Necker and the new Constitution. They fled, because their lives were in danger. Others followed, after the rising of the peasants and the spoliation of August. As things grew more acute, and the settlement of feudal claims was carried out with unsparing hostility, the movement spread to the inferior *noblesse*. After the breach with the clergy and the secularisation of Church property, the prelates went into exile, and were followed by their friends. In the winter of 1790-1791 they began to organise themselves on the Rhine, and to negotiate with some of the smaller Powers, especially Sardinia, for an invasion. The later arrivals were not welcomed, for they were men who had accepted constitutional government. The purpose of the true *émigrés* was the restoration of the old order, of the ancient principles and institutions, not without reform, but without subversion. That was the bond between them, and the basis on which they sought the aid of absolute princes. They denied that the king himself, writhing in the grip of democracy, had the right to alter the fundamental laws. Some of the best and ablest and most honourable men had joined their ranks, and they were instructed and inflamed by the greatest writer in the world, who had been the best of Liberals and the purest of revolutionary statesmen, Edmund Burke. It was not as a reactionist, but as a Whig who had drunk success to Washington, who had dressed in blue and buff, who had rejoiced over the British surrender at Saratoga, who had drawn up the address to the Colonists, which is the best State paper in the language, that he told them that it was lawful to invade their own country, and to shed the blood of their countrymen.

The *émigrés* of every grade of opinion were united in dislike of the queen and in depreciation of the king, and they wished to supersede him by declaring his brother Regent. They hoped to save them both; but they thought more of principles than of persons, and were not to be diverted from their projects by consideration of what might happen at Paris. When the emperor spoke of the danger his sister and her husband were running, Castelnau replied, "What does it matter, provided the royal authority is preserved in the person of d'Artois?" They not only refused obedience to Lewis, but they assiduously compromised him, and proclaimed that he meant the contrary of what he said, making a reconciliation between him and his people impossible. Even his brothers defied him when in this extremity, he entreated them to return. It was the *émigré* policy to magnify the significance of what was done at Pilnitz; and as they have convinced posterity that it was the announcement of an intended attack, it was easy to convince their contemporaries at home. The language of menace was there, and France believed itself in danger. How little the Princes concerned meant to give effect to it remained a secret.

The French democracy might have found its advantage in the disappearance of so many nobles; but as they were working, with apparent effect, to embroil the country with its neighbours, attempts were made to compel their return, first by a threefold taxation, then by confiscation, and at last, November 9, by threatening with death those who did not return. The nonjuring clergy were associated with the *émigrés* in the public mind as enemies and conspirators who were the more dangerous because they remained at home. The First Assembly had provoked the hostility on the frontier; the Second provoked hostilities at home. The First had left nonjuring priests with a pension, and the use of parish churches where successors had not been appointed. The Legislative Assembly decreed, November 29, that in all cases where it seemed good to the authorities, they might be deprived of their pensions and sent away. The great insurrection of the West was caused by this policy. It was religious rather than political, and was appeased by the return of the priests.

The head of the war party in the Assembly was Brissot, who was reputed to know foreign countries, and who promised certain success, as no really formidable Power was ready to take the field. Meantime he endeavoured to isolate Austria, and Ségur was sent to Berlin, Talleyrand to London, to surround France with her natural allies. Brissot's text was the weakness and division of other countries; the first man who divined the prodigious resources and invincible energy of France was the declamatory Provençal Isnard. He spoke on November 29, and this was his prophetic argument: the French people exhibited the highest qualities in war when they were treated as slaves by despotic masters; there was no fear that they had degenerated in becoming free men; only let them fight for principle, not for State policy, and the force that was in them would transform the world. Hérault de Séchelles divulged the political motive of the war party. He said a foreign conflict would be desirable for internal reasons. It would lead to measures of precaution stronger than peace time would admit, and changes otherwise impossible would then be justified by the plea of public safety. It is the first shadow cast by the coming reign of terror. But neither Girondin violence nor *émigré* intrigue was the cause that plunged France into the war that was to be the most dreadful of all wars. The true cause was the determination of Marie Antoinette not to submit to the new Constitution. At first she wished that France should be intimidated by a congress of the united Powers. She warned her friends abroad not to be taken in by the mockery of her understanding with the Feuillant statesmen; and when Leopold treated the accepted Constitution seriously, as a release from his engagements, she accused him of betraying her. On September 8, just before accepting, Lewis, in confidence, wrote that he meant to tolerate no authority in France besides his own, and that he desired to recover it by foreign aid.

The idea of an armed Congress persisted until the end of November. But during the week from the 3rd to the 10th of December the king and queen wrote to the Powers, desiring them not to regard their official acts, beseeching them to resist the demands they made in public and to make war, and assuring them that France would be easily subdued and cowed. They hoped, by this treason, to recover their undivided power. All these letters were inspired, were almost dictated, by Fersen.

As Leopold began to see more clearly what it was his sister meant, he modified his pacific policy. On the 25th of October he speaks of increasing the royal authority by a counter-revolution in France. On the 17th of November he invites Prussia to help him with 20,000 men. On the 10th of December he denounces the annexation by France of the German domains in Alsace. In conformity with this gradual change, Kaunitz became more rigid, and he made known that any assault on the Elector of Treves, for the protection he gave to the warlike *émigrés*, would be resisted by the imperial forces. Each step was as short as possible. The transition from peace to war, from pointless remonstrance to vigorous defiance, was slow and gradual. It began late in October, when the real meaning of the acceptance of the Constitution became known, but down to the month of January the change was not decisive, and the tone was still ambiguous. On the 3rd of January a letter from the queen at length carried the emperor over. On the way this appeal had converted Mercy, and Mercy, on January 7, wrote a letter which compelled Kaunitz to give way. Kaunitz had grown grey in the idea of the French alliance and of rivalry with Prussia. He laughed at Mr. Burke and the theory of contagion. He desired to perpetuate a state of things which paralyzed France, by the rivalry between the king and the democracy. To restore the king's power at home was to increase it abroad. Kaunitz was willing that it should be kept in check by the legislature; but a moment came when he perceived that the progress of the opposition, of the Jacobins as men indiscriminately called them, more properly of the Girondins, had transferred the centre of gravity. What had been cast down in the Monarch rose again in the Second Assembly, and the power of the nation, the nation united with its representatives, began to appear.

Kaunitz, though he had no eye for such things, took alarm at last, and resolved that the way to depress France was to assist the king of France. On January 5, after the queen's letter of December 16 had been received, he declared that Austria would support the elector of Treves, and would repel force by force, if he was attacked for the harbouring of *émigrés*. At the same moment Leopold resolved on an offensive alliance with Prussia. He explained his change of policy by the letters which showed him the true mind of the queen. On January 16 Kaunitz still believed that the other Powers would refuse to co-operate. But Prussia was willing to accept the new alliance, if Austria abandoned the new Polish Constitution of May 3. Leopold paid the stipulated price. On February 7 he gave up the Poles, that he might be strong against France. Already, January 25, Kaunitz had taken the deciding step, passing over from the defensive to attack. He speaks no more of the king's liberty of action. He demands restitution of the papal territory at Avignon, annexed in consequence of the Pope's action against the ecclesiastical laws. He requires that the German princes shall have their Alsatian domains given back to them, and that there shall be no trespass on the imperial dominions. And in general terms he requires the restoration of monarchy. Again he wrote, in the same warlike and defiant spirit, on February 17, when the Prussian signature had been received, and when he expected English aid for the preservation of Belgium. Meantime Simolin, the Russian minister who had been helpful in procuring the fatal passport, arrived at Vienna with a last appeal from the queen. At that time she did not feel that their lives were in jeopardy, but their power. To the faithful Fersen she wrote that she hoped the enemy would strike home, so that the French, in their terror, might pray the king to intercede.

Kaunitz, having despatched his ultimatum on the international grounds of quarrel, declined to interfere in internal affairs. But Simolin saw Leopold on the 25th, and then the emperor admitted what his chancellor denied, that the cause was the common cause of all crowned heads. With those significant words he quits the stage. Five days later he was dead.

Each step forward taken by Austria aggravated the warlike feeling in the French legislature. But Delessart, through whom the government communicated with foreign powers, mitigated everything, and avoided provocation. Even the note of the 17th, which was delivered at Paris on the 27th, produced no immediate commotion. But Narbonne thought the time had come to carry into effect his policy of war, for the majority was now with him. He threatened to resign unless Bertrand retired, who was the king's nominee among the six ministers; and he only withdrew his threat at the instance of Lafayette and the other generals who were to be in command. Lewis, indignant at this intrigue, dismissed not Bertrand, but Narbonne. The Girondins, in reply, impeached Delessart, who was sent to prison, March 10, and perished there in September. The Feuillant minister resigned. Robespierre, who divined the calculations of the Court, and feared that war might strengthen the arm that bore the banner, resisted the warlike temper, and carried the Jacobins with him. On this issue Girondins and Jacobins separated into distinct parties. The Girondins inclined to an inevitable Republic, because they distrusted the king; but they accepted the Constitution, and did not reject a king at low pressure, such as had been invented by the Whigs. They were persuaded that, in case of war, Lewis would intrigue with the enemy, would be detected, and would be at their mercy. "It is well that we should be betrayed," said Brissot, "because then we shall destroy the traitors." And Vergniaud, whose dignity and elevation of language have made him a classic, pointed to the Tuileries and said, "Terror has too often issued from that palace in the name of a despot. Let it enter, to-day, in the name of the law." They suspected, and suspected truly, that the menacing note from Vienna was inspired at Paris. They formed a new ministry, with Dumouriez at the Foreign Office. Dumouriez gave Austria a fixed term to renounce its policy of coercing France by a concert of Powers; and as Kaunitz stood his ground, and upheld his former statements of policy, on April 20 Lewis declared war against his wife's nephew, Francis, king of Hungary. Marie Antoinette triumphed, through her influence on her own family. Formally it was not a war for her deliverance, but a war declared by France, which might be turned to her advantage. To be of use to her, it must be unsuccessful; and in order to ensure defeat, she betrayed to the Court of Vienna the plan of operations adopted in Council the day before.

XIV
DUMOURIEZ

As the war was more often a cause of political events than a consequence, it will be convenient to follow up the progress of military affairs to the fall of Dumouriez, postponing the catastrophe of monarchy to next week.

On the 17th of February 1792 Pitt informed the House of Commons that the situation of Europe had never afforded such assurance of continued peace. He did not yet recognise the peril that lay in the new French Constitution. Under that Constitution, no government could be deemed legitimate unless it aimed at liberty, and derived its powers from the national will. All else is usurpation; and against usurped authority, insurrection is a duty. The Rights of Man were meant for general application, and were no more specifically French than the multiplication table. They were not founded on national character and history, but on Reason, which is the same for all men. The Revolution was essentially universal and aggressive; and although these consequences of its original principle were assiduously repressed by the First Assembly, they were proclaimed by the Second, and roused the threatened Powers to intervene. Apart from this inflaming cause the motives of the international conflict were indecisive. The emperor urged the affair of Avignon, the injury to German potentates who had possessions in Alsace, the complicity of France in the Belgian troubles, and the need of European concert while the French denied the foundations of European polity.

Dumouriez offered to withdraw the French troops from the frontier, if Austria would send no more reinforcements, but at that moment the queen sent word of an intended attack on Liége. The offer seemed perfidious, and envenomed the quarrel. Marie Antoinette despatched Goguelat, the man who was not at his post on the flight to Varennes, to implore intervention. She also gave Mercy her notions as to an Austrian manifesto; and in this letter, dated April 30, there is no sign of alarm, and no suggestion yet that France might be cowed by the use of exorbitant menaces. Dumouriez, who desired war with Austria, endeavoured to detach Prussia from the alliance.

He invited the king to arbitrate in the Alsatian dispute, and promised deference to his award. He proposed that the prerogative should be enlarged, the princes indemnified, the *émigrés* permitted to return. Frederic William was unmoved by these advances. He relied on the annexation of Alsace and Lorraine to compensate both allies, and he expected to succeed, because his army was the most illustrious of all armies in Europe. He wished to restore the *émigrés*, who would support him against Austria, and the *émigrés* looked to him to set up the order of society that had fallen. "Better to lose a province," they said, "than to live under a constitution."

The allied army was commanded by the Duke of Brunswick, the most admired and popular prince of his time. His own celebrity disabled him. Many years ago Marshal Macmahon said to an officer, since in high command at Berlin, that an army is best when it is composed of soldiers who have never smelt gunpowder, of experienced non-commissioned officers, and of generals with their reputation to make. Brunswick had made his reputation under the great king, and he feared to compromise it. Want of enterprise made him unfit for his position, although nobody doubted his capacity. In France, they thought of him for the command of their armies, and even for a still higher post. In spite of the disasters I am about to describe, the Prussians believed in him, and he was again their leader when they met Napoleon. The army which he led across the Rhine fell short of the stipulated number by 35,000 men. Francis, the new emperor, did not fulfil his engagements, and entered on the expedition with divided counsels.

Kaunitz, who was eighty-two years of age, and knew the affairs of Europe better than any other man, condemned the policy of his new master. He represented that they did not know what they were going to fight for; that Lewis had never explained what changes in the Constitution would satisfy him; that nothing could be expected from disaffection, and nothing could be done for a system which was extinct. On August 2 he resigned office, and made way for men who speculated on the dismemberment of France, and expected to see a shrunken monarchy in the north and a confederate republic in the south.

The entire force brought together for the invasion amounted to about 80,000 men, of which half were Prussians. When they were assembled on the Rhine, it became necessary to explain to the French people why they were coming, and what they meant to do. Headquarters were at Frankfort, when a confidential emissary from Lewis XVI., Mallet du Pan, appeared on the scene. Mallet du Pan was neither a brilliant writer like Burke and De Maistre and Gentz, nor an original and constructive thinker like Sieyès; but he was the most sagacious of all the politicians who watched the course of the Revolution. As a Genevese republican he approached the study of French affairs with no prejudice towards monarchy, aristocracy, or Catholicism. A Liberal at first, like Mounier and Malouet, he became as hostile as they; and his testimony, which had been enlightened and wise, became morose and monotonous when his cause was lost, until the Austrian statesmen with whom he corresponded grew tired of his narrowing ideas. He settled in England, and there he died. As he was not a man likely to propose a foolish thing, he was heard with attention. He proposed that the allies should declare that they were warring on Jacobinism, not on liberty, and would make no terms until the king regained his rightful power. If he was injured, they would inflict a terrible vengeance.

Whilst Mallet's text was being manipulated by European diplomacy at Frankfort, Marie Antoinette, acting through Fersen, disturbed their counsels. The queen understood how to control her pen, and to repress the language of emotion. But after June 20 she could not doubt that another and a more violent outrage was preparing, and that the republicans aimed at the death of the king. The terms in which she uttered her belief outweighed the advice of the sober Genevese. "Save us," she wrote, "if it is yet time. But there is not a moment to lose." And she required a declaration of intention so terrific that it would crush the audacity of Paris. Montmorin and Mercy were convinced that she was right. Malouet alone among royalist politicians expected that the measure she proposed would do more harm than good. Fersen, to whom her supplications were addressed, employed an *émigré* named Limon to draw up a manifesto equal to the occasion, and Limon, bearing credentials from Mercy, submitted his composition to the allied sovereigns. He announced that the Republicans would be exterminated, and Paris destroyed. Already Burke had written: "If ever a foreign prince enters into France, he must enter it as into a country of assassins. The mode of civilised war will not be practised; nor are the French, who act on the present system, entitled to expect it." Mallet du Pan himself had declared that there ought to be no pernicious mercy, and that humanity would be a crime. In reality, the difference between his tone and the fanatic who superseded him was not a wide one.

The manifesto, which proceeded from the queen, which had the sanction of Fersen, of Mercy, of Bouillé, was accepted at once by the emperor. The Prussians introduced some alterations, and Brunswick signed it on July 25.

His mind misgave him at the time, and he regretted afterwards that he had not died before he set his hand to it. Mercy, when it was too late, wished to put another declaration in its place. The Prussian ministers would not suffer the text to be published at Berlin. They allowed the author to fall into poverty and obscurity. He had acted in the spirit of the *émigrés*.

On July 27 the Princes issued a declaration of their own, to the effect that not Paris only should suffer the extremity of martial law, but every town to which the king might be taken if he was removed from the capital. Breteuil, although he complained that the invaders exhibited an intolerable clemency, disapproved the second proclamation. But Limon demanded the destruction of Varennes, and the *émigrés* expected that severities should be inflicted on the population as they went along. The idea of employing menaces so awful as to inspire terror at a distance of 300 miles was fatal to those who suggested it; but the danger was immediate, and the consequences of inaction were certain, for the destined assailants of the Tuileries were on the march from Toulon and Brest. It was not so certain that the king would be unable to defend himself. The manifesto was a desperate resource in a losing cause, and it is not clear that wiser and more moderate words would have done better. The text was not published at Paris until August 3. The allies were too far away for their threats to be treated seriously, and they are not answerable for consequences which were already prepared and expected. But their manifesto strengthened the hands of Danton, assured the triumph of the violent sections, and suggested the use to which terror may be put in revolutions. It contributed to the fall of the monarchy, and still more to the slaughter of the royalists three weeks later. The weapon forged by men unable to employ it was adopted by their enemies, and served the cause it was intended to destroy.

The Declaration united the French people against its authors. The Republicans whom it threatened and denounced became the appointed leaders of the national defence, and the cause of the Republic became identified with the safety of the nation. In order to withstand the invasion, and to preserve Paris from the fate of Jerusalem, the army gave itself to the dominant faction. The royalist element vanished from its ranks. Lafayette made one last attempt to uphold the Constitution, but his men repulsed him. He went over to imperial territory, and was detained in prison as the guilty author of the Revolution. Dumouriez succeeded to his command, and adhered to the new government. Out of 9000 officers in the king's service, 6000 had resigned, and, for the most part, had emigrated. Their places were filled by new men. In 1791, 100,000 volunteers had been enrolled, and enjoyed the privilege of electing their own officers. This became the popular force, and recruits preferred it to the line, where discipline was sterner and elected commanders were unknown. The men who now rose from the ranks proved better professional soldiers than the fine gentlemen whom they replaced. Talent could not fail to make its way. Those volunteer officers of 1791 and 1792 included most of the men whom the long war raised to eminence. Seventeen of the twenty-six marshals of Napoleon were among them.

On the 19th of August, four months after war had been declared, the allies entered France by the line of the Moselle. There was one French army to their left at Metz, and another to their right along Vauban's chain of fortresses, with an undefended interval between. To widen the gap they laid siege to Longwy, the nearest fortified place, and took it, after a feeble resistance, on August 24. When the news spread there was a moment of alarm, and the Council of Defence proposed to retire from the capital. Danton declared that he would burn Paris to the ground rather than abandon it to the enemy. Lavergne, who made so poor a defence at Longwy, was afterwards condemned to death. He was disheartened by disaster, but his wife cried out that she would perish with him, and the judges granted her prayer. She strove to give him comfort and courage along the way, and they were guillotined together.

From Longwy the Prussians advanced upon Verdun, which surrendered September 2, after one day's bombardment, and there was not a rampart between them and the capital. A few miles beyond Verdun the roads to the west traversed the Argonne, a low wooded range of hills pierced in five places by narrow defiles, easy to defend. Then came the open country of Champagne, and the valley of the Marne, leading, without a natural or artificial obstacle, to Paris.

On the 7th of September Pitt wrote that he expected Brunswick soon to reach his goal. There was no enemy in his front, while on his flank Dumouriez clung to his frontier strongholds, persuaded that he would arrest the invasion if he threatened the Austrians at Brussels, where they were weakened by recent insurrection and civil war. The French government rejected his audacious project, and ordered him to move on Châlons, and cover the heart of France. At Sedan, Dumouriez could hear heavy firing at a distance, and knew that Verdun was attacked, and could not hold out. He quickly changed his plan, postponing Belgium, but not for long, and fell back on the passes of the forest that he was about to make so famous. "They are the Thermopylæ of France," he said, "but I mean to do better than Leonidas."

Brunswick, delaying his cumbrous march for ten days, while Breteuil organised a new administration at Verdun, gave time for the French to strengthen their position. Before moving forward, he pointed out on the map the place where he intended to halt on the 16th, and men heard for the first time the historic name, Valmy. On the 14th Clerfayt, with the Austrians, forced one of the passes, and turned the French left. At nightfall, Dumouriez evacuated his Thermopylæ more expeditiously than became a rival Leonidas, and established himself across the great road to Châlons, opposite the southern defile of the Argonne, which extends between Clermont and St. Ménehould, where Drouet rode in pursuit of the king. His infantry encountered Prussian troopers and ran away. Ten thousand men, he wrote, were put to flight by fifteen hundred hussars.

Napoleon said, at St. Helena, that he believed himself to be bolder than any general that ever lived, but he would never have dared to hold the position that Dumouriez took up. He was outnumbered, three to one. He had been outmanœuvred, and driven from his fastness by the most enterprising of the allied generals; and his recruits refused to face the enemy. He never for a moment lost confidence in himself, for the time wasted at Verdun had given him the measure of his opponents. He summoned Kellermann, with the army of Metz, and Beurnonville, with 10,000 men, from Lille, and they arrived, just in time, on the 19th. Beurnonville, when his telescope showed him a regular army in order of battle, took alarm and fell back, thinking it must be Brunswick. It proved to be Dumouriez; and on the morning of September 20 he was at the head of 53,000 men, with the allies gathering in his front. The Prussians had come through the woods by the pass he had abandoned, and as they turned to face him, they stood with their backs to the great Catalaunian plain, which was traversed by the high road to Paris. They had been for a month in France, and had met with no resistance. Lafayette had deserted. The military breakdown was so apparent that the colonel of infantry, as he marched out of Longwy, threw himself into the river, and the governor of Verdun blew out his brains.

Clerfayt's success on the 14th and the rout of the following day raised the hopes of the Germans, and they wrote on the 19th that they were turning the enemy, and were sure of destroying him, if he was rash enough to wait their attack. From his prison at Luxemburg Lafayette urged them onward, and hinted that Dumouriez might be induced to unite with them for the rescue of the king.

Therefore, on the morning of September 20, when the mist rose over the French army drawn up on the low hills before them, there was joy in the Prussian camp, and the battalions that had been trained at Potsdam, under the eye of the great king, to the admiration of Europe, received for the first time the republican fire. They were 34,000. Kellermann opposed them with 36,000 men, and 40 guns against 58. It soon appeared that things were not going as the invaders had expected. The French soldiers were not frightened by the cannonade. Beurnonville rode up to one of his regiments and told them to lie down, to make way for shot. They refused to obey whilst he exposed himself on horseback. After time had been allowed for artillery to produce its effect on republican nerve, the Prussian infantry made ready to attack. Gouvion St. Cyr, the only general of his time whom Napoleon acknowledged as his equal, believed that the French would not have stood at close quarters. But the word to advance was never given.

The secret of war, said Wellington, is to find out what is going on on the other side of the hill. When Brunswick rode over the field some days later, a staff officer asked him why he had not moved forward. He answered, "Because I did not know what was behind the hill." There was Dumouriez's reserve of 16,000 men. He had sent to the front as many as were needed to fill Kellermann's line, and left to his colleague the part for which he was fitted. For his conduct that day Kellermann was named a marshal of the Empire and duke of Valmy; but the whole world was aware that the event was due to the brain of the man in the background. When the French had lost 300 men without wavering, the Prussians ceased firing, and broke off the engagement. Their loss was only 184. Yet this third-rate and mediocre action is counted, with Waterloo and Gettysburg, among the decisive battles of history; and Goethe was not the only man there who knew that the scene before him was the beginning of a new epoch for mankind. With 36,000 men and 40 guns the French had arrested the advance of Europe, not by skilful tactics or the touch of steel, but by the moral effect of their solidity when they met the best of existing armies. The nation discovered that the Continent was at its mercy, and the war begun for the salvation of monarchy became a war for the expansion of the Republic. It was founded at Paris, and consolidated at Valmy. Yet no military event was less decisive. The French stood their ground because nobody attacked them, and they were not attacked because they stood their ground. The Prussians suffered a strategic, though not a tactical defeat. By retiring to their encampment they renounced the purposes for which they went to war, the province they occupied, and the prestige of Frederic. They no longer possessed the advantage of numbers, and without superior numbers there could be no dash for Paris.

The object of the invasion was unattainable by force, but something might be got by negotiation, if it was undertaken before force had definitely failed. They were losing heavily, by disease and want, while French recruits were pouring in. Therefore Dumouriez wished for time. The king's secretary had been captured, and he sent him with overtures, representing that the intended advance upon Paris was hopeless, and that Prussia had more interests in common with France than with Austria. Frederic William at once surrendered the original demands. He made no stipulations now regarding the future government of France or the treatment of the *émigrés*. He only demanded that Lewis should be restored, in such manner as might seem good to France, and that the propaganda of revolution should be put an end to. That propaganda was one of the weapons by which the French checked and embarrassed the champions of European absolutism, and it was obvious that it would receive encouragement from their success at Valmy. And it was a point of honour to speak for the imprisoned monarch. But it had become a vain thing. Dumouriez produced a newspaper with the decree of the new Assembly abolishing monarchy. It was hard to say what the allies were now doing on French soil. "Only do something for the king," said Brunswick, "and we will go." The Austrians would be satisfied if he was only a stadtholder. Kellermann promised that peace might be obtained if he was sent back to the Tuileries. It was all too late. The Prince, in whose behalf the allies invaded France, was now a hostage in the power of their enemies; all that they could obtain was a pledge not to carry the revolution into foreign countries. Their position grew more dangerous every day, and Dumouriez grew stronger.

At the end of September Frederic William abandoned Lewis to his fate. He had contributed to his dethronement by entering France, and he contributed to his execution by leaving it. He did not feel that he had deserved so prodigious a humiliation. If the Austrians had joined as they promised with 100,000 men, the march upon the capital would have been conceivable with energetic commanders. And the king could justly say that he had favoured spirited schemes, and had been baffled by the faltering commander-in-chief. He attempted, by throwing out hints of neutrality, to escape without further loss. Dumouriez calculated that every attack would weld the allies more closely together, and refrained from molesting them. Early in October they evacuated the conquered province, and retreated to the Rhine, pursued by a few random shots, while Dumouriez hastened to Paris, to be hailed as the saviour of his country.

The invasion of 1792 roused a crouching lion; and the French, after their easy and victorious defence, went over to the attack. Whilst the invaders were standing still, too weak to advance and too proud to withdraw, the conquest of Europe began. The king of Sardinia, as the father-in-law of the Comte d'Artois, had thrown himself into the counter-revolutionary policy, and the scheme for attacking Lyons. Of all European monarchs, since the murder of Gustavus, he was the most hostile. An army under Montesquieu occupied Savoy and Nice without resistance, and the people readily adopted the new system. A week later Custine seized the left bank of the Rhine, where diminutive secular and ecclesiastical territories, without cohesion, were an easy prey. The Declaration of Rights, said Gouverneur Morris, proved quite as effectual as the trumpets of Joshua. Mentz fell, October 21, and Custine occupied Frankfort and replenished his military chest. This excursion into the middle of the Empire was not authorised by State policy. The idea was already taking shape that the safety of France required the defensible and historic, or, as they unscientifically called it, the natural frontier of the Rhine, and that the grand conflict with Austria should be transferred to Italy. Germany was a nation of armed men, and was best let alone. In Italy, the Austrians would have only their own resources for war. Their most vulnerable point was the outlying principality of Belgium, so distant from Vienna and so near to Paris.

Dumouriez was now at liberty to deliver the stroke by which he had hoped to stop the invasion, as Scipio drove Hannibal from Italy by landing in Africa. By carrying the war in that direction he would occupy the Imperialists, and would not excite the resentment of Prussia. The country had not long been pacified, and it presented the unusual feature that Conservatives and Liberals alike were patriotic and rebellious. As a place where disaffection would assist war, it was there that the process of European revolution would properly begin. On October 19 Dumouriez assumed the command of 70,000 men, in the region he had held before his flank march to the Argonne. One of his lieutenants was the Peruvian adventurer Miranda, whose mission it was to apply the movement in Europe to the rescue of Spanish America.

The other was known as Prince Égalité, senior, whose wonderful future was already foreseen both by Dumouriez and Danton.

During the operations in Champagne the Austrians had begun the siege of Lille, and at the turning of the tide they withdrew across the frontier, and took up a strong position at Jemmapes, in front of Mons, with 13,000 men. Clerfayt, again, was at their head; and when, on November 6, he saw the French army approaching, nearly 40,000 strong, like Nelson in the hour of death he appeared in all his stars and gold lace, that his men, seeing him, might take heart. He was defeated, and the next evening, at the theatre of Mons, Dumouriez was acclaimed by the Flemish patriots. A week later he was at Brussels, and before the end of the month he was master of Belgium. Holland was undefended, and he proposed to conquer it; but Antwerp was already in the power of the French, and his government feared that England would come to the defence of the Dutch. They directed him to march upon Cologne and complete the conquest of the Rhine.

By a decree of November 19 the Convention proffered sympathy and succour to every people that struck a blow for freedom; but the cloven hoof of annexation soon appeared, and it was avowed that the war would be carried on, that the financial needs of France might be supplied, at the expense of the populations which the French arms delivered. These things offended the political, if not the moral sense of Dumouriez. He became alienated from the Convention; and as England went to war on the death of the king, there was no consideration of policy protecting Holland. The invasion was undertaken, and immediately failed. The Austrians, under the duke of Coburg, who on that day founded the great fortunes of his house, came back in force, and gave battle at Neerwinden, close to the fields of Landen and of Ramillies. Here, March 18, Clerfayt crushed Dumouriez's left wing, and recovered the Belgic provinces as suddenly as he had lost them four months earlier.

Dumouriez had already resolved to treat with the Imperialists for common action against the Regicides. Five days after his defeat he informed Coburg that, with his support, he would lead his army against Paris, disperse the Convention, and establish a constitutional monarchy without the *émigrés*. He promised that the better part of his force would follow him. The volunteers were Jacobinical; but the regulars were jealous of the volunteers, and would obey their general. As he felt his way, hostile officers watched him, and reported what was going on in the camp of the new Wallenstein. Twice the Jacobins attempted to avert the peril. They invited Dumouriez to

Paris, that he might place himself at their head and overpower the Girondin majority, and they employed men to assassinate him. At last they sent the minister of war, accompanied by four deputies, to arrest him. There was to have been a fifth, but he did not arrive in time, and his absence saved France. For Dumouriez seized the envoys of the Convention, and handed them over to Coburg, to be hostages for the life of the queen. The deputy who failed to appear was Carnot. After that, Dumouriez was deserted by his men, and fled to the Austrian camp. He survived for thirty years. He became one of the shrewdest observers of Napoleon's career, and was the confidential correspondent of Wellington on the art they understood so well. The future "king of the French," who went over with him, remained true to his chief during the strange vicissitudes of their lives; and at the Restoration he asked that he should be made a marshal. "How could you think," was the proud comment of Dumouriez, "that they have forgotten the Argonne?"

On the 20th of June in the following year Louis Philippe drove into town from Twickenham to learn the news from the Low Countries. His sons still know the spot where he found his old commander gesticulating on the pavement at Hammersmith, and learned from him how the great war, which began with their victory at Valmy, had ended under Napoleon at Waterloo.

XV
THE CATASTROPHE OF MONARCHY

The calculations of the Girondins were justified by the event. Four months after the declaration of war the throne had fallen, and the king was in prison. Next to Dumouriez the principal members of the new ministry were the Genevese Clavière, one of Mirabeau's advisers, and the promoter of the assignats, Servan, a meritorious officer, better known to us as a meritorious military historian; and Roland, whose wife shared, on a lower scale, the social influence and intellectual celebrity of Madame de Staël.

Dumouriez, the Minister of Foreign Affairs, is one of the great figures of the Revolution. He was excessively clever rather than great, agreeable, and abounding in resource, not only cool in danger, as a commander should be, but steadfast and cheerful when hope seemed lost, and ready to meet the veterans of Frederic with undisciplined volunteers, and officers who were the remnant of the royal army. Without principle or conviction or even scruple, he had none of the inhumanity of dogmatic revolutionists. To the king, whom he despised, he said, "I shall often displease you, but I shall never deceive you." He was not an accomplice of the conspiracy to compromise him and to ruin him by war, and would have saved him if the merit and the reward had been his own. He did not begin well, in the arts either of war or peace. He employed all his diplomacy, all his secret service money, in the endeavour to make Prussia neutral. Nothing availed against the indignation of the Prussians at French policy, and their contempt for French arms. The officers received orders to make ready for a march to Paris, and were privately told that it would be a mere parade. The first encounter with Austrians on Belgian soil confirmed this persuasion, for the French turned and fled, and murdered one of their generals.

Dumouriez's credit was shaken, and the Girondin leaders, who could not rely on him to make the coming campaign turn towards the execution of their schemes, revived the question of the clergy. On May 27 Vergniaud carried a decree placing nonjurors at the mercy of local authorities, and threatening them with arbitrary expulsion as public enemies in time of national peril. If the king sanctioned, he would be isolated and humiliated.

If the king vetoed, they would have the means of raising Paris against him, without waiting for the vicissitudes of war or the co-operation of Dumouriez. Madame Roland wrote a letter to the king, and her husband signed it, on June 10, representing that it was for the safety of the priests themselves that they should be sent out of the way of danger. Roland, proud of the composition, sent it to the papers. The Girondin ministry was at once dismissed. Dumouriez remained, attempted to form an administration without the Girondin colleagues, but could not overcome the king's resistance to the act of banishment. On June 15 he resigned office, and took a command on the frontier. The majority in the Assembly was still faithful to the Constitution of 1791, and opposed to further change; but the rejection of their decree against the royalist clergy alienated them at the critical moment. Lewis had lost ground with his friends; he had angered the Girondins; and he had lost the services of the last man who was strong enough to save him.

On June 15 a high official in the administration of the department was at Maubeuge, on a visit to Lafayette. His name was Roederer, and we shall meet him again. He rose high under Napoleon, and is one of those to whom we owe our knowledge of the Emperor's character, as well as of the events I am about to relate. His interview with the general was interrupted by a message from Paris. Lafayette was called away; and Roederer, from the next room, heard the joyful exclamations of the officers. The news was the fall of the Girondin ministry; and Lafayette, to strengthen the king's hands, wrote to the Assembly remonstrating against the illiberal and unconstitutional tendencies of the hour. His letter was read on the 18th. A new ministry had been forming, consisting of Feuillants and men friendly to Lafayette, one of whom, Terrier de Montciel, enjoyed the confidence of the king. On the opposition side were the Girondins angry and alarmed at their fall from power, the more uncompromising Jacobins, Pétion at the head of the Commune, and behind Pétion, the real master of Paris, Danton, surrounded by a group of his partisans, Panis and Sergent in the police, Desmoulins and Fréron in the press, leaders of the populace, such as Santerre and Legendre, and above them all, the Alsatian soldier, Westermann.

With Danton and his following we reach the lowest stage of what can still be called the conflict of opinion, and come to bare cupidity and vengeance, to brutal instinct and hideous passion. All these elements were very near the surface in former phases of the Revolution. At this point they are about to prevail, and the man of action puts himself forward in the place of contending theorists. Robespierre and Brissot were politicians who did not shrink from crime, but it was in the service of some form of the democratic system. Even Marat, the most ghastly of them all, who demanded not only slaughter but torture, and whose ferocity was revolting and grotesque, even Marat was obedient to a logic of his own. He adopted simply the state of nature and the primitive contract, in which thousands of his contemporaries believed. The poor had agreed to renounce the rights of savage life and the prerogative of force, in return for the benefits of civilisation; but finding the compact broken on the other side, finding that the upper classes governed in their own interest, and left them to misery and ignorance, they resumed the conditions of barbaric existence before society, and were free to take what they required, and to inflict what punishment they chose upon men who had made a profit of their sufferings. Danton was only a strong man, who wished for a strong government in the interest of the people, and in his own. In point of doctrine, he cared for little but the relief of the poor by taxing the rich. He had no sympathy with the party that was gathering in the background, whose aim it was not only to reduce inequalities, but to institute actual equality and the social level. There was room beyond for more extreme developments of the logic of democracy; but the greatest change in the modern world was wrought by Danton, for it was he who overthrew the Monarchy and made the Republic.

When Lewis dismissed his ministers, Danton exclaimed that the time had come to strike terror, and on June 20 he fulfilled his threat. It was the anniversary of the Tennis Court. A monster demonstration was organised, to plant a tree of liberty or to present a petition—in reality to overawe the Assembly and the king. There was an expectation that the king would perish in the tumult, but nothing definite was settled, and no assassin was designated. It was enough that he should give way, abandon his priests, and receive his ministers from the populace. That was all the Girondins required, and they would assent to no more. The king would have to choose between them and their temporary confederates, the Cordeliers. If he gave way, he would be spared; if he resisted, he would be slain. It was not to be apprehended that he would resist and would yet come out alive. The king understood the alternative before him, made his choice, and prepared to die. After putting his house in order, he wrote, on the 19th, that he had done with this world.

Lewis XVI. had not ability to devise a policy or vigour to pursue it, but he had the power of grasping a principle. He felt at last that the ground beneath his feet was firm. He would drift no longer, sought no counsel, and admitted no disturbing inquiries. If he fell, he would fall in the cause of religion and for the rights of conscience. The proper name for the rights of conscience is liberty, and therefore he was true to himself, and was about to end as he had begun, in the character of a liberal and reforming king. When the morning came, there was a moment of hesitation. The pacific rioters asked what would happen if the guards fired upon them. Santerre, who was at their head, replied, "March on, and don't be afraid; Pétion will be there." They presented their petition, defiled before the Assembly, and made their way to the palace. It was not to be thought of that, after they had been admitted by the representatives of the nation, an inferior power should deny them access. One barrier after another yielded, and they poured into the room where the king awaited them, in the recess of a window, with four or five guards in front of him. They shielded him well, for although there were men in the crowd who struck at him with sword and pike, he was untouched. Their cry was that he should restore Roland and revoke his veto, for this was the point in common between the Girondins and their violent associates. Legendre read an insulting address, in which he called the king a traitor. The scene lasted more than two hours. Vergniaud and Isnard appeared after some time, and their presence was a protection. At last Pétion came in, borne aloft on the shoulders of grenadiers. He assured the mob that the king would execute the will of the people, when the country had shown that it agreed with the capital; he told them that they had done their duty, and then, with lenient arts, turned them out.

That trying humiliation marks the loftiest moment in the reign of Lewis XVI. He had stood there, with the red cap of liberty on his powdered head, not only fearless, but cheerful and serene. He had been in the power of his enemies and had patiently defied them. He made no surrender and no concession while his life was threatened. The Girondins were not recalled, and the movement failed. For the moment the effect was injurious to the revolutionary party, and useful to the king. It was clear that menace and outrage would not move him, and that more was wanted than the half-hearted measures of the Gironde.

The outrage of June 20 was a contumelious reply to Lafayette's letter of the 16th, and the time had come for more than the writing of letters. His letter had been well received, and the Assembly had ordered it to be printed. The Girondins, by pretending that it could not be authentic, had prevented a vote on the question of sending it to the departments. He could count on the Feuillant majority, on the ministry composed of his partisans, on his popularity with the National Guard. As he was at the head of an army, his advice to the king to adopt a policy of resistance implied that he would support him in it. He now wrote once more, that he could never maintain his ground against the Prussians unless there was a change in the state of things in the capital. On the morning of June 28, immediately after his letter, he appeared in the Assembly, and denounced the sowers of disorder who were disorganising the State. Having obtained a vote of approval, by 339 to 234, he appealed to the National Guard to stand by him against his Jacobins. He summoned a meeting of his friends, but the influence of the Court caused it to fail, and he was compelled to return to his camp, having accomplished nothing. He imagined one chance more. He now put forward his colleague, General Luckner, who was incompetent but, not being a politician, was not distrusted, and they were jointly to rescue the king, and bring him to a city of refuge.

The revolutionists could now lay their plans without fear of the army. They summoned *fédérés* from the departments for the anniversary of July 14, and it was arranged that sturdy men should be sent from Brest and Marseilles to be at their orders when they struck the final blow. Paris could not be relied on. The failure there had been complete. On June 21, and on the 25th, the Cordeliers attempted to renew, with better effect, the attack which had been baffled by a divided purpose on the 20th. But their men would not move. The minister, Montciel, gave orders that the departments should not send *fédérés* to Paris, and he succeeded in stopping all but a couple of thousand. Nothing could be done until the contingents from the seaports arrived. The crisis was postponed, and some weeks of July were spent in parliamentary warfare. Here the Girondins had the lead; but the Feuillants were the majority in the Assembly, while the Jacobins were supreme in Paris. The Girondins were driven into a policy both tortuous and weak. The Republic would give power to one of their enemies as the Monarchy gave it to the other. All they could do was to increase hostile pressure on the king, in the hope of bringing him to terms with them. They oscillated between open attack and secret negotiation and offers of defence.

Lewis was inclined to accept a scheme for his deliverance which was arranged by his ministers in conjunction with the generals. He was to have been taken to Compiégne, within reach of the army. But the army meant Lafayette, and Lafayette would only consent to restore the king as the hereditary chief of a commonwealth, who should reign, but should not govern. The queen refused to reign under such conditions, or to be saved by such hands. The security for her was in power, not in limitations to power. The sacred thing was the ancient Crown, not the new Constitution. Lally Tollendal came over from England, conferred with Malouet and Clermont Tonnerre, and exhorted her to consent. Morris, whose ready pen had put the American Constitution into final shape five years before, aided them in drawing up an amended scheme of government to be proclaimed when they should be free. But the strong will and stronger passion of the queen prevailed. When all was accurately combined, and the Swiss troops were on the march to the rendezvous, the king revoked his orders, and on July 10 the Feuillant ministry resigned, and the Girondins saw power once more within their grasp. They had vehemently denounced the king as the cause of all the troubles of the State, and on July 6 the assault had been interrupted for a moment by a scene of emotion, when the bishop of Lyons obtained a manifestation of unanimous feeling in the presence of the enemy.

On July 11 the Assembly passed a vote declaring the country in danger, and on the 22nd it was proclaimed, to the sound of cannon. It was a call to arms, and placed dictatorial power in the hands of government. Different plans were proposed to keep that power distinct from the executive, and the idea which afterwards developed into the Committee of Public Safety now began to be familiar. On July 14 the anniversary of the Bastille and of the Federation of 1790 was celebrated on the Champ de Mars; the king went up to the altar, where he swore fidelity to the Constitution, with a heavy heart; and the people saw him in public for the last time until they saw him on the scaffold. It was near the end of July when the Girondins saw that the king would not take them back, and that the risk of a Jacobin insurrection, as much against them as against the throne, was fast approaching. Their last card was a regency, to be directed by them in the name of the Dauphin. Vergniaud suggested that the king should summon four conspicuous members of the Constituent Assembly to his Council, without office, to make up for the obscurity of his new ministers. At that moment Brunswick's declaration became known, some of the forty-eight sections in which the people of Paris deliberated demanded the dethronement of the king, and the Marseillais, arriving on the 30th, five or six hundred strong, made it possible to accomplish it.

These events, coinciding almost to a day, conveyed power from the Assembly to the municipality, and from the Girondins to the Jacobins, who had the municipality in their hands, and held the machinery that worked the sections. In a letter written to be laid before the king, Vergniaud affirmed that it was impossible to dissociate him from the allies who were in arms for his sake, and whose success would be so favourable to his authority. That was the argument to which no royalist could reply. The country was in danger, and the cause of the danger was the king. The Constitution had broken down on June 20. The king could not devote himself to the maintenance of a system which exposed him to such treatment, and enabled his adversaries to dispose of all forces in a way that left him at the mercy of the most insolent and the most infamous of the rabble. He had not the instincts of a despot, and would easily have been made content with reasonable amendments. But the limit of the changes he sought was unknown, unsettled, unexplained, and he was identified simply with the reversal of the Constitution he was bound by oath to carry out.

The queen, a more important person than her husband, was more openly committed to reaction. The failure of the great experiment drove her back to absolutism. As she repudiated the *émigrés* in 1791, so she now repudiated the constitutionalists, and chose rather to perish than to owe her salvation to their detested aid. She looked for deliverance only to the foreigners slowly converging on the Moselle. Her agents had excluded a saving allusion to constitutional liberty in the manifesto of the Powers; and she had dictated the threats of vengeance on the inhabitants of Paris.

The king himself had called in the invaders. His envoy, concealed in the uniform of a Prussian major, rode by the side of Brunswick. His brothers were entering France with the heavy baggage of the enemies, and Breteuil, the agent whom he trusted more than his brothers, was preparing to govern, and did in September govern, the provinces they occupied, under the shelter of their bayonets. For him the blow was about to fall—not for his safety, but for his plenary authority. The purpose of the allied sovereigns, and of the *émigrés* who prompted them, stood confessed. They were fighting for unconditional restoration, and both as invaders and as absolutists the king was their accomplice. The country could not make war with confidence, if the military power was in the hands of traitors. The king could protect them from the horrors with which they were threatened on his account, not as the head of the executive, but as a hostage. He was a danger in his palace; he would be a security in prison. All this was obvious at the time, and the effect it had was to disable and disarm the friends of the constitutional king, so that no resistance was offered when the attack came, although it was the act of a very small part of the population. The Girondins no longer displayed a distinct policy, and scarcely differed from their former associates, of June, except by their wish to suspend the king, and not to dethrone him. The final question, as to monarchy, regency, or republic, was to be left to the Convention that was to follow. Pétion was persuaded that he would soon be the Regent of France. He received a large sum of money from the Court; and it was in reliance on him, and on some less conspicuous men, that the king and queen remained obstinately in Paris. At the last moment Liancourt offered them a haven in Normandy; but Liancourt was a Liberal of the Constituante, and therefore unforgiven. Marie Antoinette preferred to trust to Pétion and Santerre.

Early in August the most revolutionary section of Paris decided that the king should be deposed. The Assembly rescinded the vote. Then the people of that section and some others made known that they would execute their own decree, unless the Assembly itself made it unnecessary and accomplished legally what would otherwise be done by the act of the sovereign people, superseding all powers and standing above law. Time was to be allowed until August 9. If the king was still on the throne upon the evening of that day, the people of Paris would sound the tocsin against him.

On August 8 the Assembly came to a vote on the conduct of Lafayette, in abandoning his army in time of war to threaten his enemies at home. He was justified by 406 votes to 224. It was the last appearance of the Liberal party. Four hundred deputies, a majority of the entire body, kept out of the way in the moment of danger, and allowed the Girondin and republican remnant to proceed without them. The absolution of Lafayette proclaimed the resolve not to dethrone the king. The Gironde had no constitutional remedy for its anxieties. The next step would be taken by the democracy of Paris, and their victory would be a grave danger to the Gironde and a triumph for the extreme revolutionary faction. Up to this time they had struggled for mastery; they would now have to struggle for existence. They accepted what was inevitable. After the flight of the Feuillants, the Gironde, now supreme in the legislature, capitulated to the revolution which they dreaded, and appeared without initiative or policy.

On August 9 the Jacobin leaders settled their plan of action. Their partisans in each section were to elect three commissaries to act with the Commune for the public good, and to strengthen, and, if necessary, eventually to supersede, the existing municipality. About one-half of Paris sent them, and they assembled in the course of the night at the Hôtel de Ville, apart from the legal body. In the political science of the day the constituency suspended the constituted authorities and resumed all delegated powers. The revolutionary town-councillors, who now came to the front, are the authors of the atrocities that afflicted France during the next two years. They were creatures of Danton. And as we now enter the company of malefactors and the Chamber of Horrors, we must bear this in mind, that our own laws punish the slightest step towards absolute government with the same supreme penalty as murder; so that morally the difference between the two extremes is not serious. The agents are ferocious ruffians, and the leaders are no better; but they are at the same time influenced by republican convictions, as respectable as those of the *émigrés*. The function of this supplementary Commune was not to lead the insurrection or direct the attack, but to disable the defence; for the commander of the National Guard received his orders from the Hôtel de Ville, and he was a loyal soldier.

The forces of the Revolution were not overwhelming. The men from Marseilles and Brest were intent on fighting, and so were some from the departments. But when the tocsin rang from the churches soon after midnight, the Paris combatants assembled slowly, and the event might be doubtful. Ammunition was supplied to the insurgent forces from the Hôtel de Ville, but not to the National Guard. It is extremely dangerous, said Pétion, to oppose one public force to another. At the Tuileries there were less than a thousand Swiss mercenaries, who were sure to do their duty; one or two hundred gentlemen, come to defend the king; and several thousand National Guards of uncertain fidelity and valour. Pétion showed himself at the palace, and at the Assembly, and then was seen no more. By a happy inspiration he induced Santerre to place him under arrest, with a guard of four hundred men to protect him from the dangers of responsibility. He himself tells the story, and is mean enough to boast of his ingenuity. But if the mayor was a traitor and a coward, the commanding general, Mandat, knew his duty, and was resolved to do it. He prepared for the defence of the palace, and there was great probability that his men would fight. If they did, they were strong enough to repulse attack. Therefore, early in the morning of August 10, Mandat was summoned by his lawful superiors to the Hôtel de Ville. He appeared before them, made his report, and was then taken to the revolutionary committee sitting separately. He declared that he had orders to repel force by force, and that it would be done. They required him to sign an order removing half of the National Guard from the place they were to defend. Mandat refused to save his life by an act of treachery, and by Danton's order he was shot dead. He was in flagrant insurrection against the people themselves and abetting constituted authorities in resistance to their master. By this first act of bloodshed the defence of the palace was deprived of half its forces. The National Guards were without a commander, and, left to themselves, it was uncertain how many would fire on the people of Paris.

Having disposed of the general commanding, the new Commune appointed Santerre to succeed him, and then took the place of the former Commune. There was no obstacle now to the concentration and advance of the insurgents, and they appeared in the space between the Louvre and the

Tuileries, which was crowded with private houses. It was between seven and eight in the morning. All night long the royal family expected to be attacked, and the king did nothing. Some thousands of Swiss were within reach, at Courbevoie, and were not brought up in time. At last, surrounded by his family, the king made a forlorn attempt to rouse his guards to combat. It was an occasion memorable for all time, for it was the last stand of the monarchy of Clovis. His wife, his children, his sister were there, their lives depending on the spirit which, by a word, by a glance, he might infuse into the brave men before him. The king had nothing to say, and the soldiers laughed in his face. When the queen came back, tears of rage were bursting from her eyes. "He has been deplorable," she said, "and all is lost." Others soon came to the same conclusion. Roederer went amongst the men, and found them unwilling to fight in such a cause. He was invested with authority as a high official; and although the ministers were present, it was he who gave the law. The disappearance of Mandat and the hesitation of the artillery convinced him that there was no hope for the defenders.

There was a looker-on who lived to erect a throne in the place of the one that fell that day, and to be the next sovereign who reigned at the Tuileries. In 1813 Napoleon told Roederer that he had watched the scene from a window on the Carrousel, and assured him that he had made a fatal mistake. Many of the National Guard were staunch, and the royal forces were superior to those with which he himself conquered in Vendémiaire. He thought that the defence ought to have been victorious. I do not suppose he seriously resented the blunder to which he owed so much. Roederer was a clever man, and there is some reason to doubt whether he was singleminded in desiring to prevent the uncertain conflict. The queen was eager to fight, and spoke brave words to every one. Afterwards, when she heard the cannonade from her refuge in the reporter's box, she said to d'Hervilly: "Well, do you think now that we were wrong to remain in Paris?" He answered, "God grant, madam, that you may not repent of it!" Roederer had detected what was passing in her mind. Defeat would be terrible, for nothing could save the royal family. But victory would also be a perilous thing for the revolution, for it would restore the monarchy in its power, and the old nobles collected in the palace would gain too much by it. They were indeed but a residue: 7000 had been expected to appear at the supreme moment; there were scarcely 120. Charette, the future hero of Vendée, was among them, unconscious yet of his extraordinary gifts for war.

Roederer, vigorously backed by his colleagues of the department, informed the king of what he had seen and heard, assured him that the

Tuileries could not be defended with the forces present, and that there was no safety except in the Assembly, the only authority that was regarded. It was but two days since the deputies, by an immense majority, had approved the act of Lafayette. He thought they might be trusted to protect the king. As there was nothing left to fight for, he affirmed that those who remained behind would be in no danger. He would not allow the garrison to retire, and he left the Swiss, without orders, to their fate. Marie Antoinette resisted vehemently, and Lewis was not easy to convince. At last he said that there was nothing to be done, and gave orders to set out. But the queen in a fury turned upon him, and exclaimed: "Now I know you for what you are!" Lewis told his valet to wait his return; but as they crossed the garden, where the men were sweeping the gravel, he remarked: "The leaves are falling early this year." Roederer heard, and understood.

A newspaper had said that the throne would not last to the fall of the leaf; and it was by those trivial but significant words that the fallen monarch acknowledged the pathetic solemnity of the moment, and indicated that the footsteps which took him away from his palace would never be retraced. A deputation met him at the door of the Assembly, and he entered, saying that he came there to avert a great crime. The Feuillants were absent. The Girondins predominated, and the president, Vergniaud, received him with stately sentences. From his retreat in the reporter's box he placidly watched the proceedings. Vergniaud also moved that he be suspended, as he had been before, and that a Convention should be convoked, to pronounce on the future government of France. It was decided that the elections should be held without a property qualification. Roland and the other Girondin ministers returned to their former posts, and Danton was appointed Minister of Justice by 222 votes. For Danton was the victor. While Pétion kept out of the way, it was he who issued commands from the Hôtel de Ville, and when Santerre faltered, it was Danton's friend Westermann who brought up his men to the tryst at the Carrousel. After the king was gone they made their way into the Tuileries, holding parley with the defenders. If there had been anybody left to give orders, bloodshed might have been averted. But the tension was extreme; the Swiss refused to surrender their arms; a shot was fired, and then they lost patience and fell upon the intruders. In ten minutes they cleared the palace and the courtyard. But the king heard the fusillade, and sent orders to cease firing. The bearer of the order was d'Hervilly; but he had the heart of a soldier; and finding the position by no means desperate, he did not at once produce it. When he did, it was too late. The insurgents had penetrated by the long gallery of the Louvre, near the river, and then there was no escape for the Swiss. They were killed in the palace, and in the gardens, and their graves are under the tall chestnuts. Of the women, some were taken to prison, and some to their homes. The conquerors slaked their thirst in the king's wine, and then flooded the cellars, lest some fugitive aristocrat should be lurking underground. Their victims were between 700 and 800 men, and about 140 of the assailants had fallen.

The royalists did not at first perceive that the monarchy was at an end. They imagined that the king was again in the same condition as after Varennes, only occupying the Luxembourg instead of the Tuileries, and that he would be again restored, as the year before. The majority of the Legislature was loyal, and it was hoped that France would resent the action of the capital. But Paris, represented by the intruding municipality, held its prey. The allowance promised by the Assembly was suppressed, and the Temple was substituted for the Luxembourg which was deemed unsafe because of the subterranean galleries. A sum of £20,000 was voted for expenses, until the Convention in September disposed of the king.

With no severer effort than the signing of an order, Lewis might have called up other regiments of Swiss, who would have made the stronghold of monarchy impregnable. And it would have been in his power, before sunset that day, to march out of Paris at the head of a victorious army, and at once to proclaim reforms which enlightened statesmen had drawn up. His queen was active and resolute; but she had learnt, in adversity, to think more of the claims of authority and the historic right of kings. She shared Burke's passionate hatred for men whose royalism was conditional. At every step downward they were the authors of their own disaster. The French Republic was not a spontaneous evolution of social elements. The issue between constitutional monarchy, the richest and most flexible of political forms, and the Republic one and indivisible (that is, not federal), which is the most rigorous and sterile, was decided by the crimes of men, and by errors more inevitably fatal than crime. There is another world for the expiation of guilt; but the wages of folly are payable here below.

XVI
THE EXECUTION OF THE KING

The constitutional experiment, first tried on the Continent under Lewis XVI., failed mainly through distrust of the executive and a mechanical misconstruction of the division of power. Government had been incapable, the finances were disordered, the army was disorganised; the monarchy had brought on an invasion which it was now the mission of the Republic to repel. The instinct of freedom made way for the instinct of force, the Liberal movement was definitely reversed, and the change which followed the shock of the First European Coalition was more significant, the angle more acute, than the mere transition from royal to republican forms. Unity of power was the evident need of the moment, and as it could not be bestowed upon a king who was in league with the enemy, it had to be sought in a democracy which should have concentration and vigour for its dominant note. Therefore supremacy was assured to that political party which was most alert in laying its grasp on all the resources of the State, and most resolute in crushing resistance. More than public interests were at stake. Great armies were approaching, guided by vindictive *émigrés*, and they had announced the horrors they were prepared to inflict on the population of Paris.

Beyond the rest of France the Parisians were interested in the creation of a power equal to the danger, and were ready to be saved even by a dictatorship. The need was supplied by the members of the new municipality who expelled the old on the night of August 9. They were instituted by Danton. They appointed Marat their organ of publicity. Robespierre was elected a member of the body on August 11. It was the stronghold of the Revolution. Strictly, they were an illegal assembly, and their authority was usurped; but they were masters of Paris, and had dethroned the king. The *Législative*, having accepted their action, was forced to obey their commandments, and to rescind its decrees at their pleasure. By convoking the constituencies to elect a Convention, it had annulled itself. It was no more than a dying assembly whose days were exactly numbered, and whose credit and influence were at an end.

Between a king who was deposed and an assembly that abdicated, the Commune alone exhibited the energy and force that were to save the country. Being illegitimate, they could quell opposition only by violence; and they made it clear what violence they meant to use when they gave an office to Marat. This man had been a writer on science, and Goethe celebrates his sagacity and gift of observation in a passage which is remarkable for the absence of any allusion to his public career. But he considered that the rich have no right to enjoyments of which the masses are deprived, and that the guilt of selfishness and oppression could only be expiated by death. A year before he had proposed that obnoxious deputies should be killed by torture, and their quarters nailed to the walls as a hint to their successors. He now desired to reconcile mercy with safety, and declared himself satisfied if the Assembly was decimated. For royalists, and men who had belonged to privileged orders, he had no such clemency. If, he said, the able-bodied men become soldiers and are sent to guard the frontier, who is to protect us from traitors at home? Either thousands of fighting men must be kept away from the army in the field, or the internal enemy must be put out of the way. On August 10 Marat began to employ this argument, and a company of recruits protested against being sent to the front whilst their families were at the mercy of the royalists. The cry became popular that France would be condemned to fight her enemies with one arm, if she had to guard the traitors with the other. And this was the plea provided to excuse the crimes that were about to follow. It was the plea, but not the motive. If the intended destruction of royalists could be represented as an act of war, as a necessity of national defence, moderate men would be unable to prevent it without incurring reproach as unpatriotic citizens.

When the Jacobins prepared the massacre in the prisons, their purpose was to fill France with terror and to secure their majority in the Convention. That is the controlling idea that governed the events of the next few weeks. After the decree which assigned the Luxemburg palace as a residence to the king, the Commune claimed him; and he was delivered up to them, and confined in the Temple, the ancient fortress in which the Valois kept their treasure. They proceeded to suppress the newspapers that were against them, disfranchised the voters who had signed opposing or reactionary petitions, and closed the barriers. They threw their enemies into prison, erected a new tribunal for the punishment of crimes against the Revolution, and supplied it with a new and most efficient instrument which executed its victims painlessly, expeditiously, and on terms conforming to the precept of equality. From the moment of his appearance at the Hôtel de

Ville, the day after the fight was over, Robespierre became the ruling spirit and the organiser, and it was felt at once that, behind the declamations and imprecations of Marat, there was a singularly methodical, consistent, patient, and systematic mind at work, directing the action of the Commune.

The fall of Longwy was known at Paris on August 26. On that day the Minister of Justice, Danton, revised the list of prisoners; domiciliary visits were carried out, all over the city, to search for arms, and for suspected persons. Nearly 3000 were arrested by the 28th, and a thing still more ominous was that many prisoners were released. Nobody doubted, nobody seriously denied, the significance of these measures. The legislature, seeing that this was not the mere frenzy of passion, but a deliberate and settled plan, dissolved the Commune, August 30, and ordered that it should be renewed by a fresh election. They also restored the governing body of the department, as a check on the municipality. They had the law and constitution on their side, and their act was an act of sovereignty. It was the critical and deciding moment in the struggle between the Girondins and the Hôtel de Ville. On the following day, August 31, the Assembly revoked the decree. Tallien read an address, drawn up by Robespierre, declaring that the Commune, just instituted by the people of Paris, with a fresh and definite mandate, could not submit to an assembly which had lost its powers, which had allowed the initiative to pass away from it. The Assembly was entirely helpless, and was too much compromised by its complicity since the 10th of August to resist its master. Robespierre, at the Commune, threatened the Girondins with imprisonment, and, to complete their discomfiture, Brissot's papers were examined, and Roland, Minister of the Interior, was subjected to the same indignity.

In the last days of August, whilst every house was being searched for fugitives, the primary elections were held. The Jacobins were much opposed to the principle of indirect election, but they did not succeed in abolishing it. They instituted universal suffrage for the first stage, and they gave to the primary assemblies a veto on the choice of the second. For the rest, they relied on intimidation. The 800 electors met at the bishop's palace on September 2. But here there was no stranger's gallery, and it was requisite that the nominees of the people should act in the presence of the public that nominated them to do its work. Robespierre proposed that the electoral body should hold its sittings at the Jacobin Club, in the full enjoyment of publicity. On the following day they met at the same place, and proceeded to the Jacobins. Their way led them over the bridge, where a spectacle awaited them which was carefully calculated to assist their deliberations.

They found themselves in the presence of a great number of dead men, deposited from the neighbouring prison.

For this is what had happened. On the 2nd of September Verdun had fallen. This was not yet known at Paris; but it was reported that the Prussians had appeared before the fortress, and that it could not hold out. Verdun was the last barrier on the road to Paris, and the first scene of the war in Belgium made it doubtful whether the new levies would stand their ground against battalions that had been drilled by Frederic. Alarm guns were fired, the tocsin sounded, the black flag proclaimed that the country was in danger, and the men of Paris were summoned by beat of drum to be enrolled for the army of national defence.

Danton, who knew English, and read English books, seems to have remembered a passage in Spenser, when he declared that France must be saved at Paris, and told his terrified hearers to be bold, to be bold, and again to be bold. Then he went off to see to the enrolments, and left the agents of the Commune to accomplish the work appointed for the day. Twenty-four prisoners at the Mairie were removed to the Abbaye, which was the old Benedictine monastery of St. Germain, in hackney coaches; twenty-two of them were priests. Lewis XVI. had fallen because he refused to proscribe the refractory clergy who were accused of spreading discontent. Beyond all men they were identified with the lost cause, and it had been decided that they should be banished. They were imprisoned in large numbers, as a first step towards their expulsion. That group, escorted by Marseilles from the Mairie to the Abbaye, were the first victims. The people, who did not love them, let them pass through the streets without injury; but when they reached their destination, the escorting Marseillais began to plunge their swords into the carriages, and all but three were killed. Two made their way into a room where a commission was sitting, and, by taking seats among the rest, escaped. Sicard, the teacher of the deaf and dumb, was recognised and saved: and it is through him that we know the deeds that were done that day. They were directed by Maillard who proceeded from the abbey to the Carmelites, a prison filled with ecclesiastics, where he sent for the Register, and had them murdered orderly and without tumult. There was a large garden, and sixteen of the prisoners climbed over the wall and got away; fourteen were acquitted; 120 were put to death, and their bones are collected in the chapel, and show the sabre cuts by which they died.

During the absence of Maillard, which lasted three hours, certain unauthorised and self-constituted assassins appeared at the Abbaye and proposed to go on with the work of extermination which he had left unfinished. The gaolers were obliged to deliver up a few prisoners, to save time. When Maillard returned, he established a sort of tribunal for the trial of prisoners, while the murderers, in all something under 200, waited outside and slaughtered those that were given up to them. In the case of the clergy, and of the Swiss survivors of the 4th of August, little formality was observed. At the Abbaye, and at La Force, there were many political prisoners, and of these a certain number were elaborately absolved. Several prisons were left unvisited; but at Bicêtre and the Saltpêtrière, where only the most ignoble culprits were confined, frightful massacres took place.

As this was utterly pointless and unmeaning, it has given currency to the theory that all the horrors of that September were the irrational and spontaneous act of some hundreds of gaolbirds, whose eyes were stained with the vision of blood, and who ran riot in their impunity. So that criminal Paris, not revolutionary Paris, was to blame. In reality, the massacres were organised by the Commune, paid for by the Commune, and directed by its emissaries. We know how much the various agents received, and what was the cost of the whole, from the 2nd of September to the 5th. At first, all was deliberate and methodical, and the women were spared. Several were released at the last moment; some were dismissed by the tribunal before which they appeared. The exception is the Princess de Lamballe, who was the friend of the queen. But as Madame de Tourzel was spared, the cause of her death remains unexplained. Her life had not been entirely free from reproach; and it has been supposed that she was in possession of secrets injurious to the duke of Orleans.

But the problem is not to know why murderers were guilty of murder, but how they allowed many of their captives to be saved. One man made friends with a Marseillais by talking in his native patois. When asked what he was, he replied, "A hearty royalist!" Thereupon Maillard raised his hat and said, "We are here to judge actions, not opinions," and the man was received with acclamation outside by the thirsty executioners. Bertrand, brother of the royalist minister, had the same reception. Two men interrupted their work to see him home. They waited outside whilst he saw his family, and then went away, thanking him for the sight of so much happiness, and refusing a reward. Another prisoner was taken to his house in a cab, with half a dozen dripping patriots crowded on the roof, and hanging on behind. They would accept nothing but a glass of spirits. Few men were in greater danger than Weber, the foster-brother of the queen. He had been on guard at the Tuileries, and was by her side on the funereal march across the gardens from palace to prison. As he well knew what she was leaving, and to what she was going, he was so overcome that Princess Elizabeth whispered to him to control his feelings and be a man. Yet he was one of those who lived to tell the tale of his appearance before the dread tribunal of Maillard. When he was acquitted, the expectant cut-throats were wild with enthusiasm. They cheered him; they gave him the fraternal accolade; they uncovered as he passed along the line; and a voice cried, "Take care where he walks! Don't you see he has got white stockings on?"

One acquittal is remembered beyond all the rest. In every school and in every nursery of France the story continues to be told how Sombreuil, the governor of the Invalides, was acquitted by the judges, but would have been butchered by the mob outside if his daughter had not drunk to the nation in a glass filled with the warm blood of the last victim. They were taken home in triumph. Sombreuil perished in the Reign of Terror. His daughter married, and died at Avignon in 1823, at the height of the royalist reaction. The fame of that heroic moment in her life filled the land, and her heart was brought to Paris, to be laid in the consecrated ground where she had worshipped as a child, and it rests under the same gilded canopy that covers the remains of Napoleon. Many people believe that this is one of the legends of royalism which should be strung with the mock pearls of history. No contemporary mentions it, and it does not appear before 1801. Mlle. de Sombreuil obtained a pension from the Convention, but this was not included in the statement of her claims. An Englishman, who witnessed the release of Sombreuil, only relates that father and daughter were carried away swooning from the strain of emotion. I would not dwell on so well-worn an anecdote if I believed that it was false. The difficulty of disbelief is that the son of the heroine wrote a letter affirming it, in which he states that his mother was never afterwards able to touch a glass of red wine. The point to bear in mind is that these atrocious criminals rejoiced as much in a man to save as in a man to kill. They were servants of a cause, acting under authority.

Robespierre, among the chiefs, seems to have aimed mainly at the destruction of the priests. Others proposed that the prisoners should be confined underground, and that water should be let in until they were drowned. Marat advised that the prisons should be burnt, with their inmates. "The 2nd of September," said Collot d'Herbois, "is the first article of the creed of Liberty. Without it there would be no National Convention." "France," said Danton, in a memorable conversation, "is not republican. We can only establish a Republic by the intimidation of its enemies." They had crushed the Legislature, they had given warning to the Germans that they would not save the king by advancing on the capital when it was in the hands of men capable of such deeds, and they had secured a Jacobin triumph at the Paris election. Marat prepared an address exhorting the departments to imitate their example, and it was sent out under cover from the Ministry of Justice. Danton himself sent out the same orders. Only one copy seems to have been preserved, and it might have been difficult to determine the responsibility of Danton, if he had not avowed to Louis Philippe that he was the author of the massacres of September.

The example of Paris was not widely followed, but the State prisoners at Orleans were brought to Versailles, and there put to death. The whole number killed was between thirteen and fourteen hundred. We have touched low-water mark in the Revolution, and there is nothing worse than this to come. We are in the company of men fit for Tyburn. I need spend no words in impressing on you the fact that these republicans began at once with atrocities as great as those of which the absolute monarchy was justly accused, and for which it justly perished. What we have to fix in our thoughts is this, that the great crimes of the Revolution, and crimes as great as those in the history of other countries, are still defended and justified in almost every group of politicians and historians, so that, in principle, the present is not altogether better than the past.

The massacre was successful at Paris, but not in the rest of France. Under its influence none but Jacobins were elected in the capital. President and vice-president of the Electoral Assembly were Robespierre and Collot d'Herbois, with Marat for secretary. Robespierre was the first deputy returned, Danton was second, Collot third, Manuel fourth, Billaud-Varennes fifth, Camille Desmoulins sixth, and Marat seventh, with a majority over Priestley, who was chosen in two departments, but refused the seat. The twentieth and last of the deputies for Paris was the duke of Orleans.

While the people of Paris sanctioned and approved the murders, it was not the same in the country. In many places the proceedings began with mass, and concluded with a Te Deum. Seventeen bishops were sent to the Convention, and thirty-one priests. Tom Paine, though he could not speak French, was elected in four places. Two-thirds were new members, who had not sat in the previous assemblies. Four-fifths of the primary electors abstained.

The Convention began its sittings, September 20, in the Riding School, where the Législative had met; in the month of May 1793 it adjourned to the Tuileries. There were about fifty or sixty Jacobins. The majority, without being Girondins, were prepared generally to follow, if the Girondins led. Pétion was at once elected president, and all the six secretaries were on the same side. The victory of the Gironde was complete. It had the game in its hands. The party had little cohesion and, in spite of the whispered counsels of Sieyès, no sort of tactics. Excepting Buzot, and perhaps Vergniaud, they scarcely deserve the interest they have excited in later literature, for they had no principles. Embarrassed by the helpless condition of the Législative, they made no resistance to the massacres. When Roland, Condorcet, Gorsas, spoke of them in public, they described them as a dreadful necessity, an act of rude but inevitable justice. Roland, Minister of the Interior, had some of the promoters to dine with him while the bloodshed was going on, and he proposed to draw a decent veil over what had passed. Such men were unfit to compete with Robespierre in ruthless villainy, but they were equally unfit to denounce and to expose him. That was the policy which they attempted, and by which they perished.

The movement towards a permanent Republic was not pronounced, beyond the barrier of Paris. The constituencies made no demand for it, except the Jura. Two others declared against monarchy. Thirty-four departments gave no instructions; thirty-six gave general or unlimited powers. Three, including Paris, required that constitutional decrees should be submitted to popular ratification. The first act of the Convention was to adopt that new principle. By a unanimous vote, on the motion of Danton, they decided that the Constitution must be accepted by the nation in its primary assemblies. But some weeks later, October 16, when Manuel proposed to consult the people on the question of a Republic, the Convention refused. The abolition of monarchy was carried, September 21, without any discussion; for the history of kings, said Bishop Grégoire, is the martyrology of nations. On the 22nd the Republic was proclaimed, under the first impression of the news from Valmy, brought by the future king of the French. The repulse of the invasion provoked by the late government coincided with the establishment of the new.

The Girondins, who were in possession, began with a series of personal attacks on the opposite leaders. They said, what everybody knew, that Marat was an infamous scoundrel, that Danton had not made his accounts clear when he retired from office on entering the Convention, that Robespierre was a common assassin. Some suspicion remained hanging about Danton, but the assailants used their materials with so little skill that they were worsted in the encounter with Robespierre. The Jacobins expelled them from their Club, and Louvet's motion against Robespierre was rejected on November 5. Thus they were weakened already when, on the following day, the question of the trial of the king came on. It was not only the first important stage in the strife of the parties, but it was the decisive one. The question whether Lewis should live or die was no other than the question whether Jacobin or Girondin should survive and govern.

A mighty change occurred in the position of France and in the spirit of the nation, between the events we have just contemplated and the tragedy to which we are coming. In September the German armies were in France, and at first met with no resistance. The peril was evidently extreme, and the only security was the life of the king. Since then the Prussians and Austrians had been ignominiously expelled; Belgium had been conquered; Savoy had been overrun; the Alps and the Rhine as far as Mentz were the frontiers of the Republic. From the German Ocean to the Mediterranean not an army or a fortress had been able to resist the revolutionary arms. The reasonable alarm of September had made way for an exorbitant confidence. There was no fear of all the soldiery of Europe. The French were ready to fight the world, and they calculated that they ran no graver risk than the loss of the sugar islands. It suited their new temper to slay their king, as it had been their policy to preserve him as a hostage. On the 19th of November they offered aid and friendship to every people that determined to be free. This decree, really the beginning of the great war, was caused by remonstrances from Mentz where the French party feared to be abandoned. But it was aimed against England, striking at the weakest point, and reducing its warlike power by encouraging Irish disaffection.

On the 12th of August Rebecqui had proposed that the king should be tried by the Convention that was to meet, and that there should be an appeal to the people. On October 1 the question was brought before the Convention, and a Commission of twenty-four was appointed to examine the evidence. They reported on the 6th of November; and from that moment the matter did not rest. On the following day, Mailhe, in the name of the jurists, reported that there was no legal obstacle, from the inviolability acknowledged by the Constitution. Mousson replied that since Lewis was deposed, he had no further responsibility. A very young member sprang suddenly into notoriety, on the 13th, by arguing that there was no question of justice and its forms; a king deserved death not for what he did, but for what he was. The speaker's name was St. Just. On November 20, before the debate had gone either way, Roland appeared, with news of an important discovery. The king had an iron safe in his palace, which the locksmith had betrayed. Roland had found that it contained 625 documents. A committee of twelve was directed to examine them, and they found the proofs of a great scheme of corruption, and of the venality of Mirabeau. On December 3 it was resolved that the king should be tried by the Convention; the order of proceedings was determined on the 6th, and on the 10th the indictment was brought in. On the next day Lewis appeared before his judges, and was interrogated by the President. He said, in his replies, that he knew nothing of an iron safe, and had never given money to Mirabeau, or to any deputy. When he got back to prison the unhappy man exclaimed, "They asked questions for which I was so little prepared that I denied my own hand." Ten days were allowed to prepare the defence. He was assisted by Malesherbes, by the famous jurist Tronchet, and by Desèze, a younger man, who made the speech. It was unconvincing, for the advocates perceived, no better than their client, where the force and danger of the accusation lay.

Everybody believed that Lewis had brought the invader into the country, but it was not proved in evidence. If the proofs since published had been known at the time, the defence must have been confined to the plea that the king was inviolable; and the answer would have been that he is covered by the responsibility of ministers, but responsible for what he does behind their back. At the last moment several Girondins proposed that sentence should be pronounced by the nation, in primary assemblies — an idea put forward by Faure on November 29. This was contrary to the spirit of representative democracy, which consults the electors as to men, and not as to measures properly the result of debate. It was consistent with the direct action of Democracy, which was the theory of Jacobinism. But the Jacobins would not have it. By compelling the vote on the capital question, they would ruin their adversaries. If the Girondins voted for death, they would follow the train of the party that resolutely insisted on it. If they voted against, they could be accused of royalism. When the question "Guilty or not guilty?" was put, there was no hesitation; 683 voted guilty, one man, Lanjuinais, answering that he was a legislator, not a judge. The motion, to leave the penalty to the people, which was made in the interest of the Girondins, not of the king, failed by 423 to 281, and ruined the party that contrived it. The voting on the penalty began on the evening of January 17, and as each man gave his voice from the tribune, it lasted far into the following day. Vergniaud declared the result; he said that there was a majority of five for death. Both parties were dissatisfied, and suspected fraud. A scrutiny was held, and it then appeared that those who had voted simply for the capital penalty were 361, and that those who had voted otherwise were 360. Majority, 1. But when the final vote was taken on the question of delay, there was a majority of 70 for immediate execution.

That the decision was the result of fear has been stated, even by Brissot and Carnot. The duke of Orleans had written to the President that he could not vote at the trial of his kinsman. The letter was returned to him. He promised his son that he would not vote for death, and when they met again exclaimed, "I am not worthy to be your father!" At dinner, on the fatal day, Vergniaud declared that he would defend the king's life, even if he stood alone. A few hours later he voted for death. Yet Vergniaud was soon to prove that he was not a man whom intimidation influenced. The truth is, that nobody had a doubt as to guilt. Punishment was a question rather of policy than of justice.

The army was inclined to the side of mercy. Custine had offered, November 23, to save Lewis, if Prussia would acknowledge the Republic. The offer was made in vain. Dumouriez came to Paris in January, and found that there was nothing to be done. He said afterwards, "It is true he was a perfidious scoundrel, but it was folly to cut his head off." The Spanish Bourbons made every effort to save the head of the house. They offered neutrality and mediation, and they empowered their agent to spend hundreds of thousands of pounds in opportune bribery. They promised, if Lewis was delivered up to them, that they would prevent him from ever interfering in French affairs, and would give hostages for his good behaviour. They entreated George III. to act with them in a cause which was that of monarchy and of humanity. Lansdowne, Sheridan, and Fox urged the government to interpose. Grenville made known that peace would be preserved if France gave up her conquests, but he said not a word for the king. Information was brought to Pitt, from a source that could be trusted, that Danton would save him for £40,000. When he made up his mind to give the money, Danton replied that it was too late. Pitt explained to the French diplomatist Maret, afterwards Prime Minister, his motive for hesitation. The execution of the king of France would raise such a storm in England that the Whigs would be submerged.

Lewis was resigned to his fate, but he expected that he would be spared, and he spoke of retiring to the Sierra Morena, or of seeking a retreat for his old age among the faithful republicans of Switzerland. When his advocates came to tell him that there was no hope, he refused to believe them. "You are mistaken," he said; "they would never dare." He quickly recovered his composure, and declined to ask permission to see his family. "I can wait," he said; "in a few days they will not refuse me." A priest who applied for leave to attend him was sent to prison. As a foreigner was less likely to be molested, the king asked for the *abbé* Edgeworth, of Firmount, who had passed his life in France, but might be considered an Irishman. Garat, the Minister of the Interior, went to fetch him. On their way he said, "He was weak when in power; but you will see how great he is, now that he is in chains."

On the following day Lewis was taken through a vast parade of military and cannon to the scaffold in the Place de la Concorde, a little nearer to the Champs Elysées than the place where the obelisk of Luxor stands. He was nearly an hour on the way. The Spanish envoy had not made terms with the agents who were attracted by the report of his unlimited credit, and he spent his doubloons in a frantic attempt at rescue as the prisoner passed, at a foot pace, along the Boulevard. An equivocal adventurer, the Baron de Batz, who helped to organise the rising of Vendémiaire, which only failed because it encountered Bonaparte, had undertaken to break the line, with four or five hundred men. They were to make a rush from a side street. But every street was patrolled and every point was guarded as the coach went by carrying the prisoner. De Batz was true to the rendezvous, and stood up waving a sword and crying, "Follow me and save the king!" It was without effect; he vanished in the crowd; one companion was taken and guillotined, but the police were able to report that no incident had occurred on the way.

Not the royalists but the king served the royal cause on that 21st of January. Unequal to his duties on the throne, he found, in prison and on the scaffold, a part worthy of the better qualities of his race, justifying the words of Louis Blanc, "None but the dead come back." To absolve him is impossible, for we know, better than his persecutors, how he intrigued to recover uncontrolled authority by bringing havoc and devastation upon the people over whom he reigned. The crowning tragedy is not that which Paris witnessed, when Santerre raised his sword, commanding the drums to beat, which had been silenced by the first word of the dying speech; it is that Lewis XVI. met his fate with inward complacency, unconscious of guilt, blind to the opportunities he had wasted and the misery he had caused, and died a penitent Christian but an unrepentant king.

XVII
THE FALL OF THE GIRONDE

The Constitution of 1791 had failed because it carried the division of powers and the reaction against monarchical centralisation so far as to paralyse the executive. Until the day when a new system should be organised, a series of revolutionary measures were adopted, and by these the Convention governed to the end. Immediately after the death of Lewis XVI. they began to send out representatives with arbitrary powers to the departments. The revolutionary tribunal was appointed in March to judge political cases without appeal; and the Secret Committee of Public Safety in April, on the defeat and defection of Dumouriez. All this time, the Girondins had the majority. The issue of the king's trial had been disastrous to them, because it proved their weakness, not in numbers, but in character and counsel. Roland at once resigned, confessing the defeat. But they stood four months before their fall. During that memorable struggle, the question was whether France should be ruled by violence and blood, or by men who knew the passion for freedom. The Girondins at once raised the real issue by demanding inquiry into the massacres of September. It was a valid but a perilous weapon. There could be no doubt as to what those who had committed a thousand murders to obtain power would be capable of doing in their own defence.

The Girondins calculated badly. By leaving crime unpunished they could have divided their adversaries. Almost to the last moment Danton wished to avoid the conflict. Again and again they rejected his offers. Open war, said Vergniaud, is better than a hollow truce. Their rejection of the hand that bore the crimson stain is the cause of their ruin, but also of their renown. They were always impolitic, disunited, and undecided; but they rose, at times, to the level of honest men. Their second line of attack was not better chosen. Party politics were new, and the science of understanding the other side was not developed; and the Girondins were persuaded that the Montagnards were at heart royalists, aiming at the erection of an Orleanist throne. Marat received money from the Palais Royal; and Sieyès to the last regarded him as a masked agent of monarchy. Danton himself assured the young Duc de Chartres that the Republic would not last, and advised him to hold himself in readiness to reap, some day, what the Jacobins were sowing.

The aim of the Jacobins was a dictatorship, which was quite a new substitute for monarchy, and the Orleans spectre was no more than an illusion on which the Gironde spent much of its strength. In retaliation, they were accused of Federalism, and this also was a false suspicion. Federal ideas, the characteristic of America, had the sanction of the greatest names in the political literature of France—Montesquieu and Rousseau, Necker and Mirabeau. The only evident Federalist in the Convention is Barère. A scheme of federation was discussed at the Jacobins on September 10, and did not come to a vote. But the idea was never adopted by the Girondin party, or by any one of its members, with the exception of Buzot. They favoured things just as bad in Jacobin eyes. They inclined to decentralisation, to local liberties, to restraint on the overwhelming activity of Paris, to government by representatives of the sovereign people, not by the sovereign itself. All this was absolutely opposed to the concentration of all powers, which was the prevailing purpose since the alarm of invasion and treason, and was easily confounded with the theory of provincial rights and divided authority, which was dreaded as the superlative danger of the time. That which, under the title of Federalism, was laid to their charge, must be counted to their credit; for it meant that, in a limited sense, they were constitutional, and that there were degrees of power and oppression, which even a Girondin would resist.

The Jacobins had this superiority over their fluctuating opponents, that they fell back on a system which was simple, which was intelligible, and which the most famous book of the previous generation had made known to everybody. For them there was no uncertainty, no groping, and no compromise. They intended that the mass of the people should at all times assert and enforce their will, over-riding all temporary powers and superseding all appointed agents. As they had to fight the world with a divided population, they required that all power should be concentrated in the hands of those who acted in conformity with the popular will, and that those who resisted at home, should be treated as enemies. They must put down opposition as ruthlessly as they repelled invasion. The better Jacobin would not have denied liberty, but he would have defined it differently. For him it consisted not in the limitation, but the composition of the governing power. He would not weaken the state by making its action uncertain, slow, capricious, dependent on alternate majorities and rival forces; but he would find security in power exercised only by the whole body of the nation, united in the enjoyment of the gifts the Revolution had bestowed on the peasant. That was the most numerous class, the class whose interests were the same, which was identified with the movement against privilege, which would inevitably be true to the new institutions. They were a minority in the Convention, but a minority representing the unity and security of the Republic, and supported by the majority outside. They drew to themselves not the best or the most brilliant men, but those who devoted themselves to the use of power, not to the manipulation of ideas. Many good administrators belonged to the party, among whom Carnot is only the most celebrated. Napoleon, who understood talent and said that no men were so vigorous and efficient as those who had gone through the Revolution, gave office to 127 regicides, most of whom were Montagnards.

The Girondins, vacillating and divided, would never have made the Republic triumph over the *whole* of Europe and the half of France. They were immediately confronted by a general war and a formidable insurrection. They were not afraid of war. The great military powers were Austria and Prussia, and they had been driven to the Rhine by armies of thirty or forty thousand men. After that, the armies of Spain and England did not seem formidable. This calculation proved to be correct. The audacity of the French appeared in their declaration of war against the three chief maritime powers at once—England, Spain, and Holland. It was not until 1797, not for four years, that the superiority of the British fleet was established. They had long hoped that war with England could be avoided, and carried on negotiations through a succession of secret agents. There was a notion that the English government was revolutionary in character as it was in origin, that the execution of the king was done in pursuance of English examples, that a Protestant country must admire men who followed new ideas. Brissot, like Napoleon in 1815, built his hopes on the opposition. Mr. Fox could not condemn the institution of a Republic; and a party that had applauded American victories over their own countrymen might be expected to feel some sympathy with a country which was partly imitating England and partly America.

War with continental absolutism was the proper price of revolution; but the changes since 1789 were changes in the direction of a Whig alliance. When the Convention were informed that George III. would not have a regicide minister in the country, they did not debate the matter, but passed it over to a committee. They acted not only from a sense of national dignity, but in the belief that the event was not very terrible. The Girondins thought that the war would not be popular in England, that the Whigs, the revolutionary societies, and the Irish, would bring it to an early termination. Marat, who knew this country, affirmed that it was an illusion. But there was no opposition to the successive declarations of war with England, Holland, and the Spanish and Neapolitan Bourbons, which took place in February and March. Eight hundred million of *assignats* were voted at once, to be secured on the confiscated property of the *émigrés*. France, at that moment, had only 150,000 soldiers in the field. On February 24, a decree called out 300,000 men, and obliged each department to raise its due proportion. The French army that was to accomplish such marvels in the next twenty years, begins on that day. But the first consequence was an extraordinary diminution in the military power of the State. The Revolution had done much for the country people, and had imposed no burdens upon them. The compulsory levy was the first. In most places, with sufficient pressure, the required men were supplied. Some districts offered more than their proper number.

On March 10, the Conscription was opened in the remote parishes of Poitou. The country had been agitated for some time. The peasants, for there were no large towns in that region, had resented the overthrow of the nobility, of the clergy, and of the throne. The expulsion of their priests caused constant discontent. And now the demand that they should go out, under officers whom they distrusted, and die for a government which persecuted them, caused an outbreak. They refused to draw their numbers, and on the following day they gathered in large crowds and fell upon the two sorts of men they detested—the government officials, and the newly established clergy. Before the middle of March about three hundred priests and republican officials were murdered, and the war of La Vendée began. And it was there, and not in Paris, that liberty made its last stand in revolutionary France.

But we must see first what passed in the Convention under the shadow of the impending struggle. A committee had been appointed, October 11, to draw up a constitution for the Republic. Danton was upon it, but he was much away, with the army in Belgium. Tom Paine brought illumination from America, and Barère, generally without ideas of his own, made others' plausible. The majority were Girondins, and with them Sieyès was closely associated. On February 15, Condorcet produced the report. It was the main attempt of the Girondins to consolidate their power, and for three months it occupied the leisure of the Convention. The length of the debate proved the weakness of the party. Robespierre and his friends opposed the work of their enemies, and talked it out. They devoted their arguments to the preamble, the new formula of the Rights of Man, and succeeded so well that no part of the Constitution ever came to a vote. The most interesting portion of the debate turned upon the principle of religious liberty, which the draft affirmed, and which was opposed by Vergniaud. Whilst this ineffectual discussion proceeded, the fight was waged decisively elsewhere, and the Jacobins delivered a counterstroke of superior force.

Dumouriez's reverses had begun, and there was new urgency in the demand for concentration. Danton came to an understanding with Robespierre, and they decided on establishing the revolutionary tribunal. It was to consist of judges appointed by the Convention to try prisoners whom the Convention sent before it, and to judge without appeal. Danton said that it was a necessary measure, in order to avert popular violence and vengeance. He recommended it in the name of humanity. When the Convention heard Danton speak of humanity there was a shudder, and in the midst of a dead silence Lanjuinais uttered the word "September." Danton replied that there would have been no massacres if the new tribunal had been instituted at the time. The Convention resolved that there should be trial by jury, and that no deputies should be tried without their permission. The object of Robespierre was not obtained. He had meant that the revolutionary tribunal should judge without a jury, and should have jurisdiction over the deputies. The Girondins were still too strong for him. Danton next addressed himself to them. They agreed that there should be a strong committee to supervise and control the government. On March 25 they carried a list of twenty-five, composed largely of their own friends, and, by thus subjecting the Assembly at large to a committee, they once more recovered supreme power. Immediately after, the defection of Dumouriez was reported at Paris, and the Convention rightly believed that they had narrowly escaped a great danger. For Dumouriez had intended to unite all the forces he could collect in the Dutch and Belgian Netherlands, and to march into France at their head, to establish a government of his own. He had been in close communication with Danton, and the opportunity of attacking Danton was too good to be lost. On April 1 Lasource accused him of complicity in the treason. The truce between them was at an end, and the consequences were soon apparent. The committee of twenty-five was too bulky, and was made up from different parties. A proposal was made to reduce the number, and on April 6 a new committee of nine, the real Committee of Public Safety, was elected, and no Girondins were included in it. On the same day the first execution took place of a prisoner sentenced by the new tribunal. The two chief instruments of the revolutionary government were brought into action at the same time. But they did not enable the Jacobins to reach their enemies in the Assembly, for the deputies were inviolable. Everybody else was at the mercy of the public accuser.

The Girondins, having failed in their attack on Danton, now turned against Marat, and by 220 to 132 votes sent him before the revolutionary tribunal to be tried for sedition. On the 24th he was acquitted. Meantime his friends petitioned against the Girondins, and demanded that twenty-two of them should be expelled. The petition was rejected, after a debate in which Vergniaud refused to have the fate of his party decided by primary assemblies, on the ground that it would lead to civil war. Vendée was in flames, and the danger of explosion was felt in many parts of France.

Down to the month of May, the Girondins had failed in their attacks on individual deputies, but their position in the Assembly was unshaken. By their divisions, and by means of occasional majorities, especially by the uncertain and intermittent help of Danton, Robespierre had carried important measures—the Revolutionary Tribunal, the Committee of Public Safety, the employment of commissaries from the Convention to enforce the levies in each department. By a series of acceptable decrees in favour of the indigent, he had established himself and his friends as the authors of a new order of society, against the representatives of the middle class. The people of Paris responded by creating an insurrectionary committee to accomplish, by lawful pressure or otherwise, the purpose of the deputation which had demanded the exclusion of the twenty-two. On May 21 a commission of twelve was appointed to vindicate the supremacy of the Convention against the municipality. The Girondins obtained the majority. Their candidates received from 104 to 325 votes. No Jacobin had more than 98. It was their last parliamentary victory. There was no legal way of destroying them. The work had to be left to agitators like Marat, and the committee of insurrection. When this came to be understood, the end was very near. The committee of twelve, the organ of the Convention and of the moderate part of it, arrested several of the most violent agitators. On May 26, Robespierre summoned the people of Paris against the traitorous deputies. Next day they appeared, made their way into the Convention, and stated their demands. The men were released, and the commission of twelve was dissolved. But on the 28th the Assembly, ashamed of having yielded tamely to a demonstration which was not overwhelming, renewed the commission, by 279 votes to 239.

A more decisive action was now resolved upon, and the Jacobins prepared what they called a moral insurrection. They desired to avoid bloodshed, for the tenure by which the Revolutionary Tribunal existed was that it prevented the shedding of blood otherwise than by legal forms. The Girondins, after expulsion, could be left to the enjoyment of all the securities of a trial by jury. Meanwhile, the Girondin scheme of Constitution was dropped, and five new members were appointed to draw up a new one; and on May 30, for the first time, a president was taken from the deputies of the Mountain. On May 31 the insurrectionary masses invaded the Assembly. There was no actual violence, and no resistance. The Girondins did nothing to defend their cause, and their commission of twelve was again dissolved. The deputies remained uninjured; but Roland fled, and his wife was sent to prison. Two days later, June 2, the victory of moral force was completed. The Tuileries were surrounded with cannon, the deputies were not permitted to go out, and some of the Girondins agreed to resign their seats in order to prevent an outbreak. It was called a voluntary ostracism.

In the extreme weakness of the party Lanjuinais alone spoke and acted with courage and decision. Legendre went up to the Tribune while he was speaking, and threatened to kill him. As Legendre was a butcher, Lanjuinais replied, "First decree that I am a bullock." When Chabot, who had been a Capuchin, reviled the fallen statesmen, Lanjuinais exclaimed, "The ancients crowned their victims with flowers, and the priest did not insult them." This brave man lived through it all, lived to witness the destruction of his enemies, to be the elect of many departments, and to preside over the Chamber that decreed the downfall of Napoleon. At the last moment, an obscure supporter of the Girondins saw Danton, and called on him to interfere to save the Convention from violence. Danton answered that he could do nothing, for they had no confidence in him. It is a redeeming testimony. On the evening of June 2 the more conspicuous Girondins, without being sent to prison, were placed under arrest. In the capital, the victory of the Jacobins was complete. They had conquered by the aid of the insurrectionary committee, to which no man was admitted who did not swear approval of the September murders.

Rout and extermination ensued upon the fall of the Gironde. They had been scrupulous not to defend themselves by force, and preferred the Republic to their party. While some remained as hostages in the power of the foe, others went away to see what France would think of the mutilation of its parliament. Their strength was in departments, and in several departments the people were arming. In the west there was no hope for them, for they had made the laws against which La Vendée rebelled. They turned to the north. In Normandy the royalists were forming an army, under the famous intriguer, Puisaye. Between such a man and Buzot no understanding could subsist. There was no time for them to quarrel, for the movement broke down at once. The people of Normandy were quite indifferent. But there was one among them who had spirit, and energy, and courage, and passion enough to change the face of France. This extraordinary person was the daughter of M. d'Armont, and she passed into the immortality of history as Charlotte Corday. She was twenty-four. Her father was a royalist, but she had read Raynal, and had the classical enthusiasm which was bred by Plutarch in those as well as in other days. She had refused the health of Lewis XVI., because, she said, he was a good man, but a bad king. She preferred to live with a kinswoman, away from her own family, and her mind was made up never to marry. Her bringing up had been profoundly religious, but that influence seems to have been weakened in her new home. There is no trace of it during the five days on which a fierce light beats. In her room they found her Bible lying open at the story of Judith. From the 31st of May she had learnt to regard Marat as the author of the proscription of the Girondins, some of whom had appeared at Caen in a patriotic halo. When the troops were paraded, on July 7, those who volunteered for the march against Paris were so few that the hope of deeds to be done by armed men utterly vanished. It occurred to Charlotte that there may be something stronger than the hands and the hearts of armed men. The Girondins were in the power of assassins, of men against whom there was no protection in France but the dagger. To take a life was the one way of saving many lives. Not a doubt ever touched her that it is right to kill a murderer, an actual and intending murderer, on condition of accepting the penalty. She told no one of the resolution in her mind, and said nothing that was pathetic, and nothing that was boastful. She only replied to Pétion's clumsy pleasantries: "Citizen, you speak like that because you do not understand me. One day, you will know." Under a harmless pretext she went to Paris, and saw one of the Girondin deputies. In return for some civility, she advised him to leave at once for Caen. His friends were arrested, and his papers were already seized, but he told her that he could not desert the post of duty. Once more, she cried, "Believe me, fly before to-morrow night!" He did not understand, and he was one of the famous company that mounted the scaffold with

Vergniaud. Next morning, Saturday July 13, Charlotte purchased her dagger, and called on Marat. Although he was in the bath where he spent most of his time, she made her way in, and explained her importunity by telling him about the conspirators she had seen in Normandy. Marat took down their names, and assured her that in a few days he would have them guillotined. At that signal she drove her knife into his heart. When the idiotic accuser-general intimated that so sure a thrust could only have been acquired by practice, she exclaimed, "The monster! He takes me for a murderess." All that she felt was that she had taken one life to preserve thousands. She was knocked down and carried through a furious crowd to prison. At first she was astonished to be still alive. She had expected to be torn in pieces, and had hoped that the respectable inhabitants, when they saw her head displayed on a pike, would remember it was for them that her young life was given. Of all murderers, and of all victims, Charlotte Corday was the most composed. When the executioner came for the toilette, she borrowed his shears to cut off a lock of her hair. As the cart moved slowly through the raging streets, he said to her, "You must find the way long." "No," she answered, "I am not afraid of being late." They say that Vergniaud pronounced this epitaph: "She has killed us, but she has taught us all how to die."

After the failure in Normandy, of which this is the surviving episode, Buzot and his companions escaped by sea to the Gironde. Having been outlawed, on July 28, they were liable to suffer death without a trial, and had to hide in out-houses and caverns. Nearly all were taken. Barbaroux, who had brought the Marseillais, shot himself at the moment of capture, but had life enough to be carried to the scaffold. Buzot and Pétion outlived their downfall for a year. Towards the end of the Reign of Terror, snarling dogs attracted notice to a remote spot in the south-west. There the two Girondins were found, and recognised, though their faces had been eaten away. Before he went out to die, Buzot placed in safety the letters of Madame Roland. Seventy years later they came to light at a sale, and the suspected secret of her life told in her *Memoirs*, but suppressed by the early editors, was revealed to the world. She had been executed on November 10, 1793, four days after the Duke of Orleans, and the cheerful dignity of her last moments has reconciled many who were disgusted with her declamatory emphasis, her passion, and her inhumanity. Her husband was safe in his place of concealment near Rouen; but when he heard, he ran himself through with a sword-cane. The main group had died a few days earlier. Of 180 Girondin deputies, 140 were imprisoned or dispersed, and 24 of these managed to escape; 73 were arrested at Paris, October 3, but were not brought to trial; 21, among whom were many celebrities, went before the revolutionary tribunal, October 24, and a week later they were put to death. Their trial was irregular, even if their fate was not undeserved. With Vergniaud, Brissot, and their companions the practice began of sending numbers to the guillotine at once. There were 98 in the five months that followed.

During the agony of his party, Condorcet found shelter in a lodging-house at Paris. There, under the Reign of Terror, he wrote the little book on Human Progress, which contains his legacy to mankind. He derived the leading idea from his friend Turgot, and transmitted it to Comte. There may be, perhaps, a score or two dozen decisive and characteristic views that govern the world, and that every man should master in order to understand his age, and this is one of them. When the book was finished, the author's part was played, and he had nothing more to live for. As his retreat was known to one, at least, of the Montagnards, he feared to compromise those who had taken him in at the risk of their life. Condorcet assumed a disguise, and crept out of the house with a Horace in one pocket and a dose of poison in the other. When it was dark, he came to a friend's door in the country. What passed there has never been known, but the fugitive philosopher did not remain. A few miles outside Paris he was arrested on suspicion and lodged in the gaol. In the morning they found him lying dead. Cabanis, who afterwards supplied Napoleon in like manner, had given him the means of escape.

This was the miserable end of the Girondin party. They were easily beaten and mercilessly destroyed, and no man stirred to save them. At their fall liberty perished; but it had become a feeble remnant in their hands, and a spark almost extinguished. Although they were not only weak but bad, no nation ever suffered a greater misfortune than that which befell France in their defeat and destruction. They had been the last obstacle to the Reign of Terror, and to the despotism which then by successive steps centred in Robespierre.

XVIII
THE REIGN OF TERROR

The liberal and constitutional wave with which the Revolution began ended with the Girondins; and the cause of freedom against authority, of right against force was lost. At the moment of their fall, Europe was in arms against France by land and sea; the royalists were victorious in the west; the insurrection of the south was spreading, and Précy held Lyons with 40,000 men. The majority, who were masters in the Convention, had before them the one main purpose of increasing and concentrating power, that the country might be saved from dangers which, during those months of summer, threatened to destroy it. That one supreme and urgent purpose governed resolutions and inspired measures for the rest of the year, and resulted in the method of government which we call the Reign of Terror. The first act of the triumphant Mountain was to make a Constitution. They had criticized and opposed the Girondin draft, in April and May, and only the new declaration of the Rights of Man had been allowed to pass. All this was now re-opened. The Committee of Public Safety, strengthened by the accession of five Jacobins, undertook to prepare a scheme adapted to the present conditions, and embodying the principles which had prevailed. Taking Condorcet's project as their basis, and modifying it in the direction which the Jacobin orators had pointed to in debate, they achieved their task in a few days, and they laid their proposals before the Convention on June 10. The reporter was Hérault de Séchelles; but the most constant speaker in the ensuing debate was Robespierre. After a rapid discussion, but with some serious amendments, the Republican Constitution of 1793 was adopted, on June 24. Of all the fruits of the Revolution this is the most characteristic, and it is superior to its reputation.

The Girondins, by their penman Condorcet, had omitted the name of God, and had assured liberty of conscience only as liberty of opinion. They elected the executive and the legislative alike by direct vote of the entire people, and gave the appointment of functionaries to those whom they were to govern. Primary assemblies were to choose the Council of Ministers, and were to have the right of initiating laws. The plan restricted the power of the State in the interest of decentralisation. The Committee, while retaining much of the scheme, guarded against the excess of centrifugal forces. They elected the legislature by direct universal suffrage, disfranchised domestic servants, and made the ballot optional, and therefore illusory. They resolved that the supreme executive council of twenty-four should be nominated by the legislature from a list of candidates, one chosen by indirect voting in each department, and should appoint and control all ministers and executive officers; the legislature to issue decrees with force of law in all necessary matters; but to make actual laws only under popular sanction, given or implied. In this way they combined direct democracy with representative democracy. They restricted the suffrage, abolished the popular initiative, limited the popular sanction, withdrew the executive patronage from the constituency, and destroyed secret voting. Having thus provided for the composition of power, they proceeded in the interest of personal liberty. The Press was to be free, there was to be entire religious toleration, and the right of association. Education was to become universal, and there was to be a poor law; in case of oppression, insurrection was declared a duty as well as a right, and usurpation was punishable with death. All laws were temporary, and subject to constant revision. Robespierre, who had betrayed socialist inclinations in April, revoked his earlier language, and now insisted on the security of property, proportionate and not progressive taxation, and the refusal of exemptions to the poor. In April, an unknown deputy from the Colonies had demanded that the Divinity be recognised in the preamble, and in June, after the elimination of the Girondins, the idea was adopted. At the same time, inverting the order of things, equality was made the first of the Rights of Man, and Happiness, instead of Liberty, was declared the supreme end of civil society. In point of spiritual quality, nothing was gained by the invocation of the Supreme Being.

Hérault proposed that a Grand Jury should be elected by the entire nation to hear complaints against the government or its agents, and to decide which cases should be sent for trial. The plan belonged to Sieyès, and was supported by Robespierre. When it was rejected, he suggested that each deputy should be judged by his constituency, and if censured, should be ineligible elsewhere. This was contrary to the principle that a deputy belongs to the whole nation, and ought to be elected by the nation, but for the practical difficulty which compels the division into separate constituencies. The end was, that the deputies remained inviolable, and subject to no check, although the oldest member, a man so old that he might very well have remembered Lewis XIV., spoke earnestly in favour of the Grand Jury.

The Constitution wisely rescinded the standing offer of support to insurgent nations, and renounced all purpose of intervention or aggression. When the passage was read declaring that there could be no peace with an invader, a voice cried, "Have you made a contract with victory?" "No," replied Bazire; "we have made a contract with death." A criticism immediately appeared, which was anonymous, but in which the hand of Condorcet was easily recognised. He complained that judges were preferred to juries, that functionaries were not appointed by universal suffrage, that there was no fixed term of revision, that the popular sanction of laws was reduced to a mere form. Condorcet believed that nearly all inequality of fortune, such as causes suffering, is the effect of imperfect laws, and that the end of the social art is to reduce it. There were others who objected that the Constitution did not benefit the poor. In regard to property, as in other things, it was marked by a pronounced Conservatism. It was adopted by a national vote of 1,801,918 to 11,610, and, with solemn rites, was inaugurated on August 10. No term was fixed for it to come into operation. The friends of Danton spoke of an early dissolution, but the Convention refused to be dissolved, and the Constitution was never executed. Although other acts of the legislature at that time are still good law, French jurists do not appeal to the great constitutional law of June 24 and August 10, 1793. In the course of the autumn, October 10 and December 4, it was formally suspended, and was never afterwards restored. France was governed, not by this instrument, but by a series of defining enactments, which created extraordinary powers, and suppressed opposition.

After the integrity of the Assembly, the next thing to perish was the liberty of the Press. The journalists could not claim the sanctity which had been violated in the representatives, and gave way. Marat remained, and exercised an influence in Paris which his activity on June 2 increased. He had his own following, in the masses, and his own basis of power, and he was not a follower of either Danton or Robespierre. By his share in the fall of the Girondins he became their equal. When he died, the vacant place, in the Press and in the street, was at once occupied by a lesser rival, Hébert. In a little time, Hébert acquired enormous power. Marat's newspaper had seldom paid its way; but Hébert used to print 600,000 copies of the *Père Duchesne*. Through his ally Chaumette, he controlled the municipality of Paris, and all that depended from it. Through Bouchotte and Vincent, he managed the War Office, with its vast patronage and command of money, and distributed his journal in every camp. To a man of order and precision like Robespierre, the personage was odious, for he was anarchical and corrupt, and was the urgent patron of incapable generals; but Robespierre could not do without his support in the Press, and was obliged to conciliate him. Between Hébert and Danton there was open war, and Danton had not the best of it. He had been weakened by the overthrow of the Girondins whom he wished to save, and was forced to abandon. In the Convention, he was still the strongest figure, and at times could carry all before him. But when he lost his seat on the governing Committee, and was without official information, he was no match at last for Robespierre. All through the summer he was evidently waning, whilst the Confederates, Chaumette, Hébert, and Vincent, became almost invincible.

On the 10th of July the Committee of Public Safety, after acting as a Committee of Legislation, was recomposed as an executive body. There had been fourteen members, there were now nine. Barère had the highest vote, 192; St. Just had only 126; and Danton was not elected. The influence of Robespierre was supreme; he himself became a member, on a vacancy, July 27. The fortunes of France were then at their lowest. The Vendeans were unconquered, Lyons was not taken, and the Austrians and English had broken through the line of fortresses, and were making slowly for Paris. A few months saw all this changed, and those are the earlier months of the predominance of Robespierre, with his three powerful instruments, the Committee of Public Safety, the Revolutionary Tribunal, and the Jacobin Club, which made him master of the Convention. On July 27, the day before he was elected to the Committee, an important change occurred. For the first time, an order was sent from the Tuileries to the army on the frontier, in a quarter of an hour. This was the beginning of the semaphore telegraph, and science was laying hold of the Revolution. On August 1, the metrical system was introduced, and the republican calendar followed; but we shall speak of it in another connection.

In the middle of August, Prieur, an engineer officer, was elected to the Committee, to conduct the business of war; but Prieur protested that he was the wrong man, and advised them to take Carnot. Therefore, August 15, very much against the wish of Robespierre, the organiser of victory joined the government. The Hébertists had proposed that the entire population should be forced into the army, more particularly the richer class. Danton modified the proposal into something reasonable, and on August 23, Carnot drew up the decree which was called the *levée en masse*. It turned France into a nominal nation of soldiers. Practically, it called out the first class, from eighteen to twenty-five, and ordered the men of the second class, from twenty-five to thirty, to be ready. It is to Danton and Carnot that France owed the army which was to overrun the Continent; and by the end of the year the best soldiers in the world, Hoche, Moreau, Masséna, Bonaparte, were being raised to command.

On August 9, an event occurred in the civil order which influenced the future of mankind as widely as the creation of the French army. While the Committee of Public Safety was busy with the Constitution, the Committee of Legislation was employed in drawing up a Code of Civil Law, which was the basis of the Code Napoleon. Cambacérès, who, with the same colleagues, afterwards completed the work, presented it in its first form on that day. Lastly, August 24, Cambon, the financial adviser of the Republic, achieved the conversion and unification of the Public Debt.

These were the great measures, undertaken and accomplished by the men who accepted the leadership of Robespierre, in the first weeks of his government. We come to those by which he consolidated his power.

At the beginning of September, the Committee was increased by the admission of Billaud-Varennes, and of Collot d'Herbois, of whom one afterwards overthrew Danton, and the other, Robespierre. The appointment of Collot was a concession to Hébert. The same party were persuaded that the hands of government were weak, and ought to be strengthened against its enemies. Danton himself said that every day one aristocrat, one villain, ought to pay for his crimes with his head. Two measures were at once devised which were well calculated to achieve that object. September 5, the Revolutionary Tribunal was remodelled, and instead of one Revolutionary Tribunal, there were four. And on September 17 the Law of Suspects was passed, enabling local authorities to arrest whom they pleased, and to detain him in prison even when acquitted. In Paris, where there had been 1877 prisoners on September 13, there were 2975 on October 20. On September 25, the mismanagement of the Vendean War, where even the Mentz garrison had been defeated, led to a sharp debate in the Convention. It was carried away by the attack of the Dantonists; but Robespierre snatched a victory, and obtained a unanimous vote of confidence. From that date to the 26th of July 1794, we count the days of his established reign, and the Convention makes way for the Committee of Public Safety, which becomes a Provisional government.

The party of violence insisted on the death of those whom they regarded as hostages, the Girondins, for the rising in the south, the queen for the rising in the west. An attempt to save the life of Marie Antoinette had been made by the government, with the sanction of Danton. Maret was sent to negotiate the neutrality of minor Italian States by offering to release her. Austria, not wishing the Italians to be neutral, seized Maret and his companion Sémonville, in the passes of the Grisons, and sent them to a dungeon at Mantua. The queen was sent to the Conciergerie, which was the last stage before the Tribunal; and as her nephew, the emperor, did not relent, in October she was put on her trial, and executed. The death of the queen is revolting, because it was a move in a game, a concession by which Robespierre paid his debts to men at that time more violent than himself, and averted their attack. We have already seen that the advice she gave in decisive moments was disastrous, that she had no belief in the rights of nations, that she plotted war and destruction against her own people. There was cause enough for hatred. But if we ask ourselves who there is that comes forth unscathed from the trials that befell kings and queens in those or even in other times, and remember how often she pleaded and served the national cause against royalist and *émigré*, even against the great Irishman[2] whose portrait of her at Versailles, translated by Dutens, was shown to her by the Duchess of Fitzjames, we must admit that she deserved a better fate than most of those with whom we can compare her.

[2] Burke, *Reflections on the French Revolution*.

That month of October, 1793, with its new and unprecedented development of butchery, was a season of triumph to the party of Hébert. The policy of wholesale arrest, rapid judgment, and speedy execution was avowedly theirs; and to them Robespierre seemed a lethargic, undecided person who only moved under pressure. He was at last moving as they wished; but the merit was theirs, and theirs the reward. One of them, Vincent, was of so bloodthirsty a disposition that he found comfort in gnawing the heart of a calf as if it was that of a royalist. But the party was not made up of ferocious men only. They had two enemies, the aristocrat and the priest; and they had two passions, the abolition of an upper class and the abolition of religion. Others had attacked the clergy, and others again had attacked religion. The originality of these men is that they sought a substitute for it, and wished to give men something to believe in that was not God. They were more eager to impose the new belief than to destroy the old. Indeed, they were persuaded that the old was hurrying towards extinction, and was inwardly rejected by those who professed it. While Hébert was an anarchist, Chaumette was the glowing patriarch of irreligious belief. He regarded the Revolution as essentially hostile to Christian faith, and conceived that its inmost principle was that which he now propounded. The clergy had been popular, for a day, in 1789; but the National Assembly refused to declare that the country was Catholic. In June 1792 the Jacobin Club rejected a proposal to abolish the State-Church, and to erect Franklin and Rousseau in the niches occupied by Saints, and in December a member speaking against divine worship met with no support. On May 30, 1793, during the crisis of the Gironde, the procession of Corpus Christi moved unmolested through the streets of Paris; and on August 25, Robespierre presiding, the Convention expressly repudiated a petition to suppress preaching in the name of Almighty God.

On September 20, Romme brought the new calendar before the Assembly, at a moment when, he said, equality reigned in heaven as well as on earth. It was adopted on November 24, with the sonorous nomenclature devised by Fabre d'Eglantine. It signified the substitution of Science for Christianity. Winemonth and fruitmonth were not more unchristian than Julius and Augustus, or than Venus and Saturn; but the practical result was the abolition of Sundays and festivals, and the supremacy of reason over history, of the astronomer over the priest. The calendar was so completely a weapon of offence, that nobody cared about the absurdity of names which were inapplicable to other latitudes, and unintelligible at Isle de France or Pondicherry. While the Convention wavered, moving sometimes in one direction and then retracing its steps, the Commune advanced resolutely, for Chaumette was encouraged by the advantage acquired by his friends in September and October. He thought the time now come to close the churches, and to institute new forms of secularised worship. Supported by a German more enthusiastic than himself, Anacharsis Cloots, he persuaded the bishop of Paris that his Church was doomed like that of the Nonjurors, that the faithful had no faith in it, that the country had given it up. Chaumette was able to add that the Commune wanted to get rid of him. Gobel yielded. On November 7, he appeared, with some of his clergy, at the bar of the Convention, and resigned to the people what he had received from the people. Other priests and bishops followed, and it appeared that some were men who had gone about with masks on their faces, and were glad to renounce beliefs which they did not share. Sieyès declared what everybody knew, that he neither believed the doctrines nor practised the rites of his Church; and he surrendered a considerable income. Some have doubted whether Gobel was equally disinterested. They say that he offered his submission to the Pope in return for a modest sum, and it is affirmed that he received compensation through Cloots and Chaumette, to whom his solemn surrender was worth a good deal. The force of his example lost somewhat, when the bishop of Blois, Grégoire, as violent an enemy of kings as could be found anywhere, stood in the tribune, and refused to abandon his ecclesiastical post. He remained in the Convention to the end, clad in the coloured robes of a French prelate.

Three days after the ceremony of renunciation, Chaumette opened the Cathedral of Notre Dame to the religion of Reason. The Convention stood aloof, in cold disdain. But an actress, who played the leading part, and was variously described as the Goddess of Reason or the Goddess of Liberty, and who possibly did not know herself which she was, came down from her throne in the church, proceeded to the Assembly, and was admitted to a seat beside the President, who gave her what was known as a friendly accolade amid loud applause. After that invasion, the hesitating deputies yielded, and about half of them attended the goddess back to her place under the Gothic towers. Chaumette decidedly triumphed. He had already forbidden religious service outside the buildings. He had now turned out the clergy whom the State had appointed, and had filled their place with a Parisian actress. He had overcome the evident reluctance of the Assembly, and made the deputies partake in his ceremonial. He proceeded, November 23, to close the churches, and the Commune resolved that whoever opened a church should incur the penalties of a suspect. It was the zenith of Hébertism.

Two men unexpectedly united against Chaumette and appeared as champions of Christendom. They were Danton and Robespierre. Robespierre had been quite willing that there should be men more extreme than he, whose aid he could cheaply purchase with a few cartloads of victims. But he did not intend to suppress religion in favour of a worship in which there was no God. It was opposed to his policy, and it was against his conviction; for, like his master, Rousseau, he was a theistic believer, and even intolerant in his belief. This was not a link between him and Danton who had no such spiritualist convictions, and who, so far as he was a man of theory, belonged to a different school of eighteenth-century thought. But Danton had been throughout assailed by the Hébertist party, and was disgusted with their violence. The death of the Girondins appalled him, for he could see no good reason which would exempt him from their rate. He had no hope for the future of the Republic, no enthusiasm, and no belief. From that time in October, his thoughts were turned towards moderation. He identified Hébert, not Robespierre, with the unceasing bloodshed, and he was willing to act with the latter, his real rival, against the raging exterminators. From the end of September he was absent in his own house at Arcis. At his return he and Robespierre denounced the irreligious masquerades, and spoke for the clergy, who had as good a right to toleration as their opponents.

When Robespierre declared that the Convention never intended to proscribe the Catholic worship, he was sincere, and was taking the first step that led to the feast of the Supreme Being. Danton acted from policy only, in opposition to men who were his own enemies. Chaumette and Hébert succumbed. The Commune proclaimed that the churches were not to be closed; and early in December the worship of Reason, having lasted twenty-six days, came to an end. The wound was keenly felt. Fire and poison, said Chaumette, were the weapons with which the priests attack the nation. For such traitors, there must be no mercy. It is a question of life and death. Let us throw up between us the barrier of eternity. The Mass was no longer said in public. It continued in private chapels throughout the winter until the end of February. In April, one head of accusation against Chaumette was his interference with midnight service at Christmas.

Robespierre had repressed Hébertism with the aid of Danton. The visible sign of their understanding was the appearance in December of the *Vieux Cordelier*. In this famous journal Camille Desmoulins pleaded the cause of mercy with a fervour which, at first, resembled sincerity, and pilloried Hébert as a creature that got drunk on the drippings of the guillotine. Robespierre saw the earlier numbers in proof; but by Christmas he had enough of the bargain. The Convention, having shown some inclination towards clemency on December 20, withdrew from it on the 26th, and Desmoulins, in the last of his six numbers, loudly retracted his former argument. The alliance was dissolved. It had served the purpose of Robespierre, by defeating Hébert, and discrediting Danton. In January, the *Vieux Cordelier* ceased to appear.

Robespierre now stood between the two hostile parties—Danton, Desmoulins, and their friends, on the side of a regular government; Hébert, Chaumette, and Collot, returned from a terrible proconsulate, wishing to govern by severities. The energy of Collot gave new life to his party, whilst Danton displayed no resource. Just then, Robespierre was taken ill, and from February 19 to March 13 he was confined to his room. Robespierre was a calculator and a tactician, methodical in his ways, definite and measured in his ends. He was less remarkable for determination and courage; and thus two men of uncommon energy now took the lead. They were Billaud-Varennes and St. Just. When St. Just was with the army, his companion Baudot relates that they astonished the soldiers by their intrepidity under fire. He adds that they had no merit, for they knew that they bore charmed lives, and that cannon balls could not touch them. That was the ardent and fanatical spirit that St. Just brought back with him. During his leader's illness he acquired the initiative, and proclaimed the doctrine that all factions constitute a division of power, that they weaken the state, and are therefore treasonable combinations.

On March 4, Hébert called the people to arms against the government of Moderates. The attempt failed, and Robespierre, by a large expenditure of money, had Paris on his side. At one moment he even thought of making terms with this dangerous rival; and there is a story that he lost heart, and meditated flight to America. In this particular crisis money played a part, and Hébert was financed by foreign bankers, to finish the tyranny of Robespierre. On March 13 he was arrested, Chaumette on the 18th; and on the 17th, Hérault de Séchelles, Danton's friend, on coming to the Committee of Public Safety, was told by Robespierre to retire, as they were deliberating on his arrest. On the 19th the Dantonists caused the arrest of Héron, the police agent of Robespierre, who instantly had him released. March 24, Hébert was sent to the scaffold. On the way he lamented to Ronsin that the Republic was about to perish. "The Republic," said the other, "is immortal." Hitherto the guillotine had been used to destroy the vanquished parties, and persons notoriously hostile. It was an easy inference, that it might serve against personal rivals, who were the best of Republicans and Jacobins. The victims in the month of March were 127.

Danton did nothing to arrest the slaughter. His inaction ruined him, and deprived him of that portion of sympathy which is due to a man who suffers for his good intentions. Billaud and St. Just demanded that he should be arrested, and carried it, at a night sitting of the Committee. Only one refused to sign. Danton had been repeatedly and amply warned. Thibaudeau, Rousselin, had told him what was impending. Panis, at the last moment, came to him at the opera, and offered him a place of refuge. Westermann proposed to him to rouse the armed people. Tallien entreated him to take measures of defence; and Tallien was president of the Convention. A warning reached him from the very grave of Marat. Albertine came to him and told him that her brother had always spoken with scorn of Robespierre as a man of words. She exclaimed, "Go to the tribune while Tallien presides, carry the Assembly, and crush the Committees. There is no other road to safety for a man like you!" "What?" he replied; "I am to kill Robespierre and Billaud?" "If you do not, they will kill you." He said to one of his advisers, "The tribunal would absolve me." To another, "Better to be guillotined than to guillotine." And to a third, "They will never dare!" In a last interview, Robespierre accused him of having encouraged the opposition of Desmoulins, and of having regretted the Girondins. "Yes," said Danton, "it is time to stop the shedding of blood." "Then," returned the other, "you are a conspirator, and you own it." Danton, knowing that he was lost, burst into tears. All Europe would cast him out; and, as he had said, he was not a man who could carry his country in the soles of his shoes. One formidable imputation was to call him a bondsman of Mr. Pitt; for Pitt had said that if there were negotiations, the best man to treat with would be Danton. He was arrested, with Camille Desmoulins and other friends, on the night of March 31. Legendre moved next day that he be heard before the Convention, and if they had heard him, he would still have been master there. Robespierre felt all the peril of the moment, and the Right supported him in denying the privilege. Danton defended himself with such force that the judges lost their heads, and the tones of the remembered voice were heard outside, and agitated the crowd. The Committee of Public Safety refused the witnesses called for the defence, and cut short the proceedings. The law was broken that Danton and his associates might be condemned.

There was not in France a more thorough patriot than Danton; and all men could see that he had been put to death out of personal spite, and jealousy, and fear. There was no way, thenceforth, for the victor to maintain his power, but the quickening of the guillotine. Reserving compassion for less ignoble culprits, we must acknowledge that the defence of Danton is in the four months of increasing terror that succeeded the 5th of April 1794, when Robespierre took his stand at the corner of the Tuileries to watch the last moments of his partner in crime.

The sudden decline of Danton, and his ruin by the hands of men evidently inferior to him in capacity and vigour, is so strange an event that it has been explained by a story which is worth telling, though it is not authenticated enough to influence the narrative. In June 1793, just after the fall of the Girondins, Danton was married. His bride insisted that their union should be blessed by a priest who had not taken the oaths. Danton agreed, found the priest, and went to confession. He became unfitted for his part in the Revolution, dropped out of the Committees, and retired, discouraged and disgusted, into the country. When he came back, after the execution of the queen, of Madame Roland, and the Girondins, he took the side of the proscribed clergy, and encouraged the movement in favour of clemency. In this way he lost his popularity and influence, and refused to adopt the means of recovering power. He neglected even to take measures for his personal safety, like a man who was sick of his life. At that time, seven of the priests of Paris, whose names are given, took it by turns to follow the carts from the prison to the guillotine, disguised as one of the howling mob, for the comfort and consolation of the dying. And the abbé de Keravenant, who had married Danton, thus followed him to the scaffold, was recognised by him, and absolved him at the last moment.

XIX
ROBESPIERRE

We reach the end of the Reign of Terror, on the 9th of Thermidor, the most auspicious date in modern history. In April Robespierre was absolute. He had sent Hébert to death because he promoted disorder, Chaumette because he suppressed religion, Danton because he had sought to restrain bloodshed. His policy was to keep order and authority by regulated terror, and to relax persecution. The governing power was concentrated in the Committee of Public Safety by abolishing the office of minister, instead of which there were twelve Boards of Administration reporting to the Committee. That there might be no rival power, the municipality was remodelled and placed in the hands of men attached to Robespierre. The dualism remained between representation in the Assembly and the more direct action of the sovereign people in the Town Hall. When the tocsin rings, said a member of the Commune, the Convention ceases to exist. In other words, when the principal chooses to interfere, he supersedes his agent. The two notions of government are contradictory, and the bodies that incorporated them were naturally hostile. But their antagonism was suspended while Robespierre stood between.

The reformed Commune at once closed all clubs that were not Jacobin. All parties had been crushed: Royalists, Feuillants, Girondins, Cordeliers. What remained of them in the scattered prisons of France was now to be forwarded to Paris, and there gradually disposed of. But though there no longer existed an opposing party, there was still a class of men that had not been reduced or reconciled. This consisted chiefly of deputies who had been sent out to suppress the rising of the provinces in 1793. These Commissaries of the Convention had enjoyed the exercise of enormous authority; they had the uncontrolled power of life and death, and they had gathered spoil without scruple, from the living and the dead. On that account they were objects of suspicion to the austere personage at the head of the State; and they were known to be the most unscrupulous and the most determined of men.

Robespierre, who was nervously apprehensive, saw very early where the danger lay, and he knew which of these enemies there was most cause to dread. He never made up his mind how to meet the peril; he threatened before he struck; and the others combined and overthrew him. He had helped to unite them by introducing a conflict of ideas at a time when, apparently, and on the surface, there was none. Everybody was a Republican and a Jacobin, but Robespierre now insisted on the belief in God. He perished by the monstrous imposture of associating divine sanction with the crimes of his sanguinary reign. The scheme was not suggested by expediency, for he had been always true to the idea. In early life he had met Rousseau at Ermenonville, and he had adopted the indeterminate religion of the "vicaire Savoyard." In March 1792 he proposed a resolution, that the belief in Providence and a future life is a necessary condition of Jacobinism. In November, he argued that the decline of religious conviction left only a residue of ideas favourable to liberty and public virtue, and that the essential principles of politics might be found in the sublime teaching of Christ. He objected to disendowment, because it is necessary to keep up reverence for an authority superior to man. Therefore, on December 5, he induced the Club to break in pieces the bust of Helvétius.

Although Rousseau, the great master, had been a Genevese Calvinist, nobody thought of preserving Christianity in a Protestant form. The Huguenot ministers themselves did nothing for it, and Robespierre had a peculiar dislike of them. Immediately after the execution of Danton and before the trial of Chaumette, the restoration of religion was foreshadowed by Couthon. A week later it was resolved that the remains of Rousseau, the father of the new church, should be transferred to the Pantheon.

On May 7, Robespierre brought forward his famous motion that the Convention acknowledge the existence of a Supreme Being. His argument, stripped of parliamentary trappings, was this. The secret of the life of a Republic is public and private virtue, that is, integrity, the consciousness of duty, the spirit of self-sacrifice, submission to the discipline of authority. These are the natural conditions of pure democracy; but in an advanced stage of civilisation they are difficult to maintain without the restraint of belief in God, in eternal life, in government by Providence. Society will be divided by passion and interest, unless it is reconciled and controlled by that which is the universal foundation of religions. By this appeal to a higher power Robespierre hoped to strengthen the State at home and abroad. In the latter purpose he succeeded; and the solemn renunciation of atheism impressed the world. It was very distinctly a step in the Conservative direction, for it promised religious liberty. There was to be no favour to churches, but also no persecution. Practically, the advantage was for the Christian part of the population, and irreligion, though not proscribed, was discouraged. The Revolution appeared to be turning backwards, and to seek its friends among those who had acquired their habits of life and thought under the fallen order. The change was undoubted; and it was a change imposed by the will of one man, unsupported by any current of opinion.

A month later, June 8, the Feast of the Supreme Being was held with all the solemnity of which Paris was capable. Robespierre walked in procession from the Tuileries to the Champ de Mars, at the head of the Convention. As the others fell back, he marched alone with his hair powdered, a large nosegay in his hands, wearing the sky-blue coat and nankeens by which he is remembered, for they reappeared in the crisis of Thermidor. He had attained the loftiest summit of prosperity and greatness that was ever given to man. Not a monarch in Europe could compare with him in power. All that had stood in his way during the last five years had been swept to destruction; all that survived of the Revolution followed obedient at his heels. At the last election of a President in the Convention there had been 117 votes; but 485 had voted for Robespierre, that he might parade at their head that day. It was there, in that supreme and intoxicating moment, that a gulf opened before him, and he became aware of the extremity of his peril. For he could hear the hostile deputies in the front rank behind him, muttering curses and sneering at the enthusiasm with which he was received. Those fierce proconsuls who, at Lyons, Nevers, Nantes, Toulon, had crushed all that they were now forced to venerate by their master, vowed vengeance for their humiliation. They said that this was to be a starting-point for divine right, and the excuse for a new persecution. They felt that they were forging a weapon against themselves, and committing an act of suicide. The decree of the month before would have involved no such dire consequences; but the elaborate and aggressive ceremonial was felt as a declaration of war.

Experienced observers at once predicted that Robespierre would not last long. He lost no time in devising a precaution equal to the danger. He prepared what is known as the law of the 22nd of Prairial, which was presented by Couthon, and carried without a division on June 10, two days after the procession. It is the most tyrannical of all the acts of the Revolution, and is not surpassed by anything in the records of absolute monarchy. For the decree of Prairial suppressed the formalities of law in political trials. It was said by Couthon, that delays may be useful where only private interests are at stake, but there must be none where the interest of the entire public is to be vindicated. The public enemy has only to be identified. The State despatches him to save itself. Therefore the Committee was empowered to send whom it chose before the tribunal, and if the jury was satisfied, no time was to be lost with witnesses, written depositions, or arguments. Nobody whom Robespierre selected for execution would be allowed to delay judgment by defence; and that there might be no exception or immunity from arbitrary arrest and immediate sentence, all previous decrees in matter of procedure were revoked. That article contained the whole point, for it deprived the Convention of jurisdiction for the protection of its own members. Robespierre had only to send a deputy's name to the public accuser, and he would be in his grave next day. The point had been so well concealed that nobody perceived it. Afterwards, the deputies, warned by the great jurist Merlin, saw what they had done, and on June 11, they stipulated that no member should be arrested without leave of the Convention. Couthon and Robespierre were not present. On the 12th, by threatening that the Committees would resign, they caused the decree of the previous day to be rescinded, but they assured the Assembly that it was superfluous, and their design had been misunderstood. They maintained their text, and gained their object; but the success was on the other side. The scheme had been exposed, and the Convention had resisted, for the first time. The opposing deputies had received warning, and showed that they understood. From that moment they were on the watch, and their enemy shrank from employing against them a clause the validity of which he had denied. He gave them time to combine. Over the rest of the nation he exerted his new power without control. The victims increased rapidly in number. Down to the middle of June, in fourteen months, the executions had been about 1200. In seven weeks, after the law of Prairial, they were 1376; that is, an average of 32 in a week rose to an average of 196. But the guillotine was removed to a distant part of the city, where a deep trench was dug to carry away such quantities of blood.

During this time the Tribunal was not acting against men actually in public life, and we are not compelled to study its judgments, as if they were making history. Whilst inoffensive people were suffering obscurely, the enemies of the tyrant were plotting to save themselves from the dreadful fate they saw so near them. Nothing bound them together but fear and a common hatred for the obtrusive dogmatist at the head of affairs; and it was not evident to each that they were acting in the same cause. But there was a man among them, still somewhat in the background, but gifted with an incredible dexterity, who hurled Napoleon from power in 1815 and Robespierre in 1794.

Fouché, formerly an Oratorian, had been one of the most unscrupulous deputies on missions, and had given the example of seizing the treasure of churches. For he said there were no laws, and they had gone back to the state of nature. After the execution of Hébert he was recalled from Lyons; and Robespierre, whose sister he had asked in marriage, defended him at the Jacobins on April 10. Being an unfrocked ecclesiastic, he was elected president of the Club on June 6, as a protest against the clerical tendencies of Robespierre. On the 11th, immediately after the procession, and the law of Prairial, Fouché attacked him in a speech in which he said that it is to do homage to the Supreme Being to plunge a sword into the heart of a man who oppresses liberty. This was the first opening of hostilities, and it seems to have been premature. Fouché was not supported by the club at the time, and some weeks later, when Robespierre called him the head of the conspiracy against him, he was expelled. He was a doomed man, carrying his life in his hand, and he adopted more subtle means of combat. July 19, five days after his expulsion, Collot was elected President of the Convention. He and Fouché were united in sacred bands of friendship, for they had put 1682 persons to death at Lyons. About the same day others joined the plotters, and on July 20, Barère, the orator of the Committee, who watched the turning of the tide, made an ambiguous declaration portending a breach. No plan of operations had been agreed upon, and there was yet time for Robespierre, now fully awake to the approaching danger, to strike an irresistible blow.

During the last few weeks the position of the country had undergone a change. On the 1st of June, Villaret Joyeuse had given battle to the English off Ushant. It was the beginning of that long series of fights at sea, in which the French were so often successful in single combat, and so often defeated in general actions. They lost the day, but not the object for which they fought, as the supplies of American grain were brought safely into port. That substantial success and the opportune legend of the Vengeur saved the government from reproach. At the end of the month St. Just brought news of the French victory over the Austrians at Fleurus, the scene of so many battles. It was due to Jourdan and his officers, and would have been lost if they had obeyed St. Just; but he arrived in time to tell his own story.

Many years were to pass before an enemy's guns were again heard on the Belgian frontier. St. Just entreated his colleague to seize the opportunity, and to destroy his enemies while the people were rejoicing over victory. It appeared, afterwards, that the battle of Fleurus, the greatest which the French had won since the reign of Lewis XIV., rendered no service to the government under whom it was fought. The soil of France was safe for twenty years, and with the terror of invasion, the need for terror at home passed away. It had been borne while the danger lasted; and with the danger, it came to an end.

The Committee of Public Safety resented the law of Prairial; and when asked to authorise the proscription of deputies refused. Robespierre did nothing to conciliate the members, and had not the majority. And he threatened and insulted Carnot. As the powers were then constituted he was helpless against his adversaries. The Commune and the Jacobins were true to him; but the Convention was on its guard, and the two Committees were divided. Lists of proscription had been discovered, and those who knew that their names were upon them made no surrender.

Two days after the speech which showed that Barère was wavering, when Collot had been chosen President, and Fouché was at work underground, a joint sitting of both Committees was called at night. St. Just proposed that there should be a dictator. Robespierre was ready to accept, but there were only five votes in favour—three out of eleven on one Committee, two out of twelve on the other. The Jacobins sent a deputation to require that the Convention should strengthen the executive; it was dismissed with words by Barère. One resource remained. It might still be possible, disregarding the false move of Prairial, to obtain the authority of the Convention for the arrest, that is, for the trial and execution of some of its members. They had delivered up Danton and Desmoulins, Hérault and Chaumette. They would perhaps abandon Cambon or Fouché, Bourdon or Tallien, four months later.

The Committees had refused Robespierre, and were in open revolt against his will. His opponents there would oppose him in the Assembly. But the mass of the deputies, belonging not to the Mountain but to the Plain, were always on his side. They had no immediate cause for fear, and they had something to hope for. Seventy of their number had been under arrest ever since October, as being implicated in the fall of the Girondins. Robespierre had constantly refused to let them be sent to trial, and they owed him their lives. They were still in prison, still in his power. To save them, their friends in the Assembly were bound to refuse nothing that he asked for. They would not scruple to deliver over to him a few more ruffians as they had delivered over the others in the spring. That was the basis of his calculation. The Mountain would be divided; the honest men of the Plain would give him the majority, and would purge the earth of another hatch of miscreants. On his last night at home he said to the friends with whom he lived, "We have nothing to fear, the Plain is with us."

Whilst Robespierre, repulsed by the committees which had so long obeyed him, sat down to compose the speech on which his victory and his existence depended, his enemies were maturing their plans. Fouché informed his sister at Nantes of what was in preparation. On the 21st of July he is expecting that they will triumph immediately. On the 23rd he writes: "Only a few days more, and honest men will have their turn.—Perhaps this very day the traitors will be unmasked." It is unlike so sagacious a man to have written these outspoken letters, for they were intercepted and sent to Paris for the information of Robespierre. But it shows how accurately Fouché timed his calculation, that when they arrived Robespierre was dead.

The importance of the neutral men of the Plain was as obvious to one side as to the other, and the Confederates attempted to negotiate with them. Their overtures were rejected; and when they were renewed, they were rejected a second time. The Plain were disabled by consideration for their friends, hostages in the grasp of Robespierre, and by the prospect of advantage for religion from his recent policy. They loaded him with adulation, and said that when he marched in the procession, with his blue coat and nosegay, he reminded them of Orpheus. They even thought it desirable that he should live to clear off a few more of the most detestable men in France, the very men who were making advances to them. They believed that time was on their side. Tallien, Collot, Fouché were baffled, and the rigid obstinacy of the Plain produced a moment of extreme and certain danger.

Whilst they hesitated, Tallien received a note in a remembered handwriting. That bit of paper saved unnumbered lives, and changed the fortune of France, for it contained these words: "Coward! I am to be tried to-morrow." At Bordeaux, Tallien had found a lady in prison, whose name was Madame de Fontenay, and who was the daughter of the Madrid banker Cabarrus. She was twenty-one, and people who saw her for the first time could not repress an exclamation of surprise at her extraordinary beauty. After her release, she divorced her husband, and married Tallien. In later years she became the Princesse de Chimay; but, for writing that note, she received the profane but unforgotten name of Notre Dame de Thermidor.

On the night of July 26, Tallien and his friends had a third Conference with Boissy d'Anglas and Durand de Maillane, and at last they gave way. But they made their terms. They gave their votes against Robespierre on condition that the Reign of Terror ended with him. There was no condition which the others would not have accepted in their extremity, and it is by that compact that the government of France, when it came into the hands of these men of blood, ceased to be sanguinary. It was high time, for, in the morning, Robespierre had delivered the accusing speech which he had been long preparing, and of which Daunou told Michelet that it was the only very fine speech he ever made. He spoke of heaven, and of immortality, and of public virtue; he spoke of himself; he denounced his enemies, naming scarcely any but Cambon and Fouché. He did not conclude with any indictment, or with any demand that the Assembly would give up its guilty members. His aim was to conciliate the Plain, and to obtain votes from the Mountain, by causing alarm but not despair. The next stroke was reserved for the morrow, when the Convention, by voting the distribution of his oration, should have committed itself too far to recede. The Convention at once voted that 250,000 copies of the speech should be printed, and that it should be sent to every parish in France. That was the form in which acceptance, entire and unreserved acceptance, was expressed. Robespierre thus obtained all that he demanded for the day. The Assembly would be unable to refuse the sacrifice of its black sheep, when he reappeared with their names.

Then it was seen that, in naming Cambon, the orator had made a mistake. For Cambon, having had the self-command to wait until the Convention had passed its approving vote, rose to reply. He repelled the attack which Robespierre had made upon him, and turned the entire current of opinion by saying, "What paralyses the Republic is the man who has just spoken."

There is no record of a finer act of fortitude in all parliamentary history. The example proved contagious. The Assembly recalled its vote, and referred the speech to the Committee. Robespierre sank upon his seat and murmured, "I am a lost man." He saw that the Plain could no longer be trusted. His attack was foiled. If the Convention refused the first step, they would not take the second, which he was to ask for next day. He went to the Jacobin Club, and repeated his speech to a crowded meeting. He told them that it was his dying testament. The combination of evil men was too strong for him. He had thrown away his buckler, and was ready for the hemlock. Collot sat on the step below the president's chair, close to him. He said, "Why did you desert the Committee? Why did you make your views known in public without informing us?" Robespierre bit his nails in silence. For he had not consulted the Committee because it had refused the extension of powers, and his action that day had been to appeal to the Convention against them. The Club, divided at first, went over to him, gave him an ovation, and expelled Collot and Billaud-Varennes with violence and contumely. Robespierre, encouraged by his success, exhorted the Jacobins to purify the Convention by expelling bad men, as they had expelled the Girondins. It was his first appeal to the popular forces. Coffinhal, who was a man of energy, implored him to strike at once. He went home to bed, after midnight, taking no further measures of precaution, and persuaded that he would recover the majority at the next sitting.

Collot and Billaud, both members of the supreme governing body, went to their place of meeting, after the stormy scene at the Club, and found St. Just writing intently. They fell upon him, and demanded to know whether he was preparing accusations against them. He answered that that was exactly the thing he was doing. When he had promised to submit his report to the Committee of Public Safety before he went to the Assembly, they let him go. In the morning, he sent word that he was too much hurt by their treatment of him to keep his promise. Barère meanwhile undertook to have a report ready against St. Just.

Before the Assembly began business on the morning of Sunday the 9th of Thermidor, Tallien was in the lobby cementing the alliance which secured the majority; and Bourdon came up and shook hands with Durand, saying, "Oh! the good men of the Right." When the sitting opened, St. Just at once mounted the tribune and began to read. Tallien, seeing him from outside, exclaimed, "Now is the moment, come and see. It is Robespierre's last day!" The report of St. Just was an attack on the committee. Tallien broke in, declaring that the absent men must be informed and summoned, before he could proceed. St. Just was not a ready speaker, and when he was defied and interrupted, he became silent. Robespierre endeavoured to bring him aid and encouragement; but Tallien would not be stopped, Billaud followed in the name of the government; Barère and Vadier continued, while Robespierre and St. Just insisted vainly on being heard. The interrupters were turbulent, aggressive, out of order, being desperate men fighting for life. Collot d'Herbois, the President, did not rebuke them, and having surrendered his place to a colleague whom he could trust, descended to take part in the fray. If the Convention was suffered once more to hear the dreaded voice of Robespierre, nobody could be sure that he would not recover his ascendency. These tactics succeeded. Both parties to the overnight convention were true to it, and Robespierre was not allowed to make his speech. The galleries had been filled from five in the morning. Barère moved to divide the command of Hanriot, the general of the Commune, on whose sword the triumvirs relied; and the Convention outlawed him and his second in command as the excitement increased. This was early in the afternoon; and it was on learning this that the Commune called out its forces, and Paris began to rise.

All this time Robespierre had not been personally attacked. Decrees were only demanded, and passed, against his inferior agents. The struggle had lasted for hours; he thought that his adversaries faltered, and made a violent effort to reach the tribune. It had become known in the Assembly that his friends were arming, and they began to cry, "Down with the tyrant!" The President rang his bell and refused to let him speak. At last his voice failed him. A Montagnard exclaimed, "He is choking with the blood of Danton." Robespierre replied, "What! It is Danton you would avenge?" And he said it in a way that signified "Then why did you not defend him?" When he understood what the Mountain meant, and that a motive long repressed had recovered force, he appealed to the Plain, to the honest men who had been so long silent, and so long submissive. They had voted both ways the day before, but he knew nothing of the memorable compact that was to arrest the guillotine. But the Plain, who were not prepared with articulate arguments for their change of front, were content with the unanswerable cry, "Down with the tyrant!" That was evidently decisive; and when that declaration had been evoked by his direct appeal the end came speedily. An unknown deputy moved that Robespierre be arrested, nobody spoke against it; and his brother and several friends were taken into custody with him. None made any resistance or protest. The conflict, they knew, would be outside. The Commune of Paris, the Jacobin Club, the revolutionary tribunal were of their party; and how many of the armed multitude, nobody could tell. All was not lost until that was known. At five o'clock the Convention, weary with a heavy day's work, adjourned for dinner.

The Commune had its opportunity, and began to gain ground. Their troops collected slowly, and Hanriot was arrested. He was released, and brought back in triumph to the Hôtel de Ville, where the arrested deputies soon assembled. They had been sent to different prisons, but all the gaolers but one refused to admit them. Robespierre insisted on being imprisoned, but the turnkey at the Luxembourg was unmoved, and turned him out. He dreaded to be forced into a position of illegality and revolt, because it would enable his enemies to outlaw him. Once outlawed, there was nothing left but an insurrection, of which the issue was uncertain. There was less risk in going before the revolutionary tribunal, where every official was his creature and nominee, and had no hope of mercy from his adversaries, when he ceased to protect. The gaoler who shut the prison door in his face sealed his fate; and it is supposed, but I do not know, that he had his instructions from Voulland, on the other side, in order that the prisoner might be driven into contumacy, against his will. Expelled from gaol, Robespierre still refused to be free, and went to the police office, where he was technically under arrest.

St. Just, who had seen war, and had made men wonder at his coolness under heavy fire, did not calculate with so much nicety, and repaired, with the younger Robespierre, to the municipality, where a force of some thousands of men were assembled. They sent to summon their leader, but the leader declined to come. He felt safer under arrest; but he advised his friends at the Commune to ring the tocsin, close the barriers, stop the Press, seize the post, and arrest the deputies. The position of the man of peace encouraging his comrades to break the law, and explaining how to do it, was too absurd to be borne. Coffinhal, who was a much bigger man, came and carried him away by friendly compulsion.

About ten o'clock the arrested deputies were united. Couthon, who was a cripple, had gone home. The others sent for him, and Robespierre signed a letter by which he was informed that the insurrection was in full activity. This message, and the advice which he forwarded from his shelter with the police prove that he had made up his mind to fight, and did not die a martyr to legality. But if Robespierre was ready, at the last extremity, to fight, he did not know how to do it. The favourable moment was allowed to slip by; not a gun was fired, and the Convention, after several hours of inaction and danger, began to recover power. By Voulland's advice the prisoners out of prison were outlawed, and Barras was put at the head of the faithful forces. Twelve deputies were appointed to proclaim the decrees all over Paris. Mounted on police chargers, conspicuous in their tricolor scarves, and lighted by torches, they made known in every street that Robespierre was now an outlaw under sentence of death. This was at last effective, and Barras was able to report that the people were coming over to the legal authority. An ingenious story was spread about that Robespierre had a seal with the lilies of France. The western and wealthier half of Paris was for the Convention but parts of the poorer quarters, north and east, went with the Commune. They made no fight. Legendre proceeded to the Jacobin Club, locked the door, and put the key in his pocket, while the members quietly dispersed. About one in the morning, Bourdon, at the head of the men from the district which had been the stronghold of Chaumette made his way along the river to the Place de Grève. The insurgents drawn up before the Hôtel de Ville made no resistance, and the leaders who were gathered within knew that all was over.

The collapse was instantaneous. A little earlier, a messenger sent out by Gaudin, afterwards Duke of Gaëta and Napoleon's trusted finance minister, reported that he had found Robespierre triumphing and receiving congratulations. Even in those last moments he shrank from action. A warlike proclamation was drawn up, signed by his friends, and laid before him. He refused to sign unless it was in the name of the French people. "Then," said Couthon, "there is nothing to be done but to die." Robespierre, doubtful and hesitating, wrote the first two letters of his name. The rest is a splash of blood. When Bourdon, with a pistol in each hand, and the blade of his sword between his teeth, mounted the stairs of the Hôtel de Ville at the head of his troops, Lebas drew two pistols, handed one to Robespierre, and killed himself with the other. What followed is one of the most disputed facts of history. I believe that Robespierre shot himself in the head, only shattering the jaw. Many excellent critics think that the wound was inflicted by a gendarme who followed Bourdon. His brother took off his shoes and tried to escape by the cornice outside, but fell on to the pavement. Hanriot, the general, hid himself in a sewer, from which he was dragged next morning in a filthy condition. The energetic Coffinhal alone got away, and remained some time in concealment. The rest were captured without trouble.

Robespierre was carried to the Tuileries and laid on a table where, for some hours, people came and stared at him. Surgeons attended to his wound, and he bore his sufferings with tranquillity. From the moment when the shot was fired he never spoke; but at the Conciergerie he asked, by signs, for writing materials. They were denied him, and he went to death taking his secret with him out of the world. For there has always been a mysterious suspicion that the tale has been but half told, and that there is something deeper than the base and hollow criminal on the surface. Napoleon liked him, and believed that he meant well. Cambacérès, the archchancellor of the

Empire, who governed France when the Emperor took the field, said to him one day, "It is a cause that was decided but was never argued."

Some of those who felled the tyrant, such as Cambon and Barère, long after repented of their part in his fall. In the north of Europe, especially in Denmark, he had warm admirers. European society believed that he had affinity with it. It took him to be a man of authority, integrity, and order, an enemy of corruption and of war, who fell because he attempted to bar the progress of unbelief, which was the strongest current of the age. His private life was inoffensive and decent. He had been the equal of emperors and kings; an army of 700,000 men obeyed his word; he controlled millions of secret service money, and could have obtained what he liked for pardons, and he lived on a deputy's allowance of eighteen francs a day, leaving a fortune of less than twenty guineas in depreciated assignats. Admiring enemies assert that by legal confiscation, the division of properties, and the progressive taxation of wealth, he would have raised the revenue to twenty-two millions sterling, none of which would have been taken from the great body of small cultivators who would thus have been for ever bound to the Revolution. There is no doubt that he held fast to the doctrine of equality, which means government by the poor and payment by the rich. Also, he desired power, if it was only for self-preservation; and he held it by bloodshed, as Lewis XIV. had done, and Peter the Great, and Frederic. Indifference to the destruction of human life, even the delight at the sight of blood, was common all round him, and had appeared before the Revolution began. The transformation of society as he imagined, if it cost a few thousand heads in a twelvemonth, was less deadly than a single day of Napoleon fighting for no worthier motive than ambition. His private note-book has been printed, but it does not show what he thought of the future. That is the problem which the guillotine left unsolved on the evening of June 28, 1794. Only this is certain, that he remains the most hateful character in the forefront of history since Machiavelli reduced to a code the wickedness of public men.

XX
LA VENDÉE

The remorseless tyranny which came to an end in Thermidor was not the product of home causes. It was prepared by the defeat and defection of Dumouriez; it was developed by the loss of the frontier fortresses in the following July; and it fell when the tide of battle rolled away after the victory of Fleurus. We have, therefore, to consider the series of warlike transactions that reacted so terribly on the government of France. At first, and especially in the summer of 1793, the real danger was not foreign, but civil war. During four years the Revolution always had force on its side. The only active opposition had come from emigrant nobles who were a minority, acting for a class. Not a battalion had joined Brunswick when he occupied a French province; and the mass of the country people had been raised, under the new order, to a better condition than they had ever known. For the hard kernel of the revolutionary scheme, taken from agrarian Rome, was that those who till the land shall own the land; that they should enjoy the certainty of gathering the fruits of their toil for themselves; that every family should possess as much as it could cultivate. But the shock which now made the Republic tremble was an insurrection of peasants, men of the favoured class; and the democracy which was strong enough to meet the monarchies of Europe, saw its armies put to flight by a rabble of field labourers and woodmen, led by obscure commanders, of whom many had never served in war.

One of Washington's officers was a Frenchman who came out before Lafayette, and was known as Colonel Armand. His real name was the Marquis de La Rouerie. His stormy life had been rich in adventure and tribulation. He had appeared on the boards of the opera; he had gone about in company with a monkey; he had fought a duel, and believing that he had killed his man had swallowed poison; he had been an inmate of the monastery of La Trappe, after a temporary disappointment in love; and he had been sent to the Bastille with other discontented Bretons. On his voyage out his ship blew up in sight of land, and he swam ashore. But this man who came out of the sea was found to be full of audacity and resource. He rose to be a brigadier in the Continental army; and when he came home, he became the organiser of the royalist insurrection in the west. Authorised by the Princes, whom he visited at Coblenz, he prepared a secret association in Brittany, which was to co-operate with others in the central provinces.

While La Rouerie was adjusting his instruments and bringing the complicated agency to perfection, the invaders came and went, and the signal for action, when they were masters of Châlons, was never given. When volunteers were called out to resist them, men with black cockades went about interrupting the enrolment, and declaring that no man should take arms, except to deliver the king. Their mysterious leader, Cottereau, the first to bear the historic name of Jean Chouan, was La Rouerie's right hand. When the prospect of combination with the Powers was dissolved by Dumouriez, the character of the conspiracy changed, and men began to think that they could fight the Convention single-handed, while its armies were busy on the Rhine and Meuse. Brittany had 200 miles of coast, and as the Channel Islands were in sight, aid could come from British cruisers.

La Rouerie, who was a prodigy of inventiveness, and drew his lines with so firm a hand that the Chouannerie, which broke out after his death, lasted ten years and only went to pieces against Napoleon, organised a rising, almost from Seine to Loire, for the spring of 1793. Indeed it is not enough to say that they went down before the genius of Napoleon. The "Petite Chouannerie," as the rising of 1815 was called, contributed heavily to his downfall; for he was compelled to send 20,000 men against it, whose presence might have turned the fortune of the day at Waterloo.

But in January 1793 La Rouerie fell ill, the news of the king's death made him delirious, and on the 30th he died. That the explosion might yet take place at the appointed hour, they concealed his death, and buried him in a wood, at midnight, filling the grave with quicklime. The secret was betrayed, the remains were discovered, the accomplices fled, and those who were taken died faithful to their trust.

The Breton rising had failed for the time, and royalists north of the Loire had not recovered from the blow when La Vendée rose. The corpse in the thicket was found February 26; the papers were seized March 3; and it was March 12, at the moment when Brittany was paralysed, that the conscription gave the signal of civil war. The two things are quite separate. In one place there was a plot which came to nothing at the time; in the other, there was an outbreak which had not been prepared. La Vendée was not set in motion by the wires laid north of the Loire. It broke out spontaneously, under sudden provocation. But the Breton plot had ramified in that direction also, and there was much expectant watching for the hour of combined action. Smugglers, and poachers, and beggar men had carried the whispered parole, armed with a passport in these terms: "Trust the bearer, and give him aid, for the sake of Armand"; and certain remote and unknown country gentlemen were affiliated, whose names soon after filled the world with their renown. D'Elbée, the future commander-in-chief, was one of them; and he always regarded the tumultuous outbreak of March, the result of no ripened design, as a fatal error. That is the reason why the gentry hung back at first, and were driven forward by the peasants. It seemed madness to fight the Convention without previous organisation for purposes of war, and without the support of the far larger population of Brittany, which had the command of the coast, and was in touch with the great maritime Power. Politics and religion had roused much discontent; but the first real act of rebellion was prompted by the new principle of compulsory service, proclaimed on February 23.

The region which was to be the scene of so much glory and so much sorrow lies chiefly between the left bank of the Loire and the sea, about 100 miles across, from Saumur to the Atlantic, and 50 or 60 from Nantes towards Poitiers. Into the country farther south, the Vendeans, who were weak in cavalry and had no trained gunners, never penetrated. The main struggle raged in a broken, wooded, and almost inaccessible district called the Bocage, where there were few towns and no good roads. That was the stronghold of the grand army, which included all that was best in Vendean virtue. Along the coast there was a region of fens, peopled by a coarser class of men, who had little intercourse with their inland comrades, and seldom acted with them. Their leader, Charette, the most active and daring of partisans, fought more for the rapture of fighting than for the sake of a cause. He kept open communication by sea, negotiated with England, and assured the Bourbons that, if one of them appeared, he would place him at the head of 200,000 men. He regarded the other commanders as subservient to the clergy, and saw as little of them as he could.

The inhabitants of La Vendée, about 800,000, were well-to-do, and had suffered less from degenerate feudalism than the east of France. They lived on better terms with the landlords, and had less cause to welcome the

Revolution. Therefore, too, they clung to the nonjuring clergy. At heart, they were royalist, aristocratic and clerical, uniting anti-revolutionary motives that acted separately elsewhere. That is the cause of their rising; but the secret of their power is in the military talent, a thing more rare than courage, that was found among them. The disturbances that broke out in several places on the day of enrolment, were conducted by men of the people. Cathelineau, one of the earliest, was a carrier, sacristan in his village, who had never seen a shot fired when he went out with a few hundred neighbours and took Cholet. By his side there was a gamekeeper, who had been a soldier, and came from the eastern frontier. As his name was Christopher, the Germans corrupted it into Stoffel, and he made it famous in the form of Stofflet. While the conflict was carried on by small bands there was no better man to lead them. He and Charette held out longest, and had not been conquered when the clergy, for whom they fought, betrayed them.

The popular and democratic interval was short. After the first few days the nobles were at the head of affairs. They deemed the cause desperate, that one of them had promoted the rising, scarcely one refused to join in it. The one we know best is Lescure, because his wife's memoirs have been universally read. Lescure formed the bond between gentry and clergy, for the cause was religious as much as political. He would have been the third generalissimo, but he was disabled by a wound, and put forward his cousin, Henri de la Rochejaquelein, in preference to Stofflet. We shall presently see that a grave suspicion darkens his fame. Like Lescure, d'Elbée was a man of policy and management; but he was no enthusiast. He desired a reasonable restoration, not a reaction; and he said just before his death that when the pacification came it would be well to keep fanatics in order.

Far above all these men in capacity for war, and on a level with the best in character, was the Marquis de Bonchamps. He understood the art of manœuvring large masses of men; and as his followers would have to meet large masses, when the strife became deadly, he sought to train them for it. He made them into that which they did not want to be, and for which they were ill-fitted. It is due to his immediate command that the war could be carried on upon a large scale; and that men who had begun with a rush and a night attack, dispersing when the foe stood his ground, afterwards defeated the veterans of the Rhine under the best generals of republican France. Bonchamps always urged the need of sending a force to rouse Brittany; but the day when the army crossed the Loire was the day of his death.

La Vendée was far from the route of invading armies, and the district threatened by the Germans. There were no fears for hearth and home, no terrors in a European war for those who kept out of it. If they must fight, they chose to fight in a cause which they loved. They hated the Revolution, not enough to take arms against it, but enough to refuse to defend it. They were compelled to choose. Either they must resist oppression, or they must serve it, and must die for a Government which was at war with their friends, with the European Conservatives, who gave aid to the fugitive nobles, and protection to the persecuted priests. Their resistance was not a matter of policy. There was no principle in it that could be long maintained. The conscription only forced a decision. There were underlying causes for aversion and vengeance, although the actual outbreak was unpremeditated. The angry peasants stood alone for a moment; then was seen the stronger argument, the greater force behind. Clergy and gentry put forward the claim of conscience, and then the men who had been in the royalist plot with La Rouerie, began to weave a new web. That plot had been authorised by the princes, on the *émigré* lines, and aimed at the restoration of the old order. That was not, originally, the spirit of La Vendée. It was never identified with absolute monarchy. At first, the army was known as the Christian army. Then, it became the Catholic and royal army. The altar was nearer to their hearts than the throne. As a sign of it, the clergy occupied the higher place in the councils. Some of the leaders had been Liberals of '89. Others surrendered royalism and accepted the Republic as soon as religious liberty was assured. Therefore, throughout the conflict, and in spite of some intolerant elements, and of some outbursts of reckless fury, La Vendée had the better cause. One Vendean, surrounded and summoned to give up his arms, cried: "First give me back my God."

Bernier, the most conspicuous of the ecclesiastical leaders, was an intriguer; but he was no fanatical adherent of obsolete institutions. The restoration of religion was, to him, the just and sufficient object of the insurrection. A time came when he was very careful to dissociate La Vendée from Brittany, as the champions, respectively, of a religious and a dynastic cause. He saw his opportunity under the Consulate, came out of his hiding-place, and promoted a settlement. He became the agent and auxiliary of Bonaparte, in establishing the Concordat, which is as far removed from intolerance as from legitimacy. As bishop of Orleans he again appeared in the Loire country, not far from the scene of his exploits; but he was odious to many of the old associates, who felt that he had employed their royalism for other ends, without being a royalist.

The country gentlemen of La Vendée had either not emigrated, or had returned to their homes, after seeing what the emigration came to. As far as their own interests were concerned, they accepted the situation. With all the combative spirit which made their brief career so brilliant, few of them displayed violent or extreme opinions. La Vendée was made illustrious mainly by men who dreaded neither the essentials of the Revolution nor its abiding consequences, but who strove to rescue their country from the hands of persecutors and assassins. The rank and file were neither so farsighted nor so moderate. At times they exhibited much the same ferocity as the fighting men of Paris, and in spite of their devotion, they had the cruel and vindictive disposition which in France has been often associated with religion. It was seen from the outset among the wild followers of Charette; and even the enthusiasts of Anjou and of Upper Poitou degenerated and became bloodthirsty. They all hated the towns, where there were municipal authorities who arrested priests, and levied requisitions and men.

The insurrection began by a series of isolated attacks on all the small towns, which were seats of government; and in two months of the spring of 1793 the republicans had been swept away, and the whole country of La Vendée belonged to the Vendeans. They were without order or discipline or training of any sort, and were averse to the sight of officers overtopping them on horseback. Without artillery of their own, they captured 500 cannon. By the end of April they were estimated at near 100,000, a proportion of fighting men to population that has only been equalled in the War of Secession. When the signal was given, the tocsin rang in 600 parishes. In spite of momentary reverses, they carried everything before them, until, on the 9th of June, they took Saumur, a fortress which gave them the command of the Loire. There they stood on the farthest limit of their native province, with 40,000 soldiers, and a large park of artillery. To advance beyond that point, they would require an organisation stronger than the bonds of neighbourhood and the accidental influence of local men. They established a governing body, largely composed of clergy; and they elected a commander-in-chief. The choice fell on Cathelineau, because he was a simple peasant, and was trusted by the priests who were still dominant. As they were all equal there arose a demand for a bishop who should hold sway over them. Nonjuring bishops were scarce in France; but

Lescure contrived to supply the need of the moment. Here, in the midst of so much that was tragic, and of so much that was of good report, we come to the bewildering and grotesque adventure of the bishop of Agra.

At Dol, near St. Malo, there was a young priest who took the oath to the Constitution, but afterwards dropped the cassock, appeared at Poitiers as a man of pleasure, and was engaged to be married. He volunteered in the republican cavalry, and took the field against the royalists, mounted and equipped by admiring friends. On May 5, he was taken prisoner, and as his card of admission to the Jacobins was found upon him, he thought himself in danger. He informed his captors that he was on their side; that he was a priest in orders, whom it would be sacrilege to injure; at last, that he was not only a priest, but a bishop, whom, in the general dispersion, the Pope had chosen as his vicar apostolic to the suffering Church of France. His name was Guyot, and he called himself Folleville. Such a captive was worth more than a regiment of horse. Lescure carried the republican trooper to his country house for a few days; and on May 16 Guyot reappeared in the robes proper to a bishop, with the mitre, ring, and crozier that belonged to his exalted dignity.

It was a great day in camp under the white flag; and the enemy, watching through his telescope, beheld with amazement the kneeling ranks of Vendean infantry, and a gigantic prelate who strode through them and distributed blessings. He addressed them when they went into action, promising victory to those who fought, and heaven to those who fell, in so good a cause; and he went under fire with a crucifix in his hand, and ministered to the wounded. They put him at the head of the council, and required every priest to obey him, under pain of arrest. Bernier, who had been at school with Guyot, was not deceived. He denounced him at Rome, through Maury, who was living there in the enjoyment of well-earned honours. The fraud was at once exposed. Pius VI. declared that the bishop of Agra did not exist; and that he knew nothing of the man so called, except that he was an impostor and a rogue.

From the moment when Bernier wrote, Guyot was in his power; but it was October before he translated the papal Latin to the generals. They resolved to take no notice, but the detected pretender ceased to say Mass. La Rochejaquelein intended to put him on board ship and get rid of him at the first seaport. They never reached the sea. To the last, at Granville, Guyot was seen in the midst of danger, and his girdle was among the spoils of the field. Though the officers watched him, the men never found him out. He served them faithfully during his six months of precarious importance, and he perished with them. He might have obtained hope of life by betraying the mendacity of his accomplices, and the imbecility of his dupes. He preferred to die without exposing them.

In June, when the victorious Vendeans occupied Saumur, it was time that they should have a policy and a plan. They had four alternatives. They might besiege Nantes and open communications with English cruisers. They might join with the royalists of the centre. They might raise an insurrection in Brittany, or they might strike for Paris. The great road to the capital opened before them; there were the prisoners in the Temple to rescue, and the monarch to restore. Dim reports of their exploits reached the queen, and roused hopes of deliverance. In a smuggled note, the Princess Elizabeth inquired whether the men of the west had reached Orleans; in another, she asked, not unreasonably, what had become of the British fleet. It is said that Stofflet gave that heroic counsel. Napoleon believed that if they had followed it, nothing could have prevented the white flag from waving on the towers of Notre Dame. But there was no military organisation; the troops received no pay, and went home when they pleased. The generals were hopelessly divided, and Charette would not leave his own territory. Bonchamps, who always led his men, and was hit in every action, was away, disabled by a wound. His advice was known. He thought that their only hope was to send a small corps to rouse the Bretons. With the united forces of Brittany and Vendée they would then march for Paris. They adopted a compromise, and decided to besiege Nantes, an open town, the headquarters of commerce with the West Indies, and of the African slave trade. If Nantes fell it would be likely to rouse Brittany; and it was an expedition in which Charette would take a part. This was the disastrous advice of Cathelineau. They went down from Saumur to Nantes, by the right bank of the Loire, and on the night of June 28, their fire-signals summoned Charette for the morrow. Charette did not fail. But he was beyond the river, unable to make his way across, and he resented the arrangement which was to give the pillage of the wealthy city to the pious soldiers of Anjou and Poitou, whilst he looked on from a distance.

During the long deliberations at Saumur, and the slow march down the river, Nantes had thrown up earthworks, and had fortified the hearts of its inhabitants. The attack failed. Cathelineau penetrated to the market place, and they still show the window from which a cobbler shot down the hero of Anjou. The Vendeans retreated to their stronghold, and their cause was without a future. D'Elbée was chosen to succeed, on the death of Cathelineau. He admitted the superior claims of Bonchamps, but he disliked his policy of carrying the war to the north. The others preferred d'Elbée because they had less to fear from his ascendancy and strength of will. They were not only divided by jealousy, but by enmity. Charette kept away from the decisive field, and rejoiced when the grand army passed the Loire, and left their whole country to him. Charette and Stofflet caused Marigny, the commander of the artillery, to be executed. Lescure once exclaimed that, if he had not been helpless from a wound, he would have cut down the Prince de Talmond. Stofflet sent a challenge to Bonchamps; and both Stofflet and Charette were ultimately betrayed by their comrades. Success depended on the fidelity of d'Elbée, Bonchamps, and Lescure to each other, through all divergences of character and policy. For two months they continued to hold the Republic at bay. They never reached Poitiers, and they were heavily defeated at Luçon; but they made themselves a frontier line of towns, to the south-west, by taking Thouars, Parthenay, Fontenay, and Niort. There was a road from north to south by Beaupréau, Châtillon, and Bressuire; and another from east to west, through Doué, Vihiers, Coron, Mortagne. All these are names of famous battles. At Cholet, which is in the middle of La Vendée, where the two roads cross, the first success and the final rout took place.

The advantage which the Vendeans possessed was that there was no good army to oppose them, and there were no good officers. It was the early policy of Robespierre to repress military talent, which may be dangerous in a republic, and to employ noisy patriots. He was not duped by them; but he trusted them as safe men; and if they did their work coarsely and cruelly, imitating the practice that succeeded so well at Paris, it was no harm. That was a surer way of destroying royalists *en masse* than the manœuvres of a tactician, who was very likely to be humane, and almost sure to be ambitious and suspicious of civilians. Therefore a succession of incompetent men were sent out, and the star of d'Elbée ascended higher and higher. There had been time for communication with Pitt, who was believed to be intriguing everywhere, and the dread of an English landing in the west became strong in the Committees of government at Paris.

At the end of July, a serious disaster befell the French armies. Mentz surrendered to the Prussians, and Valenciennes immediately after to the

Austrians. Their garrisons, unable to serve against the enemy abroad, were available against the enemy at home. The soldiers from Mayence were sent to Nantes. They were 8000, and they brought Kléber with them. It was the doom of La Vendée. By the middle of September the best soldiers and the best generals the French government possessed met the veterans of Bonchamps and d'Elbée. In a week, from the 18th to the 23rd, they fought five battles, of which the most celebrated is named after the village of Torfou. And with this astonishing result, that the royalists were victorious in every one of them, and captured more than 100 cannon. On one of these fields, Kléber and Marceau saw each other for the first time. But it seemed that Bonchamps was able to defeat even Kléber and Marceau, as he had defeated Westermann and Rossignol. Then a strange thing happened. Some men, in disguise, were brought into the Vendean lines. They proved to be from the Mayence garrison; and they said that they would prefer serving under the royalist generals who had beaten them, rather than under their own unsuccessful chiefs. They undertook, for a large sum of money, to return with their comrades. Bonchamps and Charette took the proposals seriously, and wished to accept them. But the money could only be procured by melting down the Church plate, and the clergy made objection. Some have thought that this was a fatal miscalculation. The other causes of their ruin are obvious and are decisive. They ought to have been supported by the Bretons, and the Bretons were not ready. They ought to have been united, and they were bitterly divided and insubordinate. They ought to have created an impregnable fastness on the high ground above the Loire; but they had no defensive tactics, and when they occupied a town, would not wait for the attack, but retired, to have the unqualified delight of expelling the enemy. Above all, they ought to have been backed by England. D'Elbée's first letter was intercepted, and four months passed before the English government stirred. The *émigrés* and their princes had no love for these peasants and stay-at-home gentry and clergy, who took so long to declare themselves, and whose primary or ultimate motive was not royalism. Puisaye showed Napier a letter in which Lewis XVIII. directed that he should be put secretly to death.

England ought to have been active on the coast very early, during the light winds of summer. But the English wanted a safe landing-place, and there was none to give them. With more enterprise, while Charette held the island of Noirmoutier, Pitt might have become the arbiter of France. When he gave definite promises and advice, it was October, and the day of hope had passed.

In the middle of October Kléber, largely reinforced, advanced with 25,000 men, and Bonchamps made up his mind that the time had come to retreat into Brittany. He posted a detachment to secure the passage of the Loire at St. Laurent, and fell back with his whole force to Cholet, whilst he sent warning to Charette of the decisive hour. There, on October 16, he fought his last fight. D'Elbée was shot through the body. He was carried in safety to Noirmoutier, and still lingered when the Republicans recovered the island in January. His last conversation with his conqueror, before he suffered death, is of the highest value for this history. Lescure had already received a bullet through the head, and at Cholet, Bonchamps was wounded mortally. But there had been a moment in the day during which fortune wavered, and the lost cause owed its ruin to the absence of Charette. Stofflet and La Rochejaquelein led the retreat from Cholet to the Loire. It was a day's march, and there was no pursuit. Bonchamps was still living when they came to the river, and still able to give one last order. Four thousand five hundred prisoners had been brought from Cholet; they were shut up in the church at St. Laurent, and the officers agreed that they must be put to death. At first, the Convention had not allowed the men whom the royalists released to serve again. But these amenities of civilised war had long been abolished; and the prisoners were sure to be employed against the captors who spared them. Bonchamps gave these men their lives, and on the same day he died. When, at the same moment, d'Elbée, Lescure and Bonchamps had disappeared, La Rochejaquelein assumed the command, Kléber, whom he repulsed at Laval, described him as a very able officer; but he led the army into the country beyond the Loire without a definite purpose. The Prince de Talmond, who was a La Tremoille, promised that when they came near the domains of his family, the expected Bretons would come in. More important was the appearance of two peasants carrying a stick. For the peasants were *émigrés* disguised, and their stick contained letters from Whitehall, in which Pitt undertook to help them if they succeeded in occupying a seaport; and he recommended Granville, which stands on a promontory not far from French Saint Michael's Mount. The messengers declined to confirm the encouragement they brought; but La Rochejaquelein, heavily hampered with thousands of women and children who had lost their homes, made his way across to the sea, and attacked the fortifications of the place. He assaulted in vain; and although Jersey listened to the cannonade, no ships came. The last hope had now gone; and the remnant of the great army, cursing the English, turned back towards their own country. Some thousands of Bretons had joined, and Stofflet still drove the republicans before him. With La Rochejaquelein and Sapinaud he crossed the Loire in a small boat. The army found the river impassable, and wandered helplessly without officers until, at Savenay, December 26, it was overtaken by the enemy, and ceased to exist. Lescure had followed the column in his carriage, until he heard of the execution of the queen. With his last breath, he said: "I fought to save her: I would live to avenge her. There must be no quarter now."

In this implacable spirit Carrier was acting at Nantes. But I care not to tell the vengeance of the victorious republicans upon the brave men who had made them tremble. The same atrocities were being committed in the south. Lyons had overthrown the Jacobins, had put the worst of them to death, and had stood a siege under the republican flag. Girondins and royalists, who were enemies at Nantes, fought here side by side; and the place was so well armed that it held out to October 9. On the 29th of August, the royalists of Toulon called in a joint British and Spanish garrison, and gave up the fleet and the arsenal to Lord Hood. The republicans laid siege to the town in October. The harbour of Toulon is deep and spacious; but there was, and still is, a fort which commands the entrance. Whoever held l'Aiguillette was master of every ship in the docks and of every gun in the arsenal. On December 18, at midnight, during a violent storm, the French attacked and carried the fort. Toulon was no longer tenable. Hastily, but imperfectly, the English destroyed the French ships they could not at once take away, leaving the materials for the Egyptian expedition, and as fast as possible evacuated the harbour, under the fire of the captured fort. The fortunes of Bonaparte began with that exploit, and the first event of his career was the spectacle of a British fleet flying before him by the glare of an immense conflagration. The year 1793 thus ended triumphantly, and the Convention was master of all France, except the marshes down by the ocean, where Charette defied every foe, and succeeded in imposing his own terms on the Republic. But the danger had come that disturbed the slumber of Robespierre, and the man was found who was to make the Revolution a stepping-stone to the power of the sword.

XXI
THE EUROPEAN WAR

The French Revolution was an attempt to establish in the public law of Europe maxims which had triumphed by the aid of France in America. By the principles of the Declaration of Independence a government which obstructs liberty forfeits the claim to obedience, and the men who devote their families to ruin and themselves to death in order to destroy it do no more than their duty. The American Revolution was not provoked by tyranny or intolerable wrong, for the Colonies were better off than the nations of Europe. They rose in arms against a constructive danger, an evil that might have been borne but for its possible effects. The precept which condemned George III. was fatal to Lewis XVI., and the case for the French Revolution was stronger than the case for the American Revolution. But it involved international consequences. It condemned the governments of other countries. If the revolutionary government was legitimate, the conservative governments were not. They necessarily threatened each other. By the law of its existence, France encouraged insurrection against its neighbours, and the existing balance of power would have to be redressed in obedience to a higher law.

The successful convulsion in France led to a convulsion in Europe; and the Convention which, in the first illusions of victory, promised brotherhood to populations striking for freedom, was impolitic, but was not illogical. In truth the Jacobins only transplanted for the use of oppressed Europeans a precedent created by the Monarchy in favour of Americans who were not oppressed. Nobody imagined that the new system of international relations could be carried into effect without resistance or sacrifice, but the enthusiasts of liberty, true or false, might well account it worth all that it must cost, even if the price was to be twenty years of war. This new dogma is the real cause of the breach with England, which did such harm to France. Intelligent Jacobins, like Danton and Carnot, saw the danger of abandoning policy for the sake of principle. They strove to interpret the menacing declaration, until it became innocuous, and they put forward the natural frontier in its stead. But it was the very essence of the revolutionary spirit, and could not be denied.

England had remained aloof from Pilnitz and the expedition under Brunswick, but began to be unfriendly after the 10th of August. Lord Gower did not at once cease to be ambassador, and drew his salary to the end of the year. But as he was accredited to the king, he was recalled when the king went to prison, and no solicitude was shown to make the step less offensive. Chauvelin was not acknowledged. He was not admitted to present his new credentials, and his requests for audience were received with coldness. Pitt and Grenville were not conciliatory. They were so dignified that they were haughty, and when they were haughty they were insolent. The conquest of Belgium, the opening of the Scheldt for navigation, and the trial of the king, roused a bitter feeling in England, and ministers, in the course of December, felt that they would be safe if they went along with it. The opening of the Scheldt was not resisted by the Dutch, and gave England no valid plea. But France was threatening Holland, and if out of English hatred to the Republic, to republican principles of foreign policy, to the annexation of the Netherlands, war was really inevitable, it was important to get possession at once of the Dutch resources by sea and land.

The idea of conciliating England by renouncing conquest, and the idea of defying England by the immediate invasion of the United Provinces, balanced each other for a time. By renunciation, the moderate or Girondin party would have triumphed. The Jacobins, who drew all the consequences of theories, and who were eager to restore the finances with the spoils of the opulent Dutchmen, carried their purpose when they voted the death of the king. That event added what was wanting to make the excitement and exasperation of England boil over. Down to the month of January the government continued ready to treat on condition that France restored her conquests, and several emissaries had been received. The most trustworthy of these was Maret, afterwards Duke of Bassano. On the 28th of January Talleyrand, who was living in retirement at Leatherhead, informed ministers that Maret was again on the way to herald the approach of Dumouriez himself, whose presence in London, on a friendly mission, would have been tantamount to the abandonment of the Dutch project. But Maret came too late, and Dumouriez on his journey to the coast was overtaken by instructions that Amsterdam, not London, was his destination.

The news from Paris reached London on the evening of the 23rd, and the audience at the theatre insisted that the performance should be stopped. There was to be a drawing-room next day. The drawing-room was countermanded. A Council was summoned, and there a momentous decision was registered. Grenville had refused to recognise the official character of the French envoy, Chauvelin. He had informed him that he was subject to the Alien Act. On the 24th he sent him his passports, with orders to leave the country. Upon that Dumouriez was recalled. On the 29th Chauvelin arrived at Paris, and told his story. And it was then, February 1, that the Convention declared war against England. With less violent counsels in London, and with patience to listen to Dumouriez, the outbreak of the war might have been postponed. But nothing that England was able to offer could have made up to France for the sacrifice of the fleet and the treasure of Holland.

Our ministers may have been wanting in many qualities of negotiators, and the dismissal of Chauvelin laid on them a responsibility that was easy to avoid. They could not for long have averted hostilities. It is possible that Fox might have succeeded, for Fox was able to understand the world of new ideas which underlay the policy of France; but the country was in no temper to follow the Whigs. They accused Pitt unjustly when they said that he went to war from the motive of ambition. He was guiltless of that capital charge. But he did less than he might have done to prevent it, perceiving too clearly the benefit that would accrue. And he is open to the grave reproach that he went over to the absolute Powers and associated England with them at the moment of the Second Partition, and applied to France the principles on which they acted against Poland. When the Prince of Coburg held his first conference with his allies in Belgium, he declared that Austria renounced all ideas of conquest. The English at once protested. They made known that they desired to annex as much territory as possible, in order to make the enemy less formidable. Our envoy was Lord Auckland, a man of moderate opinions, who had always advised his government to come to terms with the Republic. He exhorted Coburg not to rest until he had secured a satisfactory line of frontier, as England was going to appropriate Dunkirk and the Colonies, and meant to keep them. George III., on April 27, uttered the same sentiments. France, he said, must be greatly circumscribed before we can talk of any means of treating with that dangerous and faithless nation. In February Grenville definitely proposed dismemberment, offering the frontier fortresses and the whole of Alsace and Lorraine to Austria. It was the English who impressed on the operations, that were to follow, the character of a selfish and sordid rapacity.

The island kingdom alone had nothing to fear, for she had the rest of the maritime Powers on her side, and the preponderance of the naval forces was decisive. The French began the war with 76 line-of-battle ships. England had 115, with 8718 guns to 6002. In weight of metal the difference was not so great, for the English guns threw 89,000 lbs. and the French 74,000. But England had the Spanish fleet, of 56 ships-of-the-line, and the Dutch with 49—the Spaniards well built, but badly manned; the Dutch constructed for shallow waters, but with superior crews. To these must be added Portugal, which followed England, and Naples, whose king was a Bourbon, brother to the king of Spain. Therefore, in weight of metal, which is the first thing, next to brains, we were at least 2 to 1; and in the number of ships 3 to 1, or about 230 to 76. That is the reason why the insular statesmen went to war, if not with greater enterprise and energy, yet with more determination and spirit, than their exposed and vulnerable allies upon the Continent. The difference between them is that between men who are out of reach and are 2 to 1, and men whose territories are accessible to an enemy greatly superior to themselves in numbers. Therefore it was Pitt who from his post of vantage pushed the others forward, and, when they vacillated, encouraged them with money and the promise of spoil. The alliance with the maritime states was important for his policy, but it accomplished nothing in the actual struggle. The Dutch and the Spaniards were never brought into line; and the English, though they owed their safety at first to their system of alliances, owed their victories to themselves. And those victories became more numerous and splendid when, after two years of inefficacious friendship with us, the Spaniard and the Dutchman joined our enemies. England was drawn into the war, which it maintained with unflagging resolution, by the prospect of sordid gain. It brought increase of rents to the class that governed, and advantage to the trader from the conquest of dependencies and dominions over the sea.

The year 1793 brought us no profit from the sea. We occupied Toulon on the invitation of the inhabitants, and there we had in our possession half of the naval resources of France. But before the end of the year we were driven away. The French dominions in India fell at once into our hands, and in March and April 1794 we captured the Windward Islands in the West Indies, Martinique, Santa Lucia, and at last Guadeloupe. But a Jacobin lawyer came over from France and reconquered Guadeloupe, and the French held it with invincible tenacity till 1810. They lost Hayti, but it never became English, and drifted into the power of the negroes, who there rose to the highest point they have attained in history. In the summer of the same year, 1794, Corsica became a British dependency, strengthening enormously our position in the Mediterranean. We were not able to retain it. Our admirals did nothing for La Vendée. So little was known about it that on December 19 there was a question of sending an officer to serve under Bonchamps, who at that time had been dead two months.

In all this chequered and inglorious history there is one day to be remembered. On April 11, 1794, 130 merchantmen, laden with food-supplies, sailed from Chesapeake Bay for the ports of France. Lord Howe went out to intercept them; and on May 16 the French fleet left Brest to protect them. Howe divided his force. He sent Montagu to watch for the merchantmen, and led the remainder of his squadron against Villaret Joyeuse. After a brush on May 28, they met, in equal force, on the 1st of June, 400 miles from land. The French admiral had an unfrocked Huguenot divine on board, who had been to sea in his youth, and was now infusing the revolutionary ardour into the fleet, as St. Just did with the army. The fight lasted three hours and then ceased. Villaret waited until evening, but Lord Howe had several ships disabled, and would neither renew the battle nor pursue the enemy. The French had lost seven ships out of twenty-six. The most famous of these is the *Vengeur du Peuple*. It engaged the *Brunswick,* and the rigging of one ship became so entangled with the anchors of the other that they were locked together, and drifted away from the line. They were so close that the French could not fire their lower deck guns, having no space to ram the charge. The English were provided for this very emergency with flexible rammers of rope and went on firing into the portholes of the enemy, while the French captain, calling up his men from below, had the advantage on the upper deck. At last the rolling of the sea forced the unconquered enemies to part. The *Brunswick* had lost 158 out of a crew of 600 and 23 of her guns out of 74 were dismounted. She withdrew out of action disabled, and went home to refit. The *Vengeur* remained on the ground, with all her masts gone. Presently it was seen that she had been hit below the water-line. The guns were thrown overboard, but after some hours the *Vengeur* made signals that she was sinking. English boats came and rescued about 400 men out of 723. Those of the survivors who were not wounded were seen standing by the broken mast, and cried "Vive la république," as the ship went down. That is the history, not the legend, of the loss of the *Vengeur*, and no exaggeration and no contradiction can mar the dramatic grandeur of the scene.

The battle of the 1st of June is the one event by land or sea that was glorious to British arms in the war of the first Coalition. The ascendancy then acquired was never lost. Our failures in the West Indies, at Cape Verde Islands, in the Mediterranean, and on the coasts of France, and even the defection of our maritime allies, did not impair it. And later on, when all were against us, admirals more original and more enterprising than Howe increased our superiority. The success was less brilliant and entire than that which Nelson gained against a much greater force at Trafalgar, when France lost every ship. Montagu did not intercept the French merchantmen, and did not help to crush the French men-of-war. Villaret Joyeuse and the energetic minister from Languedoc lost the day, but they gained the substantial advantage. Under cover of their cannon, the ships on which the country depended for its supplies came into port. Although during those two years the French fought against great odds at sea, their loss was less than they had expected, and did not weaken their government at home. They had reason to hope that whenever their armies were brought to close quarters with Spain and the Netherlands, the fortune of war at sea would follow the event on land.

The war with which we have now to deal passed through three distinct phases. During the year 1793, the French maintained themselves with difficulty, having to contend with a dangerous insurrection. In 1794 the tide turned in their favour; and 1795 was an epoch of preponderance and triumph. The Republic inherited from the Monarchy a regular army of 220,000 men, seriously damaged and demoralised by the emigration of officers. To these were added, first, the volunteers of 1791, who soon made good soldiers, and supplied the bulk of the military talent that rose to fame down to 1815, and the like of which was never seen, either in the American Civil War, or among the Germans in 1870. The second batch of volunteers, those who responded to the Brunswick proclamation and the summons of September, when the country was in danger, were not equal to the first. The two together supplied 309,000 men. At the beginning of the general war, in March 1793, the Conscription was instituted, which provoked the rising in Vendée, and was interrupted by troubles in other departments. Instead of 300,000 men, it yielded 164,000. In the summer of 1793, when the fortresses were falling, there was, first, the levy *en masse*, and then, August 23, the system of requisition, by which the levy was organised and made to produce 425,000 men. Altogether, in a year and a half, France put 1,100,000 men into line; and at the critical moment, at the end of the second year, more than 700,000 were present under arms. That is the force which Carnot had to wield. He was a man of energy, of integrity, and of professional skill as an engineer, but he was not a man of commanding abilities. Lord Castlereagh rather flippantly called him a foolish mathematician. Once, having quarrelled with his former comrade Fouché and having been condemned to banishment, he had this conversation with him: "Where am I to go, traitor?" "Wherever you like, idiot." As an austere republican he was out of favour during the empire; but his defence of Antwerp is a bright spot in the decline of Napoleon. He became Minister of the Interior on the return from Elba, and his advice might have changed the history of the world. For he wished the emperor to fall upon the English before they could concentrate, and then to fight the Prussians at his leisure. One night, during a rubber of whist, the tears that ran down his cheek betrayed the news from Waterloo.

Carnot owed his success to two things—arbitrary control over promotion, and the cheapness of French lives. He could sacrifice as many men as he required to carry a point. An Austrian on the Sambre, 1,000 miles from home, was hard to replace. Any number of Frenchmen were within easy reach. Colonel Mack observed that whenever a combatant fell, France lost a man, but Austria lost a soldier. La Vendée had shown what could be done by men without organisation or the power of manœuvring, by constant activity, exposure, and courage. Carnot taught his men to win by a rush many times repeated, and not to count their dead. The inferior commanders were quickly weeded out, sometimes with help from the executioner, and the ablest men were brought to the front. The chief army of all, the army of Sambre et Meuse, was commanded by Kléber, Moreau, Reynier, Marceau, and Ney. Better still, on the Rhine were Hoche, Desaix, and St. Cyr. Best of all, in the Apennines, the French were led by Bonaparte and Masséna.

All these armaments had scarcely begun when the victory of Neerwinden and the flight of Dumouriez brought the Austrians up to the Belgian frontier. Carnot was not discovered, the better men had not risen to command, the levy *en masse* had not been thought of. The French could do nothing in the field while the Prince of Coburg, supported by the Dutch, and by an Anglo-Hanoverian army under the Duke of York, sat down before the fortresses. By the end of July Condé and Valenciennes had fallen, and the road to Paris was open to the victors. They might have reached the capital in overwhelming force by the middle of August. But the English coveted, not Paris but Dunkirk, and the Duke of York withdrew with 37,000 men and laid siege to it. Coburg turned aside in the opposite direction, to besiege Le Quesnoy. He proposed to conquer the fortified towns, one after another, according to Grenville's prescription, and then to join hands with the Prussians whom it was urgent to have with him when penetrating to the interior. The Prussians meanwhile had taken Mentz, the garrison, like that of Valenciennes, making a defence too short for their fame. But the Prussians remembered the invasion of the year before, and they were in no hurry. The allies, with conflicting interests and divided counsels, gave the enemy time. Some years later, when Napoleon had defeated the Piedmontese, and was waiting for them to send back the treaty he had dictated at Cherasco, duly signed, he grew excessively impatient at their delay. The Piedmontese officers were surprised at what seemed a want of self-restraint, and let him see it. His answer was, "I may often lose a battle, but I shall never lose a minute."

The French put to good account the time their enemies allowed them. Carnot took office on August 14, and on the 23rd he caused the Convention to decree what is pleasantly called the levy *en masse* but was the system of requisition, making every able-bodied man a soldier. The new spirit of administration was soon felt in the army. The forces besieging Le Quesnoy and Dunkirk were so far apart that the French came between and attacked them successively. The Dunkirk garrison opened the sluices and flooded the country, separating the English from the covering force of Hanoverians, and leaving the Duke of York no means of retreat except by a single causeway. On September 8 the French defeated the Hanoverians at Hondschooten and relieved Dunkirk. The English got away in great haste, abandoning their siege guns; but as they ought not to have got away at all, the French cut off the head of their victorious commander. Jourdan, his successor, turned upon the Prince of Coburg, and, by the new and expensive tactics, defeated him at Wattignies on October 16. Carnot, who did not yet trust his generals, arrived in time to win the day by overruling Jourdan and his staff. And every French child knows how he led the charge through the grapeshot, on foot, with his hat at the end of his sword. From that day to the peace of Bâle he held the army in his grasp. He had stopped the invasion. No one in the allied camp spoke any more of the shortest road to Paris; but they still held the places they had conquered. Two months later, Hoche, who had distinguished himself at Dunkirk, took the command in the Vosges, and stormed the lines of Weissenburg at the scene of the first action in the war of 1870. By the end of December the Prussians were shut up in Mayence, and Wurmser had retired beyond the Rhine. By that time, too, La Vendée, and

Lyons, and Toulon had fallen. The campaign of 1794 was to be devoted to foreign war.

During that autumn and winter, Carnot, somewhat unmindful of what went on near him and heedless of the signatures he gave, was organising the enormous force the requisition provided, and laying the plans that were to give him so great a name in the history of his country. He divided the troops into thirteen armies. They call them fourteen, I believe, because there were *cadres* for an army of reserve. Two were required for the Spanish war, for the Pyrenees are impassable by artillery except at the two ends, where narrow valleys lead from France to Spain near San Sebastian, and by a strip of more open country near the Mediterranean. What passed there did not influence events; but it is well to know that the Spaniards under Ricardos gained important advantages in 1794, and fought better than they ever did in the field during their struggle with Napoleon. A third army was placed on the Italian frontier, a fourth on the Rhine, and a fifth against the allies in Flanders. Carnot increased the number because he had no men who had proved their fitness for the direction of very large forces. He meant that his armies should be everywhere sufficient, but in Belgium they were to be overwhelming. That was the point of danger, and there a great body of Austrians, Dutch, English, and Hanoverians had been collected. The Emperor himself appeared among them in May; and his brother, the Archduke Charles, was the best officer in the allied camp.

At the end of April Coburg took Landrecies, the fourth of the line of fortresses that had fallen. On May 18 the French were victorious at Tourcoing, where the English suffered severely, and the Duke of York sought safety in precipitate flight. There was even talk of a court martial. The day was lost in consequence of the absence of the Archduke, who suffered from fits like Julius Cæsar, and is said to have been lying unconscious many miles away. For a month longer the allies held their ground and repeatedly repressed Jourdan in his attempts to cross the Sambre. At last, Charleroi surrendered to the French, and on the following day, June 26, they won the great battle of Fleurus. Mons fell on July 1, and on the 5th the allies resolved to evacuate Belgium. The four fortresses were recovered in August; and Coburg retired by Liége into Germany, York by Antwerp into Holland. In October Jourdan pursued the Austrians, and drove them across the Rhine. The battle of Fleurus established the ascendancy of the French in Europe as the 1st of June had created that of England on the ocean. They began the offensive, and retained it for twenty years. Yet the defeat of Fleurus, after such varying fortunes and so much alternate success does not explain the sudden discouragement and collapse of the allies. One of the great powers was about to abandon the alliance. Prussia had agreed in the spring to accept an English subsidy. For, £300,000 down, and £150,000 a month, a force of fifty to sixty thousand Prussians was to be employed in a manner to be agreed upon with England,—that meant in Belgium. Before Malmesbury's signature was dry the whole situation altered.

The Committee of Public Safety had created a diversion in the rear of the foe. Kozsiusko, with the help of French money and advice, had raised an insurrection in Poland, and the hands of the Prussians were tied. The Polish question touched them nearer than the French, and all their thoughts were turned in the opposite direction. The Austrians began to apprehend that Prussia would desert them on the Rhine, and would gain an advantage over them in Poland, while they were busy with their best army in Flanders. Pitt increased his offers. Lord Spencer was sent to Vienna to arrange for a further subsidy. But the Prussians began to withdraw. Marshal Moellendorf informed the French in September that the Austrians were about to attack Treves. He promised that he would do no more than he could help for his allies. On the 20th, Hohenlohe, who was not in the secret, having fought Hoche at Kaiserslautern and defeated him, the commander-in-chief sent explanations and apologies. In October, Pitt stopped the supplies, and the Prussians disappeared from the war.

The winter of 1794-95 was severe, and even the sea froze in Holland. In January, Pichegru marched over the solid Rhine, and neither Dutch nor English offered any considerable resistance. The Prince of Orange fled to England; the Duke of York retreated to Bremen, and there embarked; and on the 28th the French were welcomed by the democracy of Amsterdam. A body of cavalry rode up to the fleet on the ice, and received its surrender. There was no cause left for it to defend. Holland was to be the salvation of French credit. It gave France trade, a fleet, a position from which to enter Germany on the undefended side. The tables were turned against Pitt and his policy. His Prussian ally made peace in April, giving up to France all Germany as far as the Rhine, and undertaking to occupy Hanover, if George III., as elector, refused to be neutral. Spain almost immediately followed. Manuel Godoy, lately a guardsman, but Prime Minister and Duke of Alcudia since November 1792, had declined Pitt's proposals for an alliance as long as there were hopes of saving the life of Lewis by the promise of neutrality. When those hopes came to an end, he consented. The joint occupation of

Toulon had not been amicable; and when George III. was made King of Corsica, it was an injury to Spain as a Mediterranean Power. The animosity against regicide France faded away; the war was not popular, and the Duke of Alcudia became, amid general rejoicing, Prince of the Peace.

We saw how the first invasion in 1792, brought the worst men to power. In 1793, the Reign of Terror coincided exactly with the season of public danger. Robespierre became the head of the government on the very day when the bad news came from the fortresses, and he fell immediately after the occupation of Brussels, July 11, 1794, exposed the effects of Fleurus. We cannot dissociate these events, or disprove the contention that the Reign of Terror was the salvation of France. It is certain that the conscription of March 1793, under Girondin auspices, scarcely yielded half the required amount, whilst the levies of the following August, decreed and carried out by the Mountain, inundated the country with soldiers, who were prepared by the slaughter going on at home to face the slaughter at the front. This, then, was the result which Conservative Europe obtained by its attack on the Republic. The French had subjugated Savoy, the Rhineland, Belgium, Holland, whilst Prussia and Spain had been made to sue for peace. England had deprived France of her colonies, but had lost repute as a military Power. Austria alone, with her dependent neighbours, maintained the unequal struggle on the Continent under worse conditions, and with no hope but in the help of Russia.

XXII
AFTER THE TERROR

It remains for us to pursue the course of French politics from the fall of the Terrorists to the Constitution of the year III., and the close of the Convention in October 1795. The State drifted after the storm, and was long without a regular government or a guiding body of opinion. The first feeling was relief at an immense deliverance. Prisons were opened and thousands of private citizens were released. The new sensation displayed itself extravagantly, in the search for pleasures unknown during the stern and sombre reign. Madame Tallien set the fashion as queen of Paris society. Men rejected the modern garment which characterised the hateful years, and put on tights. They buried the chin in folded neckcloths, and wore tall hats in protest against the exposed neck and the red nightcap of the enemy. Powder was resumed; but the pigtail was cut off straight, in commemoration of friends lost by the fall of the axe. Young men, representing the new spirit, wore a kind of uniform, with the badge of mourning on the arm, and a knobstick in their hands adapted to the Jacobin skull. They became known afterwards as the *Jeunesse Dorée*. The press made much of them, and they served as a body to the leaders of the reaction, hustling opponents, and denoting the infinite change in the conditions of public life.

These were externals. What went on underneath was the gradual recovery of the respectable elements of society, and the passage of power from the unworthy hands of the men who destroyed Robespierre. These, the Thermidorians, were faithful to the contract with the Plain, by which they obtained their victory. Some had been friends of Danton, who, at one moment of the previous winter, had approved a policy of moderation in the use of the guillotine. Tallien had domestic as well as public reasons for clemency. But the bulk of the genuine Montagnards were unaltered. They had deserted Robespierre when it became unsafe to defend him; but they had not renounced his system, and held that it was needful as their security against the furious enmity they had incurred when they were the ruling faction.

The majority in the Convention, where all powers were now concentrated, were unable to govern. The irresistible resources of the Reign of Terror were gone, and nothing occupied their place. There was no working Constitution, no settled authority, no party enjoying ascendancy and respect, no public men free from the guilt of blood. Many months were to pass before the ruins of the fallen parties gathered together and constituted an effective government with a real policy and the means of pursuing it. The chiefs of the Commune and of the revolutionary tribunal, near one hundred in number, had followed Robespierre to the scaffold.

The Committees of government had lost their most energetic members, and were disabled by the new plan of rapid renewal. Power fluctuated between varying combinations of deputies, all of them transient and quickly discredited. The main division was between vengeance and amnesty. And the character of the following months was a gradual drift in the direction of vengeance, as the imprisoned or proscribed minority returned to their seats. But the Mountain included the men, who by organising, and equipping, and controlling the armies had made France the first of European Powers, and they could not at once be displaced. Barère proposed that existing institutions should be preserved, and that Fouquier should continue his office. On August 19, Louchet, the man who led the assault against Robespierre, insisted that it was needful to keep up the Terror with all the rigour that had been prescribed by the sagacious and profound Marat. A month later, September 21, the Convention solemnised the apotheosis of Marat, whose remains were deposited in the Pantheon, while those of Mirabeau were cast out. Three weeks later, the master of Robespierre, Rousseau, was brought, with equal ceremony, to be laid by his side. The worst of the remaining offenders, Barère, Collot d'Herbois, and Billaud-Varennes, were deprived of their seats on the Committee of Public Safety. But in spite of the denunciations of Lecointre and of Legendre, the Convention refused to proceed against them.

All through September and a great part of October the Mountain held its ground, and prevented the reform of the government. Billaud, gaining courage, declared that the lion might slumber, but would rend his enemies on awaking. By the lion, he meant himself and his friends of Thermidor. The governing Committees were reconstructed on the principle of frequent change; the law of Prairial, which gave the right of arbitrary arrest and unconditional gaol delivery, was abrogated; and commissaries were sent out to teach the Provinces the example of Paris.

Beyond these measures, the action of the State stood still. The fall of the men who reigned by terror produced, at first, no great political result. The process of change was set in motion by certain citizens of Nantes. Carrier had sent a batch of 132 of his prisoners to feed the Paris guillotine. Thirty-eight of them died of the hardships they endured. The remainder were still in prison in Thermidor; and they now petitioned to be put on their trial. The trial took place; and the evidence given was such as made a reaction inevitable. On September 14, the Nantais were acquitted. Then the necessary consequence followed. If the victims of Carrier were innocent, what was Carrier himself? His atrocities had been exposed, and, on November 12, the Convention resolved, by 498 to 2, that he should appear before the tribunal. For Carrier was a deputy, inviolable under common law. The trial was prolonged, for it was the trial not of a man, but of a system, of a whole class of men still in the enjoyment of immunity.

Everything that could be brought to light gave strength to the Thermidorians against their enemies, and gave them the command of public opinion. On December 16 Carrier was guillotined, he had defended himself with spirit. The strength of his case was that his prosecutors were nearly as guilty as himself, and that they would all, successively, be struck down by the enemies of the Republic. He did his best to drag down the party with him. His associates, acquitted by the revolutionary tribunal on the plea that their delinquencies were not political, were then sent before the ordinary courts. On the day on which the convention resolved that the butcher of Nantes must stand his trial, they closed the Jacobin Club, and now the reaction was setting in.

On December 1, after hearing a report by Carnot, the assembly offered an amnesty to the insurgents on the Loire, and on the 8th those Girondins were recalled who had been placed under arrest. This measure was decisive. With the willing aid of the Plain they were masters of the Convention, for they were seventy-three in number, and, unlike the Plain, they were not hampered and disabled by their own iniquities. They were not accomplices of the Reign of Terror, for they had spent it in confinement. They had nothing to fear from a vigorous application of deserved penalties, and they had a terrible score to clear off. There were still sixteen deputies who had been proscribed with Buzot and the rest. They were now amnestied, and three months later, March 8, they were admitted to their seats. There they sat face to face with the men who had outlawed them, who had devoted them to death by an act the injustice of which was now proclaimed.

The cry for vengeance was becoming irresistible as the policy of the last year was reversed. In the course of that process La Vendée had its turn. On the 17th of February, at La Jaunaye, the French Republic came to terms with Charette. He was treated as an equal power. He obtained liberty for religion, compensation in money, relief from conscription, and a territorial guard of 2000 men, to be paid by the government, and commanded by himself. The same conditions were accepted soon after by Stofflet, and by the Breton leader, Cormatin. In that hour of triumph Charette rode into Nantes with the white badge of Royalism displayed; and he was received with honour by the authorities, and acclaimed by the crowd. Immediately after the treaty of La Jaunaye which, granted the free practice of religion in the west, it was extended to the whole of France. The churches were given back some months later; there is one parish, in an eastern department, where it is said that the church was never closed, and the service never interrupted.

In March the Girondins were strong enough to turn upon their foes. The extent of the reaction was tested by the expulsion of Marat from his brief rest in the Pantheon, and the destruction of his busts all over the town, by the young men stimulated by Fréron. In March, the great offenders who had been so hard to reach, Collot d'Herbois, Billaud, and Barère, were thrown into prison. Carnot defended them, on the ground that they were hardly worse than himself. The Convention resolved that they should be sent to Cayenne. Barère escaped on the way. Fouquier-Tinville came next, and his trial did as much harm to his party in the spring as that of Carrier in the preceding autumn. He pleaded that he was but an instrument in the hands of the Committee of Public Safety, and that as the three members of it, whom he had obeyed, were only transported, no more could be done to himself. The tribunal was not bound by the punishments decreed by the Assembly, and in May Fouquier was executed.

The Montagnards resolved that they would not perish without a struggle. On April 1 they assailed the Convention, and were repulsed. A number of the worst were thrown into prison. A more formidable attack was made on May 20. For hours the Convention was in the power of the mob, and a deputy was killed in attempting to protect the president. Members who belonged to the Mountain carried a series of decrees which gratified the populace. Late at night the Assembly was rescued. The tumultuous votes were declared non-existent, and those who had moved them were sent before a military commission. They had not prompted the sedition, and it was urged that they acted as they did in order to appease it, and to save the lives of their opponents. Romme, author of the republican Calendar, was the most remarkable of these men; and there is some doubt as to their guilt, and the legality of their sentence. One of them had been visited by his wife, and she left the means of suicide in his hands. As they left the court, each of them stabbed himself, and passed the knife in silence to his neighbour. Before the guards were aware of anything, three were dead, and the others were dragged, covered with blood, to the place of execution. It was the 17th of June, and the Girondins were supreme. Sixty-two deputies had been decreed in the course of the reaction, and the domination of the Jacobin mob, that is, government by equality instead of liberty, was at an end. The middle class had recovered power, and it was very doubtful whether these new masters of France were willing again to risk the experiment of a republic. That experiment had proved a dreadful failure, and it was more easy and obvious to seek relief in the refuge of monarchy than on the quicksands of fluttering majorities.

The royalists were wreaking vengeance on their enemies in the south, by what was afterwards known as the White Terror; and they showed themselves in force at Paris. For a time, every measure helped them that was taken against the Montagnards, and people used publicly to say that 8 and 9 are 17, that is, that the revolution of 1789 would end by the accession of Lewis XVII. Between Girondin and royalist there was the blood of the king, and the regicides knew what they must expect from a restoration. The party remained irreconcilable, and opposed the idea. Their struggle now was not with the Mountain, which had been laid low, but with their old adversaries the reforming adherents of Monarchy. But there were some leading men who, from conviction or, which would be more significant, from policy began to compound with the exiled princes. Tallien and Cambacérès of the Mountain, Isnard and Lanjuinais of the Gironde, Boissy d'Anglas of the Plain, the successful general Pichegru, and the best negotiator in France Barthélemy, were all known, or suspected, to be making terms with the Count of Provence at Verona. It was commonly reported that the Committee was wavering, and that the Constitution would turn towards monarchy. Breton and Vendean were ready to rise once more, Pitt was preparing vast armaments to help them; above all, there was a young pretender who had never made an enemy, whose early sufferings claimed sympathy from royalist and republican, and who shared no responsibility for *émigré* and invader, whom, for the best of reasons, he had never seen.

Meantime the Republic had improved its position in the world. Its conquests included the Alps and the Rhine, Belgium, and Holland, and surpassed the successes of the Monarchy even under Lewis XIV. The confederacy of kings was broken up. Tuscany had been the first to treat. Prussia had followed, bringing with it the neutrality of Northern Germany. Then Holland came, and Spain had opened negotiations. But with Spain there was a difficulty. There could be no treaty with a government which detained in prison the head of the House of Bourbon. As soon as he was delivered up, Spain was ready to sign and to ratify. Thus in the spring of 1795, the thoughts of men came to be riveted on the room in the Temple where the king was slowly and surely dying. The gaoler had asked the Committee what their intention was. "Do you mean to banish him?" "No." "To kill him?" "No." "Then," with an oath! "what is it you want?" "To get rid of him." On May 3, it was reported to the government that the young captive was ill. Next day, that he was very ill. But he was an obstacle to the Spanish treaty which was absolutely necessary, and twice the government made no sign. On the 5th, it was believed that he was in danger, and then a physician was sent to him. The choice was a good one, for the man was capable, and had attended the royal family. His opinion was that nothing could save the prisoner, except country air. One day he added: "He is lost, but perhaps there are some who will not be sorry." Three days later Lewis XVII. was living, but the doctor was dead, and a legend grew up on his grave. It was said that he was poisoned because he had discovered the dread secret that the boy in the Temple was not the king. Even Louis Blanc believed that the king had been secretly released, and that a dying patient from the hospital had been substituted for him. The belief has been kept alive to this day. The most popular living dramatist[3] has a play now running at Paris, in which the king is rescued in a washerwoman's linen basket, which draws crowds. The truth is that he died on June 8, 1795. The Republic had gained its purpose. Peace was signed with Spain; and the friends of monarchy on the Constitutional Committee at once declared that they would not vote for it.

[3] Sardou.

At the very moment when the Constitution was presented to the Assembly by Boissy d'Anglas, a fleet of transports under convoy appeared off the western coast. Pitt had allowed La Vendée to go down in defeat and slaughter, but at last he made up his mind to help, and it was done on a magnificent scale. Two expeditions were fitted out, and furnished with material of war. Each of them carried three or four thousand *émigrés* armed and clad by England. One was commanded by d'Hervilly, whom we have already seen, for it was he who took the order to cease firing on August 10; the other by young Sombreuil, whose father was saved in September in the tragic way you have heard. At the head of them all was the Count de Puisaye, the most politic and influential of the *émigrés*, a man who had been in touch with the Girondins in Normandy, who had obtained the ear of ministers at Whitehall, and who had been washed in so many waters that the genuine, exclusive, narrow-minded managers of Vendean legitimacy neither understood nor believed him. They brought a vast treasure in the shape of forged *assignats*; and in confused memory of the services rendered by the titular of Agra, they brought a real bishop who had sanctioned the forgery.

The first division sailed from Cowes on June 10. On the 23rd Lord Bridport engaged the French fleet and drove it into port. Four days later the *émigrés* landed at Carnac, among the early monuments of the Celtic race. It was a low promontory, defended at the neck by a fort named after the Duke de Penthièvre, and it could be swept, in places, by the guns of the fleet. Thousands of Chouans joined; but La Vendée was suspicious and stood aloof. They had expected the fleet to come to them, but it had gone to Brittany, and there was jealousy between the two provinces, between the partisans of Lewis XVIII. and those of his brother the Count d'Artois, between the priests and the politicians. The clergy restrained Charette and Stofflet from uniting with Puisaye and his questionable allies, whom they accused of seeking the crown of France for the Duke of York; and they promised that, if they waited a little, the Count d'Artois would appear among them. They effectively ruined their prospects of success; but Pitt himself had contributed his share. Puisaye declined to bring English soldiers into his country, and his scruples were admitted. But, in order to swell his forces, the frugal minister armed between 1000 and 2000 French prisoners, who were republicans, but who declared themselves ready to join, and were as glad to escape from captivity as the government was to get rid of them. The royalist officers protested against this alloy, but their objections did not prevail, and when they came to their own country these men deserted. They pointed out a place where the republicans could pass under the fort at low water, and enter it on the undefended side. At night, in the midst of a furious tempest, the passage was attempted. Hoche's troops waded through the stormy waters of Quiberon bay, and the tricolor was soon displayed upon the walls.

The royalists were driven to the extremity of the peninsula. Some, but not many, escaped in English boats, and it was thought that our fleet did not do all that it might have done to retrieve a disaster so injurious to the fame and the influence of England. Sombreuil defended himself until a republican officer called on him to capitulate. He consented, for there was no hope; but no terms were made, and it was in truth an unconditional surrender. Tallien, who was in the camp, hurried to Paris to intercede for the prisoners. Before going to the Convention, he went to his home. There his wife told him that she had just seen Lanjuinais, that Sieyès had brought back from Holland, where he had negotiated peace, proofs of Tallien's treasonable correspondence with the Bourbons, and that his life was in danger. He went at once to the Convention, and called for the summary punishment of the captured *émigrés*.

Hoche was a magnanimous enemy, both by character and policy, and he had a deep respect for Sombreuil. He secretly offered to let him escape. The prisoner refused to be saved without his comrades; and they were shot down together near Auray, on a spot which is still known as the field of sacrifice. They were six or seven hundred. The firing party awakened the echoes of Vendée, for Charette instantly put his prisoners to death; and the Chouans afterwards contrived to cut down every man of the four battalions charged with the execution.

The battle of Quiberon took place on July 21, and when all that ensued was over on August 25, another expedition sailed from Portsmouth with the Count d'Artois on board. He landed on an island off La Vendée, and Charette, with fifteen thousand men, marched down to the coast to receive him, among the haggard veterans of the royal cause. There, on October 10, a message came from the Prince informing the hero that he was about to sail away, and to wait in safety for better times. Five days earlier the question had been fought out and decided at Paris, and a man had been revealed who was to raise deeper and more momentous issues than the obsolete controversy between monarchy and republic. That controversy had been pursued in the constitutional debates under the fatal influence of the events on the coast of Brittany. The royalists had displayed their colours, sailing under the British flag, and the British alliance had not availed them. And they had displayed a strange political imbecility, contrasting with their spirit and intelligence in war.

The constitutional committee had been elected on April 23 under different auspices, when the Convention was making terms with Charette and Cormatin, as well as with the foreign Powers. Sieyès, of necessity, was the first man chosen; but he was on the governing committee, and he declined. So did Merlin and Cambacérès, for the same reason, and the three ablest men in the assembly did not serve.

Eleven moderate but not very eminent men were elected, and the draft was made chiefly by Daunou, and advocated by Thibaudeau. Daunou was an ancient oratorian, a studious and thoughtful if not a strong man, who became keeper of the archives, and lived down to 1840 with a somewhat usurped reputation for learning. Thibaudeau now began to exhibit great intelligence, and his writings are among our best authorities for these later years of the Republic and for the earlier years of the Empire. The general character of their scheme is that it is influenced more by experience than by theory, and strives to attach power to property. They reported on June 23; the debate began on July 4; and on the 20th Sieyès intervened. His advice turned mainly on the idea of a constitutional jury, an elective body of about one hundred, to watch over the Constitution, and to be guardians of the law against the makers of the law. It was to receive the plaints of minorities and of individuals against the legislature, and to preserve the spirit of the organic institutions against the omnipotence of the national representatives. This memorable attempt to develop in Europe something analogous to that property of the Supreme Court which was not yet matured in America, was rejected on August 5, almost unanimously.

The Constitution was adopted by the Convention on August 17. It included a declaration of duties, founded on confusion, but defended on the ground that a declaration of rights alone destroys the stability of the State. And in matters touching religion it innovated on what had been done hitherto, for it separated Church and State, leaving all religions to their own resources. The division of powers was carried farther, for the legislative was divided into two, and the executive into five. Universal suffrage was restricted; the poorest were excluded; and after nine years there was to be an educational test. The law did not last so long. The electoral body, one in two hundred of the whole constituency, was to be limited to owners of property. The directors were to be chosen by the legislature. Practically, there was much more regard for liberty, and less for equality, than in the former constitutions. The change in public opinion was shown by the vote on two Houses which only one deputy opposed.

At the last moment, that there might be no danger from royalism in the departments, it was resolved that two-thirds of the legislature must be taken from the Convention. They thus prolonged their own power, and secured the permanence of the ideas which inspired their action. At the same time they showed their want of confidence in the republican feeling of the country, and both exasperated the royalists and gave them courage to act for themselves. On September 23 the country accepted the scheme, by a languid vote, but with a large majority.

The new Constitution afforded securities for order and for liberty such as France had never enjoyed. The Revolution had begun with a Liberalism which was a passion more than a philosophy, and the first Assembly endeavoured to realise it by diminishing authority, weakening the executive, and decentralising power. In the hour of peril under the Girondins the policy failed, and the Jacobins governed on the principle that power, coming from the people, ought to be concentrated in the fewest possible hands and made absolutely irresistible. Equality became the substitute of liberty, and the danger arose that the most welcome form of equality would be the equal distribution of property. The Jacobin statesmen, the thinkers of the party, undertook to abolish poverty without falling into Socialism. They had the Church property, which served as the basis of the public credit. They had the royal domain, the confiscated estates of emigrants and malignants, the common lands, the forest lands. And in time of war there was the pillage of opulent neighbours. By these operations the income of the peasantry was doubled, and it was deemed possible to relieve the masses from taxation, until, by the immense transfer of property, there should be no poor in the Republic. These schemes were at an end, and the Constitution of the year III. closes the revolutionary period.

The royalists and conservatives of the capital would have acquiesced in the defeat of their hopes but for the additional article which threatened to perpetuate power in the hands of existing deputies, which had been carried by a far smaller vote than that which was given in favour of the organic law itself. The alarm and the indignation were extreme, and the royalists, on counting their forces, saw that they had a good chance against the declining assembly. Nearly thirty thousand men were collected, and the command was given to an experienced officer. It had been proposed by some to confer it on the Count Colbert de Maulevrier, the former employer of Stofflet. This was refused on the ground that they were not absolutists or *émigrés*, but Liberals, and partisans of constitutional monarchy, and of no other.

The army of the Convention was scarcely six thousand, and a large body of Jacobin roughs were among them. The command was bestowed on Menou, a member of the minority of nobles of 1789. But Menou was disgusted with his materials, and felt more sympathy with the enemy. He endeavoured to negotiate, and was deposed, and succeeded by Barras, the victor in the bloodless battle of Thermidor.

Bonaparte, out of employment, was lounging in Paris, and as he came out of the theatre he found himself among the men who were holding the parley. He hurried to headquarters, where the effect of his defining words upon the scared authorities was such that he was at once appointed second in command. Therefore, when morning dawned, on October 5, the Louvre and the Tuileries had become a fortress, and the gardens were a fortified camp. A young officer who became the most brilliant figure on the battlefield of Europe—Murat—brought up cannon from the country. The bridge, and the quay, and every street that opened on the palace, were so commanded by batteries that they could be swept by grape-shot. Officers had been sent out for provisions, for barrels of gunpowder, for all that belongs to hospital and ambulance. Lest retreat should be cut off, a strong detachment held the road to St. Cloud; and arms were liberally supplied to the Convention and the friendly quarter of St. Antoine. The insurgents, led by dexterous intriguers, but without a great soldier at their head, could not approach the river; and those who came down from the opulent centre of the city missed their opportunity. After a sharp conflict in the Rue St. Honoré, they fled, pursued by nothing more murderous than blank cartridge; and Paris felt, for the first time, the grasp of the master. The man who defeated them, and by defeating them kept the throne vacant, was Bonaparte, through whose genius the Revolution was to subjugate the Continent.

APPENDIX

THE LITERATURE OF THE REVOLUTION

Before embarking on the stormy sea before us, we ought to be provided with chart and compass. Therefore I begin by speaking about the histories of the Revolution, so that you may at once have some idea what to choose and what to reject, that you may know where we stand, how we have come to penetrate so far and no farther, what branches there are that already bear ripe fruit and where it is still ripening on the tree of knowledge. I desire to rescue you from the writers of each particular school and each particular age, and from perpetual dependence on the ready-made and conventional narratives that satisfy the outer world.

With the growing experience of mankind, the larger curiosity and the increased resource, each generation adds to our insight. Lesser events can be understood by those who behold them, great events require time in proportion to their greatness.

Lamartine once said that the Revolution has mysteries but no enigmas. It is humiliating to be obliged to confess that those words are no nearer truth now than when they were written. People have not yet ceased to dispute about the real origin and nature of the event. It was the deficit; it was the famine; it was the Austrian Committee; it was the Diamond Necklace, and the humiliating memories of the Seven Years' War; it was the pride of nobles or the intolerance of priests; it was philosophy; it was freemasonry; it was Mr. Pitt; it was the incurable levity and violence of the national character; it was the issue of that struggle between classes that constitutes the unity of the history of France.

Amongst these interpretations we shall have to pick our way; but there are many questions of detail on which I shall be forced to tell you that I have no deciding evidence.

After the contemporary memoirs, the first historian who wrote with authority was Droz. He was at work for thirty years, having begun in 1811, when Paris was still full of floating information, and he knew much that otherwise did not come out until long after his death. He had consulted Lally Tollendal, and he was allowed to use the memoirs of Malouet, which were in manuscript, and which are unsurpassed for wisdom and good faith in the literature of the National Assembly. Droz was a man of sense and experience, with a true if not a powerful mind; and his book, in point of soundness and accuracy, was all that a book could be in the days when it was written. It is a history of Lewis XVI. during the time when it was possible to bring the Revolution under control; and the author shows, with an absolute sureness of judgment, that the turning-point was the rejection of the first project of Constitution, in September 1789. For him, the Revolution is contained in the first four months. He meant to write a political treatise on the natural history of revolutions, and the art of so managing just demands that unjust and dangerous demands shall acquire no force. It became a history of rejected opportunities, and an indictment of the wisdom of the minister and of the goodness of the king, by a constitutional royalist of the English school. His service to history is that he shows how disorder and crime grew out of unreadiness, want of energy, want of clear thought and definite design. Droz admits that there is a flaw in the philosophy of his title-page. The position lost in the summer of 1789 was never recovered. But during the year 1790 Mirabeau was at work on schemes to restore the monarchy, and it is not plain that they could never have succeeded. Therefore Droz added a volume on the parliamentary career of Mirabeau, and called it an appendix, so as to remain true to his original theory of the fatal limit. We know the great orator better than he could be known in 1842, and the value of Droz's excellent work is confined to the second volume. It will stand undiminished even if we reject the idea which inspired it, and prefer to think that the cause might have been won, even when it came to actual fighting, on the 10th of August. Droz's book belongs to the small number of writings before us which are superior to their fame, and it was followed by one that enjoyed to the utmost the opposite fate.

For our next event is an explosion. Lamartine, the poet, was one of those legitimists who believed that 1830 had killed monarchy, who considered the Orleans dynasty a sham, and set themselves at once to look ahead of it towards the inevitable Republic. Talleyrand warned him to hold himself ready for something more substantial than the exchange of a nephew for an uncle on a baseless throne. With the intuition of genius he saw sooner than most men, more accurately than any man, the signs of what was to come. In six years, he said, we shall be masters. He was mistaken only by a few weeks. He laid his plans that, when the time came, he should be the accepted leader. To chasten and idealise the Revolution, and to prepare a Republic that should not be a terror to mankind, but should submit easily to the fascination of a melodious and sympathetic eloquence, he wrote the *History of the Girondins*. The success was the most instantaneous and splendid ever obtained by a historical work. People could read nothing else; and Alexandre Dumas paid him the shrewd compliment of saying that he had lifted history to the level of romance. Lamartine gained his purpose. He contributed to institute a Republic that was pacific and humane, responsive to the charm of phrase, and obedient to the master hand that wrote the glories of the Gironde. He always believed that, without his book, the Reign of Terror would have been renewed.

From early in the century to the other day there was a succession of authors in France who knew how to write as scarcely any but Mr. Ruskin or Mr. Swinburne have ever written in England. They doubled the opulence and the significance of language, and made prose more sonorous and more penetrating than anything but the highest poetry. There were not more than half a dozen, beginning with Chateaubriand, and, I fear, ending with Saint Victor. Lamartine became the historian in this Corinthian school of style, and his purple patches outdo everything in effectiveness. But it would appear that in French rhetoric there are pitfalls which tamer pens avoid. Rousseau compared the Roman Senate to two hundred kings, because his sensitive ear did not allow him to say three hundred—*trois cents rois*. Chateaubriand, describing in a private letter his journey to the Alps, speaks of the moon along the mountain tops, and adds: "It is all right; I have looked up the Almanac, and find that there was a moon." Paul Louis Courier says that Plutarch would have made Pompey conquer at Pharsalus if it would have read better, and he thinks that he was quite right. Courier's exacting taste would have found contentment in Lamartine. He knows very well that Marie Antoinette was fifteen when she married the Dauphin in 1770; yet he affirms that she was the child the Empress held up in her arms when the Magyar magnates swore to die for their queen, Maria Theresa. The scene occurred in 1741, fourteen years before she was born. Histories of literature give the catalogue of his amazing blunders.

In his declining years he reverted to this book, and wrote an apology, in which he answered his accusers, and confessed to some passages which he exhorted them to tear out. There was good ground for recantation. Writing to dazzle the democracy by means of a bright halo, with himself in the midst of it, he was sometimes weak in exposing crimes that had a popular motive. His republicanism was of the sort that allows no safeguard for minorities, no rights to men but those which their country gives them. He had been the speaker who, when the Chamber wavered, rejected the Regency which was the legal government, and compelled the Duchess of Orleans to fly. When a report reached him that she had been seized, and he was asked to order her release, he refused, saying, "If the people ask for her, she must be given up to them."

In his own defence he showed that he had consulted the widow of Danton, and had found a witness of the last banquet of the Girondins. In his book he dramatised the scene, and displayed the various bearing of the fallen statesmen during their last night on earth. Granier de Cassagnac pronounced the whole thing a fabrication. It was told by Nodier who was a professional inventor, and by Thiers who gave no authority, and none could be found. But there was a priest who sat outside the door, waiting to offer the last consolations of religion to the men about to die. Fifty years later he was still living, and Lamartine found him and took down his recollections. An old Girondin, whom Charlotte Corday had requested to defend her, and who died a senator of the Second Empire, Pontécoulant, assured his friends that Lamartine had given the true colour, had reproduced the times as he remembered them. In the same way General Dumas approved of Thiers's 10th of August. He was an old soldier of the American war, a statesman of the Revolution, a trusted servant of Napoleon, whose military history he wrote, and he left memoirs which we value. But I suspect that these lingering veterans were easily pleased with clever writers who brought back the scenes of their early life. There may be truth in Lamartine's colouring, but on the whole his Girondins live as literature not as history. And his four volumes on the National Assembly are a piece of book-making that requires no comment.

Before the thunder of the Girondins had rolled away, they were followed by two books of more enduring value on the same side. Louis Blanc was a socialist politician, who helped, after 1840, to cement that union of socialists and republicans which overthrew the monarchy, and went to pieces on the barricades of June 1848. Driven into exile, he settled in London, and spent several years at work in the British Museum. It was not all a misfortune, as this is what he found there: it will give you an encouraging idea of the resources that await us on our path. When Croker gave up his house at the Admiralty on the accession of the Whigs, he sold his revolutionary library of more than 10,000 pieces to the Museum. But the collector's fever is an ailment not to be laid by change of government or loss of income. Six years later Croker had made another collection as large as the first, which also was bought by the Trustees. Before he died, this incurable collector had brought together as much as the two previous lots, and the whole was at last deposited in the same place. There, in one room, we have about five hundred shelves crowded, on an average, with more than one hundred and twenty pamphlets, all of them belonging to the epoch that concerns us. Allowing for duplicates, this amounts to forty or fifty thousand Revolution tracts; and I believe that there is nothing equal to it at Paris. Half of them were already there, in time to be consulted both by Louis Blanc and Tocqueville. Croker's collection of manuscript papers on the same period was sold for £50 at his death, and went to what was once the famous library of Middle Hill.

Louis Blanc was thus able to continue in England the work he had begun at home, and he completed it in twelve volumes. It contains much subsidiary detail and many literary references, and this makes it a useful book to consult. The ponderous mass of material, and the power of the pen, do not compensate for the weary obtrusion of the author's doctrine and design.

An eminent personage once said to me that the parliament of his country was intent on suppressing educational freedom. When I asked what made them illiberal, he answered, "It is because they are liberal." Louis Blanc partook of that mixture. He is the expounder of Revolution in its compulsory and illiberal aspect. He desires government to be so constituted that it may do everything for the people, not so restricted that it can do no injury to minorities. The masses have more to suffer from abuse of wealth than from abuse of power, and need protection by the State, not against it. Power, in the proper hands, acting for the whole, must not be restrained in the interest of a part. Therefore Louis Blanc is the admirer and advocate of Robespierre; and the tone of his pleading appears at the September massacres, when he bids us remember St. Bartholomew.

Michelet undertook to vindicate the Revolution at the same time as Louis Blanc, without his frigid passion, his ostentatious research, his attention to particulars, but with deeper insight and a stronger pinion. His position at the archives gave him an advantage over every rival; and when he lost his place, he settled in the west of France and made a study of La Vendée. He is regardless of proof, and rejects as rubbish mere facts that contribute nothing to his argument or his picture. Because Arras was a clerical town, he calls Robespierre a priest. Because there are Punic tombs at Ajaccio, he calls Napoleon a countryman of Hannibal. For him the function of history is judgment, not narrative. If we submit ourselves to the event, if we think more of the accomplished deed than of the suggested problem, we become servile accomplices of success and force. History is resurrection. The historian is called to revise trials and to reverse sentences, as the people, who are the subject of all history, awoke to the knowledge of their wrongs and of their power, and rose up to avenge the past. History is also restitution. Authorities tyrannised and nations suffered; but the Revolution is the advent of justice, and the central fact in the experience of mankind. Michelet proclaims that at his touch the hollow idols were shattered and exposed, the carrion kings appeared, unsheeted and unmasked. He says that he has had to swallow too much anger and too much woe, too many vipers and too many kings; and he writes sometimes as if such diet disagreed with him. His imagination is filled with the cruel sufferings of man, and he hails with a profound enthusiasm the moment when the victim that could not die, in a furious act of retribution, avenged the martyrdom of a thousand years. The acquisition of rights, the academic theory, touches him less than the punishment of wrong. There is no forgiveness for those who resist the people rising in the consciousness of its might. What is good proceeds from the mass, and what is bad from individuals. Mankind, ignorant in regard to nature, is a righteous judge of the affairs of man. The light which comes to the learned from reflection comes to the unlearned more surely by natural inspiration; and power is due to the mass by reason of instinct, not by reason of numbers. They are right by dispensation of heaven, and there is no pity for their victims, if you remember the days of old. Michelet had no patience with those who sought the pure essence of the Revolution in religion. He contrasts the agonies with which the Church aggravated the punishment of death with the swift mercy of the guillotine, and prefers to fall into Danton's hands rather than into those of Lewis IX. or Torquemada.

With all this, by the real sincerity of his feeling for the multitude, by the thoroughness of his view and his intensely expressive language, he is the most illuminating of the democratic historians. We often read of men whose lives have been changed because a particular book has fallen into their hands, or, one might say, because they have fallen into the hands of a particular book. It is not always a happy accident; and one feels that things would have gone otherwise with them if they had examined Sir John Lubbock's List of Best Books, or what I would rather call the St. Helena library, containing none but works adequate and adapted to use by the ablest man in the full maturity of his mind. Of such books, that are strong enough, in some eminent quality, to work a change and form an epoch in a reader's life, there are two, perhaps, on our revolutionary shelf. One is Taine, and the other Michelet.

The fourth work of the revolutionary party, that was written almost simultaneously with these, is that of Villiaumé. Lamartine esteemed Vergniaud. Louis Blanc esteemed Robespierre, Michelet, Danton. Villiaumé went a step farther, and admired Marat. He had lived much in the surviving families of revolutionary heroes, and received, he says, the last breath of an expiring tradition. He had also gathered from Chateaubriand what he remembered; and Thierry, who was blind, caused his book to be read to him twice over.

The account of Marat in the 28th volume of Buchez was partly written by Villiaumé, and was approved by Albertine Marat. The great bibliographical curiosity in the literature of the Revolution is Marat's newspaper. It was printed often in hiding-places and under difficulties, and is so hard to find that, a few years ago, the Paris library did not possess a complete set. A bookseller once told me that he had sold it to an English statesman for £240. Marat's own copy, corrected in his handwriting, and enriched with other matter, was preserved by his sister. In 1835 she made it over to Villiaumé, who, having finished his book, sold it in 1859 for £80 to the collector Solar. Prince Napoleon afterwards owned it; and at last it made its way to an ancient Scottish castle, where I had the good fortune to find it.

Whilst the revolutionary historians, aided by public events, were predominating in France, the conservatives competed obscurely, and at first without success. Genoude was for many years editor of the leading royalist journal, and in that capacity initiated a remarkable phase of political thought. When the Bourbons were cast out under the imputation of incurable absolutism, the legitimists found themselves identified with a grudging liberality and a restricted suffrage, and stood at a hopeless disadvantage. In the *Gazette de France* Genoude at once adopted the opposite policy, and overtrumped the liberal Orleanists. He argued that a throne which was not occupied by right of inheritance, as a man holds his estate, could only be made legitimate by the expressed will of France. Therefore he insisted on an appeal to the nation, on the sovereignty of the people, on the widest extension of the franchise. When his friend Courmenin drew up the Constitution of 1848, it was Genoude who induced him to adopt the new practice of universal suffrage, which was unknown to the Revolution. Having lost his wife, he took orders. All this, he said one day, will presently come to an end, not through the act of a soldier or an orator, but of a Cardinal. And he drank to the memory of Richelieu.

The notion of a legitimate throne, restored by democracy, which was borrowed from Bolingbroke, and which nearly prevailed in 1873, gives some relief and originality to his work on the Revolution. You are not likely to meet with it. When Talleyrand's *Memoirs* appeared, most people learnt for the first time that he went at night to offer his services to the king, to get the better of the Assembly. The editor placed the event in the middle of July. Nobody seemed to know that the story was already told by Genoude, and that he fixed the midnight bid for power at its proper date, a month earlier.

The history of Amédée Gabourd is a far better book, and perhaps the best of its kind. Gabourd had previously written a history of France, and his many volumes on the nineteenth century, with no pretension in point of research, are convenient for the lower range of countries and events. He writes with the care, the intelligence, the knowledge of the work of other men, which distinguish Charles Knight's *Popular History of England*. I have known very deep students indeed who were in the habit of constantly using him. He says, with reason, that no writer has sought truth and justice with more perfect good faith, or has been more careful to keep aloof from party spirit and accepted judgments. As he was a constitutionalist, the revolution of February was the ruin of a system which he expected to last for ever, and to govern the last age of the world. But Gabourd remained true to his principles. He wrote: "I shall love the people, and honour the king; and I shall have the same judgment on the tyranny from above and the tyranny from below. I am not one of those who set a chasm between liberty and religion, as if God would accept no worship but that of servile hearts. I shall not oppose the results of the event which I describe, or deny the merit of what had been won at the price of so much suffering."

The Doctrinaires were of all men in the best position to understand the Revolution and to judge it rightly. They had no weakness for the ancient monarchy, none for the republic; and they accepted the results rather than the motives. They rejoiced in the reign of reason, but they required the monarchy duly limited, and the church as established by the Concordat, in order to resume the chain of history and the reposing influence of custom. They were the most intellectual group of statesmen in the country; but, like the Peelites, they were leaders without followers, and it was said of them that they were only four, but pretended to be five, to strike terror by their number. Guizot, the greatest writer among them, composed, in his old age, a history of France for his grandchildren. It was left incomplete, but his discourses on the Revolution, the topic he had thought about all his life, were edited by his family. These tales of a grandfather are not properly his work, and, like the kindred and coequal lectures of Niebuhr, give approximately the views of a man so great that it is a grief not to possess them in authentic form.

Instead of Guizot, our Doctrinaire historian is Barante. He had the distinction and the dignity of his friends, their book learning, and their experience of public affairs; and his work on the dukes of Burgundy was praised, in the infancy of those studies, beyond its merit in early life he had assisted Madame de la Rochejaquelein to bring out her *Memoirs*. His short biography of Saint Priest, Minister of the Interior in the first revolutionary year, is a singularly just and weighty narrative. After 1848 he published nine volumes on the Convention and the Directory. Like the rest of his party, Barante had always acknowledged the original spirit of the Revolution as the root of French institutions. But the movement of 1848, directed as it was against the Doctrinaires, against their monarchy and their ministry, had much developed the conservative element which was always strong within them.

In those days Montalembert succeeded Droz at the Academy, and took the opportunity to attack, as he said, not 1793 but 1789. He said that Guizot, the most eloquent of the immortals, had not found a word to urge in reply. On this level, and in opposition to the revival of Jacobin ideas and the rehabilitation of Jacobin character, Barante composed his work. It was a great occasion, as the tide had been running strongly the other way; but the book, coming from such a man, is a disappointment. In the trial of the king adverse points are slurred over, as if a historian could hold a brief. A more powerful writer of conservative history appeared about the same time in Heinrich von Sybel.

About the middle of the fifties, when Sybel's earlier volumes were coming out, the deeper studies began in France with Tocqueville. He was the first to establish, if not to discover, that the Revolution was not simply a break, a reversal, a surprise, but in part a development of tendencies at work in the old monarchy. He brought it into closer connection with French history, and believed that it had become inevitable, when Lewis XVI. ascended the throne, that the success and also the failure of the movement came from causes that were at work before. The desire for political freedom was sincere but adulterated. It was crossed and baffled by other aims. The secondary and subordinate liberties embarrassed the approach to the supreme goal of self-government. For Tocqueville was a Liberal of the purest breed—a Liberal and nothing else, deeply suspicious of democracy and its kindred, equality, centralisation and utilitarianism. Of all writers he is the most widely acceptable, and the hardest to find fault with. He is always wise, always right, and as just as Aristides. His intellect is without a flaw, but it is limited and constrained. He knows political literature and history less well than political life; his originality is not creative, and he does not stimulate with gleams of new light or unfathomed suggestiveness.

Two years later, in 1858, a work began to appear which was less new and less polished than Tocqueville's, but is still more instructive for every student of politics. Duvergier de Hauranne had long experience of public life. He remembered the day when he saw Cuvier mount the tribune in a black velvet suit and speak as few orators have spoken, and carry the electoral law which was the Reform Bill of 1817. Having quarrelled with the Doctrinaires, he led the attack which overthrew Guizot, and was one of three on whom Thiers was relying to save the throne, when the king went away in a cab and carried the dynasty with him. He devoted the evening of his life to a history of parliamentary government in France, which extends in ten volumes to 1830, and contains more profound ideas, more political science, than any other work I know in the compass of literature. He analyses every constitutional discussion, aided by much confidential knowledge, and the fullest acquaintance with pamphlets and leading articles. He is not so much at home in books; but he does not allow a shade of intelligent thought or a valid argument to escape him. During the Restoration, the great controversy of all ages, the conflict between reason and custom was fought out on the higher level. The question at that time was not which of the two should prevail, but how they should be reconciled, and whether rational thought and national life could be made to harmonise. The introductory volume covers the Revolution, and traces the progress and variation of views of government in France, from the appearance of Sieyès to the elevation of Napoleon.

Laboulaye was a man of like calibre and measurements, whom Waddington, when he was minister, called the true successor of Tocqueville. Like him he had saturated himself with American ideas, and like him he was persuaded that the revolutionary legacy of concentrated power was the chief obstacle to free institutions. He wrote, in three small volumes, a history of the United States, which is a most intelligent abstract of what he had learnt in Bancroft and Hildreth. He wrote with the utmost lucidity and definiteness, and never darkened counsel with prevaricating eloquence, so that there is no man from whom it is so easy and so agreeable to learn. His lectures on the early days of the Revolution were published from time to time in a review, and, I believe, have not been collected. Laboulaye was a scholar as well as a statesman, and always knew his subject well, and as a guide to the times we can have none more helpful than his unfinished course.

The event of the English competition is the appearance of Carlyle. After fifty years we are still dependent on him for Cromwell, and in *Past and Present* he gave what was the most remarkable piece of historical thinking in the language. But the mystery of investigation had not been revealed to him when he began his most famous book. He was scared from the Museum by an offender who sneezed in the Reading Room. As the French pamphlets were not yet catalogued, he asked permission to examine them and to make his selection at the shelves on which they stood. He complained that, having applied to a respectable official, he had been refused. Panizzi, furious at being described as a respectable official, declared that he could not allow the library to be pulled about by an unknown man of letters. In the end, the usual modest resources of a private collection satisfied his requirements. But the vivid gleam, the mixture of the sublime with the grotesque, make other opponents forget the impatient verdicts and the poverty of settled fact in the volumes that delivered our fathers from thraldom to Burke. They remain one of those disappointing stormclouds that give out more thunder than lightning.

The proof of advancing knowledge is the improvement in compendiums and school books. There are three which must be mentioned. In the middle of the century Lavallée wrote a history of France for his students at the Military College. Quoting Napoleon's remark, that the history of France must be in four volumes or in a hundred, he pronounces in favour of four. During a generation his work passed for the best of its kind. Being at St. Cyr, once the famous girls' school, for which Racine composed his later tragedies, he devoted many years to the elucidation of Madame de Maintenon, and the recovery of her interpolated letters. His Revolution is contained in 230 pages of his fourth volume. There is an abridgment of the like moderate dimensions by Carnot. He was the father of the President, and the son of the organiser of victory, who, in 1815, gave the memorable advice to Napoleon that, if he made a rush at the English, he would find them scattered and unprepared. He was a militant republican, editor of the *Memoirs* of his father, of Grégoire, and of Barère, and M. Aulard praises his book, with the sympathy of a co-religionist, as the best existing narrative. Other good republicans prefer what Henri Martin wrote in continuation of his history of France. I should have no difficulty in declaring that the seventh volume of the French history by Dareste is superior to them all; and however far we carry the process of selection and exclusion, I would never surrender it.

We have seen that there are many able works on either side, and two or three that are excellent. And there are a few sagacious and impartial men who keep the narrow path between them: Tocqueville for the origin, Droz and Laboulaye for the decisive period of 1789, Duvergier de Hauranne for all the political thinking, Dareste for the great outline of public events, in peace and war. They amount to no more than five volumes, and are less than the single Thiers or Michelet, and not half as long as Louis Blanc. We can easily read them through; and we shall find that they have made all things clear to us, that we can trust them, and that we have nothing to unlearn. But if we confine ourselves to the company of men who steer a judicious middle course, with whom we find that we can agree, our wisdom will turn sour, and we shall never behold parties in their strength. No man feels the grandeur of the Revolution till he reads Michelet, or the horror of it without reading Taine. But I have kept the best for the end, and will speak of Taine, and two or three more who rival Taine, next week.

After much partial and contentious writing, sagacious men attained a reasonable judgment on the good and evil, the truth and error, of the Revolution. The view established by constitutional royalists, like Duvergier de Hauranne, and by men equidistant from royalist or republican exclusiveness, such as Tocqueville and Laboulaye, was very largely shared by intelligent democrats, more particularly by Lanfrey, and by Quinet in his two volumes on the genius of the Revolution. At that time, under the Second Empire, there was nothing that could be called an adequate history. The archives were practically unexplored, and men had no idea of the amount of labour serious exploration implies. The first writer who produced original matter from the papers of the Paris Commune was Mortimer Ternaux, whose eight volumes on the Reign of Terror came out between 1862 and 1880. What he revealed was so decisive that it obliged Sybel to rewrite what he had written on the scenes of September.

When I describe the real study of the Revolution as beginning with Tocqueville and Ternaux, I mean the study of it in the genuine and official sources. Memoirs, of course, abounded. There are more than a hundred. But memoirs do not supply the certainty of history. Certainty comes with the means of control, and there is no controlling or testing memoirs without the contemporary document. Down to the middle of the century, private letters and official documents were rare. Then, in the early summer of 1851, two important collections appeared within a few weeks of each other.

First came the *Memoirs* of Mallet du Pan, a liberal, independent, and discerning observer, whom, apart from the gift of style, Taine compares to Burke, and who, like Burke, went over to the other side.

This was followed by Mirabeau's *Secret Correspondence with the Court*. His prevarication and double-dealing as a popular leader in the pay of the king had long been known. At least twenty persons were in the secret. One man, leaving Paris hurriedly, left one paper, the most important of all, lying about in his room. Unmistakable allusions were found among the contents of the Iron Chest. One of the ministers told the story in his *Memoirs*, and a letter belonging to the series was printed in 1827. La Marck, just before his death, showed the papers to Montigny, who gave an account of them in his work on Mirabeau, and Droz moreover knew the main facts from Malouet when he wrote in 1842. For us the interest of the publication lies not in the exposure of what was already known, but in the details of his tortuous and ingenious policy during his last year of life, and of his schemes to save the king and the constitution. For the revolutionary party, the posthumous avowal of so much treachery was like the story of the monk who, dying with the fame of a saint, rose under the shroud during the funeral service, and confessed before his brethren that he had lived and died an unrepentant hypocrite.

Still, no private papers could make up for the silence of the public archives; and the true secrets of government, diplomacy and war, remained almost intact until 1865. The manner in which they came to be exhumed is the most curious transaction in the progress of revolutionary history. It was a consequence of the passion for autographs and the collector's craze. Seventy thousand autographs were sold by auction in Paris in the twenty-eight years from 1822 to 1850. From the days of the Restoration no letters were more eagerly sought and prized than those of the queen. Royalist society regarded her as an august, heroic, and innocent victim, and attributed the ruin of the monarchy to the neglect of her high-minded counsels. It became a lucrative occupation to steal letters that bore her signature, in order to sell them to wealthy purchasers. Prices rose steadily. A letter of the year 1784, which fetched fifty-two francs in 1850, was sold for one hundred and seven in 1857, and for one hundred and fifty in 1861. In 1844 one was bought for two hundred francs, and another for three hundred and thirty. A letter to the Princess de Lamballe, which fetched seven hundred francs in 1860, went up to seven hundred and sixty in 1865, when suspicion was beginning to stir. In all, forty-one letters from the queen to Mme. de Lamballe have been in the market, and not one of them was genuine. When it became worth while to steal, it was still more profitable to forge, for then there was no limit to the supply.

In her lifetime the queen was aware that hostile *émigrés* imitated her hand. Three such letters were published in 1801 in a worthless book called *Madame de Lamballe's Memoirs*. Such forgeries came into the market from the year 1822. The art was carried to the point that it defied detection, and the credulity of the public was insatiable. In Germany a man imitated Schiller's writing so perfectly that Schiller's daughter bought his letters as fast as they could be produced. At Paris the nefarious trade became active about 1839.

On March 15, 1861, a facsimilist, Betbeder, issued a challenge, undertaking to execute autographs that it would be impossible to detect, by paper, ink, handwriting, or text. The trial came off in the presence of experts, and in April 1864 they pronounced that his imitations could not be distinguished from originals. In those days there was a famous mathematician whose name was Chasles. He was interested in the history of geometry, and also in the glory of France, and a clever genealogist saw his opportunity. He produced letters from which it appeared that some of Newton's discoveries had been anticipated by Frenchmen who had been robbed of their due fame. M. Chasles bought them, with a patriotic disregard for money; and he continued to buy, from time to time, all that the impostor, Vrain Lucas, offered him. He laid his documents before the Institute, and the Institute declared them genuine. There were autograph letters from Alexander to Aristotle, from Cæsar to Vercingetorix, from Lazarus to St. Peter, from Mary Magdalen to Lazarus. The fabricator's imagination ran riot, and he produced a fragment in the handwriting of Pythagoras, showing that Pythagoras wrote in bad French. At last other learned men, who did not love Chasles, tried to make him understand that he had been befooled. When the iniquity came to light, and the culprit was sent to prison, he had flourished for seven years, had made several thousand pounds, and had found a market for 27,000 unblushing forgeries.

About the time when this mysterious manufacture was thriving, Count Hunolstein bought one hundred and forty-eight letters from Marie Antoinette, of a Paris dealer, for £3400, and he published them in June 1864. Napoleon III. and the Empress Eugénie, whose policy it was to conciliate legitimists whom the Italian Revolution offended, exhibited a cultivated interest in the memory of the unhappy queen; and it happened that a high official of their Court, M. Feuillet de Conches, was zealous in the same cause. He began his purchases as early as 1830, and had obtained much from the Thermidorean, Courtois, who had had Robespierre's papers in his hands. Wachsmuth, who went to Paris in 1840 to prepare his historical work, reported in German reviews on the value of Feuillet's collection; and in 1843 he was described as the first of French autographophiles—the term is not of my coining. It was known that he meditated a publication on the royal family. He travelled all over Europe, and was admitted to make transcripts and facsimiles in many places that were jealously guarded against intruders. His first volume appeared two months later than Hunolstein's, and his second in September. During that summer and autumn royalism was the fashion, and enjoyed a season of triumph. Twenty-four letters were common to both collections; and as they did not literally agree, troublesome people began to ask questions.

The one man able to answer them was Arneth, then deputy keeper of the archives at Vienna, who was employed laying down the great history of Maria Theresa that has made him famous. For the letters written by Marie Antoinette to her mother and her family had been religiously preserved, and were in his custody. Before the end of the year Arneth produced the very words of the letters, as the Empress received them; and then it was discovered that they were quite different from those which had been printed at Paris.

An angry controversy ensued, and in the end it became certain that most of Hunolstein's edition, and part of Feuillet's, was fabricated by an impostor. It was whispered that the supposed originals sold by Charavay, the dealer, to Hunolstein came to him from Feuillet de Conches. Sainte Beuve, who had been taken in at first, and had applauded, thereupon indignantly broke off his acquaintance, and published the letter in which he did it. Feuillet became more wary. His four later volumes are filled with matter of the utmost value;

and his large collection of the illegible autographs of Napoleon were sold for £1250 and are now at The Durdans.

It is in this way that the roguery of a very dexterous thief resulted in the opening of the imperial archives, in which the authentic records of the Revolution are deposited. For the emperors, Joseph and Leopold, were the queen's brothers; her sister was regent in the Low Countries, the family ambassador was in her confidence, and the events that brought on the great war, and the war itself, under Clerfayt, Coburg, and the Archduke Charles, can be known there and there only. Once opened, Arneth never afterwards allowed the door to be closed on students. He published many documents himself, he encouraged his countrymen to examine his treasures, and he welcomed, and continues to welcome, the scholars of Berlin. Thirty or forty volumes of Austrian documents, which were brought to light by the act of the felonious Frenchman, constitute our best authority for the inner and outer history of the Revolution and of the time that preceded it. The French Foreign Office is less communicative. The papers of their two ablest diplomatists, Barthélemy and Talleyrand, have been made public, besides those of Fersen, Maury, Vaudreuil, and many *émigrés*; and the letters of several deputies to their constituents are now coming out.

Next to the Austrian, the most valuable of the diplomatists are the Americans, the Venetians, and the Swede, for he was the husband of Necker's illustrious daughter. This change in the centre of gravity which went on between 1865 and 1885 or 1890, besides directing renewed attention to international affairs, considerably reduced the value of the memoirs on which the current view of our history was founded. For memoirs are written afterwards for the world, and are clever, apologetic, designing and deceitful. Letters are written at the moment, and are confidential, and therefore they enable us to test the truth of the memoirs. In the first place, we find that many of them are not authentic, or are not by the reputed author. What purports to be the memoirs of Prince Hardenberg is the composition of two well-informed men of letters, Beauchamp and d'Allouville. Beauchamp also wrote the book known as the *Memoirs of Fouché*. Those of Robespierre are by Reybaud, and those of Barras by Rousselin. Roche wrote the memoirs of Levasseur de la Sarthe, and Lafitte those of Fleury. Cléry, the king's confidential valet, left a diary which met with such success that somebody composed his pretended memoirs. Six volumes attributed to Sanson, the executioner, are of course spurious.

When Weber's *Memoirs* were republished in the long collection of Baudoin, Weber protested and brought an action. The defendant denied his claim, and produced evidence to prove that the three first chapters are by Lally Tollendal. It does not always follow that the book is worthless because the title-page assigns it to a man who is not the author. The real author very often is not to be trusted. Malouet is one of those men, very rare in history, whose reputation rises the more we know him; and Dumont of Geneva was a sage observer, the confidant, and often the prompter, of Mirabeau. Both are misleading, for they wrote long after, and their memory is constantly at fault. Dumouriez wrote to excuse his defection, and Talleyrand to cast a decent veil over actions which were injurious to him at the Restoration. The Necker family are exasperating, because they are generally wrong in their dates. Madame Campan wished to recover her position, which the fall of the Empire had ruined. Therefore some who had seen her manuscript have affirmed that the suppressed passages were adverse to the queen; for the same reason that, in the Fersen correspondence, certain expressions are omitted and replaced by suspicious asterisks. Ferrières has always been acknowledged as one of the most trustworthy witnesses. It is he who relates that, at the first meeting after the oath, the deputies were excluded from the tennis-court in order that the Count d'Artois might play a match. We now find, from the letters of a deputy recently published, that the story of this piece of insolence is a fable. The clergy had made known that they were coming, and it was thought unworthy of such an occasion to receive a procession of ecclesiastics in a tennis-court; so the deputies adjourned to a neighbouring church.

Montlosier, who was what Burke called a man of honour and a cavalier, tells us that his own colleague from Auvergne was nearly killed in a duel, and kept his bed for three months. Biauzat, the fellow-townsman of the wounded man, writes home that he was absent from the Assembly only ten days. The point of the matter is that the adversary whose hand inflicted the wound was Montlosier himself.

The narrative which Madame Roland drew up in prison, as an appeal to posterity, is not a discreet book, but it does not reveal the secret of her life. It came out in 1863, when three or four letters were put up for sale at auction, and when, shortly after, a miniature, with something written on it, was found amid the refuse of a greengrocer's shop. They were the letters of Madame Roland, which Buzot had sent to a place of safety before he went out and shot himself; and the miniature was her portrait, which he had worn in his flight.

Bertrand, the Minister of Marine, relates that the queen sent to the emperor to learn what he would do for their deliverance, and he publishes the text of the reply which came back. For a hundred years that document has been accepted as the authentic statement of Leopold's intentions. It was the document which the messenger brought back, but not the reply which the emperor gave. That reply, very different from the one that has misled every historian, was discovered by Arneth, and was published two years ago by Professor Lenz, who lectures on the Revolution to the fortunate students of Berlin. Sybel inserted it in his review, and rewrote Lenz's article, which upset an essential part of his own structure.

The Marquis de Bouillé wrote his recollections in 1797, to clear himself from responsibility for the catastrophe of Varennes. The correspondence, preserved among Fersen's papers, shows that the statements in his *Memoirs* are untrue. He says that he wished the king to depart openly, as Mirabeau had advised; that he recommended the route by Rheims, which the king rejected; and that he opposed the line of military posts, which led to disaster. The letters prove that he advised secret departure, the route of Varennes, and the cavalry escort.

The general characteristic of the period I am describing has been the breakdown of the Memoirs, and our emancipation from the authority of the writers who depended on them. That phase is represented by the three historians, Sybel, Taine, and Sorel. They distanced their predecessors, because they were able to consult much personal, and much diplomatic, correspondence. They fell short of those who were to come, because they were wanting in official information.

Sybel was Ranke's pupil, and he had learnt in the study of the Middle Ages, which he disliked, to root out the legend and the fable and the lie, and to bring history within the limits of evidence. In early life he exploded the story of Peter the Hermit and his influence on the Crusades, and in the same capacity it was he who exposed the fabrication of the queen's letters. Indeed he was so sturdy a critic that he scorned to read the fictitious Hardenberg, although the work contains good material. He more than shared the unspiritual temper of the school, and fearing alike the materialistic and the religious basis of history, he insisted on confining it to affairs of state. Having a better eye for institutions than his master, and an intellect adapted to affairs, he was one of the first to turn from the study of texts to modern times and burning questions. In erudition and remote research he fully equalled those who were scholars and critics, and nothing else; but his tastes called him to a different career. He said of himself that he was three parts a politician, so that only the miserable remnant composed the professor. Sybel approached the Revolution through Burke, with essays on his French and Irish policy. He stood firmly to the doctrine that men are governed by descent, that the historic nation prevails invincibly over the actual nation, that we cannot cast off our pedigree. Therefore the growth of things in Prussia seemed to him to be almost normal, and acceptable in contrast with the condition of a people which attempted to constitute itself according to its own ideas. Political theory as well as national antagonism allowed him no sympathy with the French, and no wonder he is generally under-estimated in France. He stands aloof from the meridian of Paris, and meditates high up in Central Europe on the conflagration of 1789, and the trouble it gave to the world in general. The distribution of power in France moves him less than the distribution of power in Europe, and he thinks forms of government less important than expansion of frontier. He describes the fall of Robespierre as an episode in the partition of Poland. His endeavour is to assign to the Revolution its place in international history.

Once it was said, in disparagement of Niebuhr and other historians, that when you ask a German for a black coat he offers you a white sheep, and leaves you to effect the transformation yourself. Sybel belongs to a later age, and can write well, but heavily, and without much light or air. His introduction, published in 1853, several years before the volume of Tocqueville, has so much in common with it, that it was suggested that he might have read the earlier article by Tocqueville, which John Mill translated for the *Westminster Review*. But Sybel assured me that he had not seen it. He had obtained access to important papers, and when he became a great public personage, everything was laid open before him. In diplomatic matters he is very far ahead of all other writers, except Sorel. Having been an opposition leader, and what in Prussia is called a Liberal, he went over to Bismarck, and wrote the history of the new German Empire under his inspiration, until the Emperor excluded him from the archives, of which, for many active years, he had been the head. His five volumes, not counting various essays written in amplification or defence, stand, in the succession of histories, by dint of constant revision, at a date near the year 1880. For a time they occupied the first place. In successive editions errors were weeded out as fast as they could be found; and yet, even in the fourth, Mounier, who, as everybody knows, was elected for Dauphiné, is called the deputy from Provence. Inasmuch as he loves neither Thiers nor Sieyès, Sybel declares it absurd to compare, as Thiers has done, the Constitution of 1799 to the British Constitution. In the page alluded to, one of the most thoughtful in the Consulate and Empire, Thiers is so far from putting the work of Sieyès on the British level, that his one purpose is to display the superiority of a government which is the product of much experiment and incessant adaptation to the artificial outcome of political logic.

Sybel's view is that the Revolution went wrong quite naturally, that the new order was no better than the old, because it proceeded from the old, rose from an exhausted soil, and was worked by men nurtured in the corruption of the old *régime*. He uses the Revolution to exhibit the superiority of conservative and enlightened Germany. And as there is little to say in favour of Prussia, which crowned an inglorious war by an inglorious peace, he produced his effect by piling up to the utmost the mass of French folly and iniquity. And with all its defects, it is a most instructive work. A countryman, who had listened to Daniel Webster's Bunker Hill oration, described it by saying that every word weighed a pound. Almost the same thing might be said of Sybel's history, not for force of language or depth of thought, but by reason of the immense care with which every passage was considered and all the evidence weighed. The author lived to see himself overtaken and surpassed, for internal history by Taine, and for foreign affairs by Sorel.

Taine was trained in the systems of Hegel and Comte, and his fundamental dogma was the denial of free will and the absolute dominion of physical causes over the life of mankind. A violent effort to shape the future by intention and design, and not by causes that are in the past, seemed to him the height of folly. The idea of starting fresh, from the morrow of creation, of emancipating the individual from the mass, the living from the dead, was a defiance of the laws of nature. Man is civilised and trained by his surroundings, his ancestry, his nationality, and must be adapted to them. The natural man, whom the Revolution discovered and brought to the surface, is, according to Taine, a vicious and destructive brute, not to be tolerated unless caught young, and perseveringly disciplined and controlled.

Taine is not a historian, but a pathologist, and his work, the most scientific we possess, and in part the most exhaustive, is not history. By his energy in extracting formulas and accumulating knowledge, by the crushing force with which he masses it to sustain conclusions, he is the strongest Frenchman of his time, and his indictment is the weightiest that was ever drawn up. For he is no defender of the Monarchy or of the Empire, and his cruel judgments are not dictated by party. His book is one of the ablest that this generation has produced. It is no substitute for history. The consummate demonstrator, concentrated on the anatomy of French brains, renounces much that we need to be told, and is incompetent as to the literature and the general affairs of Europe. Where Taine failed Sorel has magnificently succeeded, and he has occupied the vacant place both at the Academy and in his undisputed primacy among writers on the Revolution. He is secretary to the Senate, and is not an abstract philosopher, but a politician, curious about things that get into newspapers and attract the public gaze. Instead of investigating the human interior, he is on the look-out across the Alps and beyond the Rhine, writing, as it were, from the point of view of the Foreign Office. He is at his best when his pawns are diplomatists. In the process of home politics, and the development of political ideas, he does not surpass those who went before him. Coming after Sybel, he is somewhat ahead of him in documentary resource. He is more friendly to the principles of the Revolution, without being an apologist, and is more cheerful, more sanguine, and pleasanter to read. A year ago I said that, Sybel and Taine being dead, Sorel is our highest living authority. To-day I can no longer use those words.

On Ranke's ninetieth birthday, Mommsen paid him this compliment: "You are probably the last of the universal historians. Undoubtedly you are the first." This fine saying was double-edged, and intended to disparage general histories; but it is with a general history that I am going to conclude what I have to say on the literature of the Revolution. In the eighth volume of the *General History*, now appearing in France, Aulard gives the political outline of the Revolution. It may be called the characteristic product of the year 1889. When the anniversary came round, for the hundredth time, and found the Republic securely established, and wielding a power never dreamed of by the founders, men began to study its history in a new spirit. Vast pains and vast sums were expended in collecting, arranging, printing, the most authentic and exact information; and there was less violence and partiality, more moderation and sincerity, as became the unresisted victor. In this new school the central figure was M. Aulard. He occupies the chair of revolutionary history at Paris; he is the head of the society for promoting it;

the editor of the review, *La Révolution*, now in its thirty-first volume; and he has published the voluminous acts of the Jacobin Club and of the Committee of Public Safety. Nobody has ever known the printed material better than he, and nobody knows the unpublished material so well. The cloven hoof of party preference appears in a few places. He says that the people wrought vengeance after the manner of their kings; and he denies the complicity of Danton in the crimes of September. As Danton himself admitted his guilt to no less a witness than the future king of the French, this is a defiance of a main rule of criticism that a man shall be condemned out of his own mouth. Aulard's narrative is not complete, and lacks detail; but it is intelligent and instructive beyond all others, and shows the standard that has been reached by a century of study.

Where then do we now stand, and what is the elevation that enables us to look down on men who, the other day, were high authorities? We are at the end, or near the end, of the supply of Memoirs; few are known to exist in manuscript. Apart from Spain, we are advanced in respect of diplomatic and international correspondence; and there is abundant private correspondence, from Fersen downwards. But we are only a little way in the movement for the production of the very acts of the government of revolutionary France.

To give you an idea of what that means. Thirty years ago the Cahiers, or Instructions, of 1789 were published in six large volumes. The editors lamented that they had not found everything, and that a dozen cahiers were missing in four provinces. The new editor, in his two volumes of introduction, knows of 120 instructions that were overlooked by his predecessors in those four regions alone; and he says that there were 50,000 in the whole of France. One collection is coming out on the Elections for Paris, another on the Paris Electors, that is, the body entrusted with the choice of deputies, who thereupon took over the municipal government of the city and made themselves permanent. Then there is the series of the acts of the Commune, of the several governing committees, of the Jacobins, of the war department, and seven volumes on Vendée alone.

In a few years all these publications will be completed, and all will be known that ever can be known. Perhaps some one will then compose a history as far beyond the latest that we possess as Sorel, Aulard, Rambaud, Flammermont are in advance of Taine and Sybel, or Taine and Sybel of Michelet and Louis Blanc; or of the best that we have in English, the three chapters in the second volume of Buckle, or the two chapters in the fifth volume of Lecky. In that golden age our historians will be sincere, and our history certain. The worst will be known, and then sentence need not be deferred. With the fulness of knowledge the pleader's occupation is gone, and the apologist is deprived of his bread. Mendacity depended on concealment of evidence. When that is at an end, fable departs with it, and the margin of legitimate divergence is narrowed.

Don't let us utter too much evil of party writers, for we owe them much. If not honest, they are helpful, as the advocates aid the judge; and they would not have done so well from the mere inspiration of disinterested veracity. We might wait long if we watched for the man who knows the whole truth and has the courage to speak it, who is careful of other interests besides his own, and labours to satisfy opponents, who can be liberal towards those who have erred, who have sinned, who have failed, and deal evenly with friend and foe—assuming that it would be possible for an honest historian to have a friend.

INDEX

Adams, John

Agra, bishop of

Aiguillon, Duc de

Alsace

Amsterdam

Anglas, Boissy d'

Archives, Austrian

Argenson, d'

Argenteau, Mercy

Armand, Colonel, the Marquis de la Rouerie

Arneth

Artois, Comte d'

Auckland, Lord

Aulard

Baillon

Bailly

Bâle, peace of

Barante,

Barbaroux,

Barentin,

Barère

Barnave

Barras

Barthélemy

Bastille

Batz, Baron de

Baudotr

Bazire

Beaumetz

Bécard

Beccaria

Belgium

Bentham

Bernier

Bertrand

Besenval

Beurnonville

Billaud-Varennes

Blanc, Louis

Bonchamps, Marquis de ff.

Bordeaux archbishop of

Bouillé, Marquis de

Bouillé, de, the younger

Bourbon House of

Bourdon

Breteuil

Bridport, Lord

Brissot

Broglie, Marshal de

Brunswick, Duke of

Brussels

Burke, Edmund

Buzot

Cabanis

Calonne

Cambacérès

Cambon

Campan, Madame

Camus

Carlyle

Carnac

Carnot

Carnot the younger

Carrier

Cassagnac, Granier de

Castlereagh, Lord

Cathelineau

Cazalès

Cérutti

Chabot,

Charette

Charleroi

Charles Archduke

Chartres, Duc de

Chateaubriand

Chatelet, Duc de

Chatham

Chaumette

Chauvelin

Choiseul, Duc de

Cholet, battle of

Chouans, Chouannerie

Clerfayt

Clermont, Count Tonnerre de

Clermont

Cloots, Anacharsis

Coburg, Prince of

Coffinhal

Collot

Condé

Condorcet

Cook Captain

Corday Charlotte

Cordeliers the

Cormatin

Corsica

Cottereau

Courier Paul Louis

Courmenin

Couthon

Croker

Custine

Cuvier

Damas

Danton

Dareste

Daunou

Delauney

Delessart

Desaix

Desèze

Desmoulins, Camille

Diderot

Domat

Dreux-Brézé

Drouet

Droz

Dumouriez

Dunkirk

Dupont de Nemours

Duport

Égalité, Prince

Eglantine, Fabre de

Elbée, de

Elizabeth, Princess

Émigrés, the

Estaing Count

Favras Marquis de

Féderés, the

Fénelon

Fersen, Count

Feuillants

Fleurus battle of

Fontenoy, Madame de her note to Tallien

Fouché, ff.

Foulon

Fouquier-Tinville

Fox

Francis, king of Hungary

Franklin

Frederic William

Fréron

Gabourd, Amédée

Garat

Genoude

George III.

Gobel

Godoy, Manuel

Goethe

Goguelat

Gouvion, General

Gower Lord

Grégoire, bishop of Blois

Grenville

Guadeloupe

Guizot

Gustavus III.

Guyot, bishop of Agra

Hamilton, Alexander

Hanriot

Hauranne, Duvergier de

Hayti, island of

Hébert

Herbois, Collot de

Hervilly, de

Hoche

Hohenlohe

Holland

Hood, Lord

Howe, Lord

Hunolstein

Isnard

Jansenists, the

Jefferson

Jourdan

Joyeuse, Villaret

Jurieu

Kaiserslautern, battle of

Kaunitz

Kellermann

Kléber

Klopstock

Korff, Madame de

Kozsiusko and the Polish insurrection

Laboulaye

Lafayette, General

Lally Tollendal

La Marck

Lamartine

Lamballe, Princess de

Lameth

Lanfrey

Langres, bishop of

La Jaunaye, treaty of

Lanjuinais

urce

Latour Maubourg

Lavallée

Lavergne

Lavoisier

Lecointre

Legendre

Léonard

Leopold

Le Quesnoy

Lescure

Lewis XIV

Lewis XVI

Lewis XVII

Lewis XVIII

Liancourt, Duc de Rochefoucauld

Limon

Longwy

Louchet

Louis Philippe

Louvet

Lubbock, Sir John

Lubersac, bishop of Chartres

Luckner, General

Luxemburg, Duke of

Lyons

Machault

Mack, Colone

Mailhe

Maillane, Durand de

Maillard

Malesherbes

Mallet du Pan

Malmesbury

Malouet

Mandat

Mantua

Manuel

Marat

Marceau

Maret

Marie Antoinette

Marigny

Martin, Henry

Masséna

Maulevrier, Count Colbert de

Maultrot

Maurepas

Maury, Cardinal

Mayence

Menou

Mentz

Mercier de la Rivière

Merlin

Michele

Mirabeau

Moellendorf, Marshal

Mons

Montagu

Montalembert

Montciel, Terrier de

Montesquieu

Montlosier

Montmédy

Montmorin

Moreau

Morris,

Mounier

Mousson

Murat

Nantes

Napier

Naples

Napoleon Bonaparte

Narbonne de Lara, Count, Minister of War

Necker

Neerwinden

Ney, Marshal

Niebuhr

Noaille

Orange, the Prince of

Orleans, the Duke of

Orleans, the Duchess of

Paine, Tom

Pamiers, bishop of

Panis

Panizzi

Paris, archbishop of

Penthièvre, Duc de

Pétion

Pichegru

Pilnitz, declaration of

Pitt

Pius VI. and the Civil Constitution of the clergy

Plain, the deputies of the

Poland

Polignac, the Duchess of

Pontécoulant

Portugal

Précy

Priestly

Prieur

Provence, the Count of

Prussia

Puisaye, Count de

Quiberon, battle of

Quinet

Ranke

Raynal, Abbé

Rebecqui

Reinhard

Reynier

Richelieu, Duc de

Rigby, Dr.

Robespierre

Rochefoucauld, La, Duke de Liancourt

Rochejaquelein, Henri de la

Roederer

Roland

Roland, Madame

Romeuf

Romilly, Sir Samuel

Romme

Rouerie, Marquis de la,

Rousseau

Royer Collard

Saint Victor

Sainte Marie, Miomandre de

Santerre

Sardinia, the king of

Sauce

Saumur

Savenay

Scheldt, opening of the

Séchelles, Hérault de

Sémonville

Sergent

Serre, De

Sieyès

Simolin

Smith, Adam

Sombreuil

Sorel

Spain

Spencer, Lord

St. Cyr

St. Just

St. Ménehould

St. Priest

Staël, Madame de

Stofflet

Swiss Guard

Sybel, Heinrich von

Taine

Talleyrand, bishop of Autun

Tallien

Tallien, Madame

Talmond, Prince de

Target

Ternaux, Mortimer

Thibaudeau

Thierry

Thiers

Thouret

Tocqueville

Torfou

Torquemada

Toulon

Toulouse, archbishop of

Tourzel, Madame de

Tronchet

Turgot

Tuscany

Ushant

Vadier

Valenciennes

Valmy

Vancouver Island

Varennes

Vendée, La

Verdun

Vergniaud

Versailles, the march to

Villaret-Joyeuse

Villiaumé

Vincent

Virieu

Volney

Voulland

Washington

Wattignies

Weber

Webster, Daniel

Weissenburg

Westermann

Wilson, James

Windward Islands

Wurmser

York, the Duke of